"Gary has done an [...] documenting a dange[...] our careers. His description of events based on excellent research is right on target and as accurate as I could imagine. 'SHOTS FIRED!' is not only a good read but an informative review of tactical procedures."*

Chief of Police Joe Gerwens (retired)
Fort Lauderdale Police Department

"Everything in this book is real, the scheming criminals, the dedicated cops, the streets they battled for possession of, the victims, and the justice system that enveloped them all. Gary Jones knows those streets, and with this book asks the reader to take a dangerous and unforgettable walk in his shoes."

Cherokee Paul McDonald
Author of "The Patch" and "Blue Truth"

"Gary Jones does an excellent job of portraying the dedication of law enforcement to protect our communities as it plays out on the street. That perspective, coupled with the mental exercises, made 'Shots Fired!' a gripping book that I could not put down until it was finished."

Sheriff John R. Armer
Gila County, Arizona

Badge 149 – "Shots Fired!"

Gary P. Jones

www.badge149.com

Copyright © 2006 by Gary P. Jones

ISBN 0-7414-3244-7

The photograph used for the cover of this book was taken by George Long and I want to thank him, and the individuals who helped him, for their assistance. The author's photograph on the back cover was taken by Dave Exterkamp and I want to thank him too.

Published by:

INFINITY
PUBLISHING.COM

1094 New DeHaven Street, Suite 100
West Conshohocken, PA 19428-2713
Info@buybooksontheweb.com
www.buybooksontheweb.com
Toll-free (877) BUY BOOK
Local Phone (610) 941-9999
Fax (610) 941-9959

Printed in the United States of America

Printed on Recycled Paper

Published December 2006

DEDICATION

This book is dedicated to the memory of Fort Lauderdale Police Officers Dimitri Walter Ilyankoff and Bryant Peney, and all of the other courageous men and women of law enforcement who have paid the ultimate price, and who have made the supreme sacrifice. Their unselfishness, and their strong devotion to duty, shall not be forgotten!

FOREWORD

Washington D.C. is home to many breathtaking monuments and memorials, but none is more inspiring than the **National Law Enforcement Officers Memorial** which sits on three acres of federal park land at Judiciary Square. Dedicated by President George Bush in 1991 this imposing Memorial honors the brave men and women of law enforcement who have made the ultimate sacrifice. The first known law enforcement fatality recorded at the Memorial occurred in 1792, in New York City. Now, more than 17,000 names of federal, state and local law enforcement officers are inscribed on the Memorial's blue-gray marble walls.

Two tree-lined "pathways of remembrance" border the Memorial's beautifully landscaped park and this is where the names of these fallen heroes are forever engraved. A statue of an adult lion, protecting its cubs, guards each pathway's entrance. These bronze statues symbolize the protective role our nation's law enforcement officers have always voluntarily accepted, sometimes at an enormous cost.

As part of this magnificent Memorial, planning for a new National Law Enforcement Museum is now in progress and funds are being raised for its eventual construction. Ground breaking is currently scheduled for 2007 and the new museum will hopefully open in 2009. With its many interesting and informative exhibits, and its historic memorabilia, museum visitors will have a much better appreciation and understanding of the law enforcement profession, and of the dedicated men and women who have unselfishly served our nation throughout its history, and who continue to serve us now.

The National Law Enforcement Museum is an important and worthwhile endeavor. It is a project that each of us in law enforcement, and all Americans outside our profession too, should eagerly embrace and support wholeheartedly. Therefore, <u>a portion of all book sale profits from the sale of this book will be donated to the National Law Enforcement Officers Memorial Fund (NLEOMF)</u>. These donations will be used to help fund the construction of this Museum.

These poignant words, inscribed on the Memorial's east wall, help to remind us that these officers did not die in vain:

"In valor there is hope."

INTRODUCTION

Every incident portrayed in this book happened just as it is written. These were all true events and I tried my best to describe them as accurately and truthfully, as possible. In most cases the original police reports documenting these events, and even some of the actual dispatch tapes too, were available to me while I researched and then wrote this book. Most of the time, when radio communications are quoted, these are the actual transmissions that were made and not just what I may recall from memory. The names of most of the bad guys, and a few of the police officers too, have sometimes been changed, for obvious reasons. But, for the most part, the names of the police officers involved in these incidents are accurate and factual.

If you are interested in learning more about the specific incidents portrayed in this book, please visit my website (www.badge149.com). Many interesting items that were not included in this book can be found there. This includes, but is not limited to, crime scene photographs, original dispatch tapes, plus much, much more. My website is still a work in progress and I plan to add additional material on a regular basis, so I would encourage you to periodically stop by to see what's new.

Thank you for your support of law enforcement and for supporting the National Law Enforcement Officers Memorial Fund.

Gary P. Jones, Captain (retired)
Fort Lauderdale Police Department
(1967-1993)

TABLE OF CONTENTS

1

JUNE 27, 1968

Both vehicles raced along Hammondville Road side by side as if engaged in some illegal and dangerous drag race. As the young driver of the teal blue Chevrolet Chevelle continued his reckless driving left of center, in the opposite lane of traffic, our own black and white Plymouth Fury remained in the right curbside lane where we belonged. A brilliant non-stop series of red and white colored flashes seemed to completely block out the heavens above; leaving the moon, the stars and the night, insignificant and meaningless by comparison. And, as if this wasn't enough, the weird psychedelic-like wail of our police car's electronic siren also terrorized the night. This frightening kaleidoscope of lights, sounds and action boldly announced our deadly presence in the area.

As I continued to match the Chevy's excessive speed I looked over and saw my partner Dave Martin reloading his Smith & Wesson revolver. For the past six minutes Dave and I had chased this stolen car north from our own northwest section in Fort Lauderdale, to Pompano Beach's downtown area. Somewhere along the way the occupants of this "Signal 10" began firing shots at us and Dave quickly returned their fire. Now, he was running low of .38 caliber ammunition. I continued to steer our Fury with my left hand and with my right I undid my ammunition pouch and handed Dave all of my extra rounds. I also gave him my back-up weapon, a small .25 caliber automatic I usually carried in my right rear pocket. I never had needed it before, but now I suspected it might just come in handy.

As we headed up Hammondville Road, away from downtown Pompano Beach, I watched the Chevelle's passenger lay down prone across the front seat as I pulled up abreast of them again. He apparently thought I was about to shoot him. Then, just as quickly as he had gone down, he suddenly bolted back upright with a dark object in his right hand! It looked very much like a gun. I drew my own .38 caliber S&W revolver and when he saw the gun in my hand he went totally prone once again. The Chevy suddenly accelerated rapidly, almost like a jet fighter turning on its afterburners. It easily pulled away from us and in a few more precious seconds it was almost one full block in front of us.

Okay Officer, It's Decision Time!

(Situation #1)

The occupants of the fleeing vehicle have definitely fired several shots at us. Therefore, we are legally justified to use deadly force and my partner Dave Martin has already fired back at the suspects in the stolen car. Under these circumstances, if you were me, and you were driving our police vehicle during this pursuit, would you fire your weapon?

Note: Although current Fort Lauderdale Police Department policy prohibits an officer from firing his weapon during a pursuit, while he/she is driving, no such policy existed in 1968 when this pursuit occurred.

What is your answer? (put an "X" in the space in front of your answer)

❑ _____ Yes! I would fire my weapon at the fleeing suspects in the stolen car.

❑ _____ No! I would not fire at this time.

An analysis of this situation appears at the end of the book

(Do <u>not</u> go there until you have finished reading this chapter)

I changed my gun from my right hand to my left hand and put it out the open driver's door window. I tried to take aim as best as I could and then I fired off three quick shots. There was no way at all for me to know if I actually hit the Chevelle and I quickly realized this was just a waste of good ammunition. Thank God I had my wits about me enough to know I'd better save my remaining three rounds for when we finally got these bastards stopped. When that happened, and I was sure it would, I didn't want to have to face these guys with an empty weapon. As Dave fired off the entire contents of my little .25 caliber auto, I holstered my own weapon and once again concentrated entirely on my driving.

When the stolen Chevy reached the intersection at Powerline Road they made a quick right turn and headed northbound. They had to slow down when they made this turn, so once again I was able to overtake them. Now they were the ones in the right-hand lane and we were driving on the wrong side of the highway. Dave leaned out his window and popped off a few more rounds in the direction of the driver. We were only about ten to fifteen feet away from him. I watched with satisfaction as he slumped forward against the steering wheel. He'd been hit! I was sure he would now lose control and probably crash the stolen Chevelle, so I instinctively took my foot off of the gas pedal.

"I think we just got the driver!" I advised the dispatcher triumphantly. But then, when he sat back upright and put his own pedal to the metal once again, I had to add, "He's still driving though."

Powerline Road. This extremely narrow and dangerous stretch of pavement cut northward through the semi-abandoned countryside; far from the glamour, congestion and chaos usually associated with Florida's infamous "Gold Coast". This often neglected portion of Broward County, located far to the northwest of the Fort Lauderdale metropolitan area, the *"Venice of America,"* had somehow miraculously escaped the rapid growth and development so

4

characteristic of most of the south Florida region. Deep placid canals, filled with richly stagnant waters, menacingly flanked both sides of the deserted highway. There were no street lights along this isolated part of Powerline Road and except for both vehicle's headlights, and our rotating red and white spinner on our roof, it was pitch black. To make matters even worse a soft fragile mist now began to slowly envelop the darkened roadway.

We continued north on Powerline Road for approximately the next nine miles. Once or twice I briefly stole a quick glance at our patrol car's speedometer and found it totally buried. Our speed was in excess of 120 miles per hour and yet the Chevelle still slowly pulled away from us. At one point it seemed to be about a half mile ahead but Dave and I weren't about to let go of these two felons without a fight. We both knew what the risks were if we continued the pursuit and I'm sure some Monday morning quarterbacks might even say chasing these guys just wasn't worth it. They'd probably call us crazy, and who knows, they might even be right. I have to admit, I really didn't want to think about what would happen if we lost control at that insane speed. If we did, I knew we'd end up in one of the canals bordering the highway. And, if that happened, we'd be finished for sure! But, I didn't intend to let that happen. Unless the two bad guys in the Chevelle made a lucky shot and hit me, I wasn't about to lose control. I didn't care how fast they wanted to go.

One major thing in our favor was the late hour. It was right around 3:30 a.m. and there was absolutely no other traffic on this long lonely stretch of Powerline Road. In a couple more hours however, this would all change. At daybreak I knew the road would again be clogged with farm vehicles, eighteen wheelers and various pieces of assorted construction equipment. But for now, the road belonged to us.

"Still north on Powerline," I advised the dispatcher.

"Any idea where you're at Jonesy?" he answered back.

"You've got to be kidding!" I thought to myself. I knew we were still in Broward County, on Powerline Road, but other than that I was totally lost.

The driver of the Chevelle appeared to have a definite destination in mind and I suspected he was trying to get home, or at least somewhere near to it.

The Chevelle made a right turn. "They're turning off of Powerline, I don't know what the street is!" I advised over the radio.

"Which way?" another voice asked.

"He doesn't know!" the dispatcher immediately shot back, a hint of irritation in his voice.

"We're going into the Deerfield Beach City Limits," I proclaimed loudly, after I saw a welcome sign announcing that fact. "I don't know what street we're on, but we're just turning off Powerline Road going east!"

"East off of Powerline into Deerfield," the dispatcher repeated.

"They're going east on Sample into Deerfield," the dispatcher dutifully reported. Dave and I didn't know where we were, and our radio room received this erroneous information from Pompano Beach P.D. Several of their marked units were right behind us and they thought this was Sample Road. In reality however, we were much farther to the north. We now headed eastbound on Hillsboro Boulevard, which happened to be the last major east/west thoroughfare before entering Palm Beach County.

"Deerfield and Boca Raton 26," the dispatcher announced almost casually.

This stretch of Hillsboro Boulevard wasn't much better than Powerline Road, but at least there weren't any deep canals to drive into. As we continued eastbound at a high rate of speed I felt just a little bit better.

Hillsboro Boulevard was only a narrow two-lane road; one lane for eastbound traffic like us, and one for westbound.

Dave and I both saw the Deerfield Beach P.D. patrol unit at about the same time. It was headed westbound towards us. When the Deerfield officer suddenly pulled his unit over to the right onto the swale neither one of us thought that much about it. After all, it seemed to be the prudent thing to do. It made sense to get out of the way of the stolen Chevelle and only a fool would want to chance a head-on collision at these extreme speeds. We watched as the Chevelle passed by the Deerfield Beach cruiser. I glanced down at the speedometer and observed our speed was in excess of 90 miles per hour. The Chevelle was going at least that fast.

Immediately after the Chevelle passed him by the Deerfield Beach unit began to slowly pull away from the right side swale portion of the roadway. Dave saw this and let out a loud warning, "Look out!"

Even though Dave thought the Deerfield Beach officer might do something stupid I still didn't think we were in any real danger. The movement by the Deerfield unit didn't seem that unusual and I suspected he was just getting ready to pull in behind us after we had passed him. I did wonder, however, what he was going to do about the two Pompano Beach units already there behind us.

"Don't worry, I got it," I said, as I tried to reassure Dave and drive our Fury at the same time.

In a reckless move that almost seemed to be suicidal the Deerfield Beach officer suddenly made a U-turn and pulled his own unit out onto Hillsboro Boulevard directly in front of us. Even though we were both now headed eastbound in the same direction the huge difference in our speeds made an accident almost inevitable. Now, while this turkey was desperately trying to accelerate from dead zero, Dave and I already had a full head of steam up! Our speed was still right around 90 m.p.h. I thought about hitting the brakes but quickly realized we were too close to this guy for that to work. If I tried to stop I knew I'd never make it and we'd climb right up his damn tail pipe! And, the Pompano Beach units behind us would probably do the same. It's amazing what one dumb shit can do if he really puts his mind to it!

Even though my eyes were glued to the area right there in front of us, with my peripheral vision I could see Dave trying with all his might to apply the brakes to stop our still charging vehicle. Problem was, the brake pedal happened to be on my side of the passenger compartment. All Dave was doing was wearing a hole in the floorboard. "Shit! We're gonna hit the bastard!" Dave yelled out.

Things were happening so quickly I really didn't have a chance to think about what we should do. I knew we couldn't stop in time so that left us only one other possible option. We had to pass him! Unfortunately however, in addition to being apparently brain dead, the Deerfield officer seemed to be a real road hog too. His unit was almost smack dab in the middle of the roadway.

"Better get out of the way sucker!" I thought to myself, "Fort Lauderdale P.D.'s coming through!"

I suspect the Deerfield officer probably realized his mistake almost immediately, but by then it was way to late. Once he was out on Hillsboro, and directly in front of us, he was totally committed and he now had very few options to choose from. If he tried to stop, he invited almost certain disaster! His only real hope lay in our ability to safely get by him. He must have realized this because he suddenly pulled all the way over to the right and we were able to shoot by him in the westbound lane of traffic. Thank God there were no other civilian vehicles in that lane heading towards us. As we passed him Dave and I both looked over at him. We really couldn't see him that well and I never did find out who he was. I'm sure he was happy about that. He was also very lucky we were so low on ammunition because I suspect Dave briefly thought abouth letting one fly in this stupid guy's direction. I'm sure the bad guys in the Chevelle wouldn't have minded.

The Pompano Beach units behind us were also able to pass the Deerfield Beach car safely and we all once again concentrated on the original task at hand. The Chevelle was now about a half mile ahead of us but we still weren't about to let them get away. For the next 2½ miles the suspects in the Chevy continued to widen the total distance between us. Then, for some unknown reason, they suddenly turned off of Hillsboro Boulevard and headed south into a residential area. I suspected they were near home and would probably bail out of their vehicle soon. After a half mile of going straight south they once again tried to make a turn. This time however, the driver's luck ran out. He lost control and the Chevelle ended up in someone's front yard. Instead of fleeing from the vehicle, as I thought they would, the driver tried to drive his way out of the yard. He apparently wasn't ready to give up just yet. The Chevelle went nowhere however and it quickly got hopelessly stuck and bogged down in a yard full of sugar sand. After nearly 20 full miles, which had taken us just twelve minutes to cover, the hectic chase was now finally over!

Even before I could get our unit totally stopped I observed someone running alongside the driver's side of our vehicle. This turned out to be one of the Pompano Beach officers who had been behind us. I never was able to figure out how he managed to get out of his own vehicle, and then run up to the suspect's Chevelle, all before I even had a chance to put our own cruiser into park. No matter, he toted a very large shotgun and I suspected the bad guys wouldn't offer any additional resistance once they observed him standing there by their driver's door. I was wrong! And, if this Pompano Beach patrolman also assumed they would give up without a fight, he was almost dead wrong!

Pompano Beach Officer William Harvey stood there by the driver's door, his shotgun at the ready. He had been the first police officer to approach the suspect's vehicle but now he was quickly joined by at least a dozen more who swarmed in from all directions. Dave and I exited our unit so damn fast neither one of us took the time to turn off our siren and now its wailing continued to fill the night with its ear-piercing screams. In fact, even though the pursuit was finally over the sounds of many sirens continued to be heard. Some were from faraway units still enroute to the scene of the stop but most of the sirens belonged to police units already there. Dave and I weren't the only ones to abandon their vehicles without turning off their siren. Now, we yelled for the two bad guys to get out of their vehicle, but they didn't move an inch. I don't know if they could even hear us above the wail of the sirens, because I was having trouble hearing myself. I suspect their problem really wasn't with their hearing however, and their failure to respond to our commands more than likely was a desperate desire to avoid getting their asses kicked, if possible.

But, out of the Chevelle they did come! I'm not really sure exactly how this exit occurred, and all I know is one moment the defiant driver was seated in the Chevelle, and the next second he was laid out prone on the ground, his face kissing the sand and the dirt in that front yard. Even though I didn't personally take him out of the Chevelle myself it was still our arrest so I felt it was my responsibility to handcuff him if I could. As Dave assisted other officers with the passenger I began to handcuff the driver by putting both his hands behind his back. I won't lie and say the driver was treated gently, with compassion and understanding. Because he wasn't! As I tried to finish handcuffing him he received a few whacks which didn't appear to do him any real damage.

<u>Okay Officer, It's Decision Time!</u>

(Situation #2)

Now that the lengthy pursuit is finally over, you are trying to take the driver into custody. Even though he is <u>not</u> physically resisting, he is <u>not</u> fully cooperating either. One of his hands is cuffed, and when you attempt to handcuff his other hand, several other officers kick and punch him a few times. If you were me, and you were faced with this violent situation, what would you do next?

What is your answer? (put an "X" in the space in front of your answer)

❑ _____ I would stop trying to handcuff the suspect and I would hit and punch him myself (the other officers may see something you don't and this is why they are kicking and hitting him).

❑ _____ I would stop trying to handcuff the suspect and I would back away from him (again, the other officers may see something you don't).

❑ _____ I would continue my efforts to handcuff the suspect.

An analysis of this situation appears at the end of the book

(Do <u>not</u> go there until you have finished reading this chapter)

I don't know for sure where all these blows and kicks came from, or why. All I know is they didn't come from me, even though I felt like killing the son-of-a-bitch! I could fully appreciate the anger and frustration that fueled such violent emotions. After all, these two guys in the Chevelle had just tried to kill us! In my young rookie's mind, these two felons did deserve a little-on-the job rehab! I knew this was more than likely the most punishment they would get!

I managed to get one of his hands completely cuffed and was just starting to cuff the other hand when a big leather boot suddenly slammed into my right hand. The sharp pain told me immediately that my hand had just been broken. I looked up and saw a Deerfield Beach sergeant standing there with a stupid-looking shit-eating grin on his face. It seemed as though he realized he had kicked me instead of the bad guy, but I don't believe he understood what had just happened. I don't think he knew that my hand was broken and at this point in time I was a little to busy to tell him. I knew I'd see him again later, so I went ahead and finished handcuffing my bad guy. When I turned around, Sergeant Stupid was gone!

After the driver and passenger had been fully subdued we were shocked to find out there had also been three young females in the back seat of the Chevelle during the pursuit. At the very beginning of the wild chase we thought we saw several other subjects in the back seat, but then these phantom figures disappeared completely and in the commotion that followed we forgot all about them. These girls had all laid down across the back seat and the floorboard and Dave and I were happy none of them had been hit by any of our rounds. The driver was a different story, however. Not only had he been hit once in the shoulder, back at Powerline Road when we saw him slump against the steering wheel, he had also been hit in the head. Fortunately for him, he either had an extremely thick skull, or Fort Lauderdale P.D. had given us some piss-poor ammunition. I suspect both were true.

The .38 caliber round entered the right side of the driver's head but when it struck bone, his skull, it failed to penetrate. Instead, it traveled along the skull, underneath the skin and around the back of his head, to a point on the left side of his head where it exited. Yes indeed, this was one lucky car thief! Since the driver was in need of medical attention we put him and the passenger in the back of our unit and headed towards the nearest hospital which happened to be on Sample Road in Pompano Beach. Another F.L.P.D. unit transported the three females for us. Even though the driver didn't have any life threatening injuries we still ran 10-18, lights and siren, just the same. This wasn't so much out of concern for the subject's welfare, instead it just seemed to be the thing to do. My right hand was hurting like hell and I wanted to get there as quickly as possible.

The hospital staff were all very helpful and friendly and when the emergency room doctor heard what had happened he asked us if we would like to do the honors and sew up the driver's left shoulder for him. The driver looked over at me with those big brown puppy dog eyes and you could see he was terrified. I must admit I was tempted and I probably would have enjoyed it. But, I knew the doctor was only joking so I politely responded with, "No thanks."
"You sure?" he answered back. Shit, maybe he wasn't kidding after all!
"Yeah, I'm sure." Even if the doctor was serious, making this asshole suffer just wasn't worth my career.

While the E.R. doctor worked on the driver other hospital personnel tended to me. I received the standard tetanus shot and a shot of penicillin. I've had penicillin many times before so when they asked me if I was allergic to this wonderful drug I immediately answered, "No." I was unaware the human body can sometimes develop a sudden allergy to this drug without any advance warning. When it comes to penicillin you can definitely get to much of a good thing! Other than these shots, and a few welcome words of encouragement, there really wasn't that much they could do for me at four in the morning. I would have to see a specialist during the day to have the broken bone set and then put in a cast.

Two totally unexpected things happened now and each was so incredible they blew my mind. I wasn't really surprised when Pompano Beach Officer William Harvey arrived at the hospital E.R. I thought he probably stopped by just to chat. But, Dave and I were shocked when we learned he'd been wounded in the ankle. Apparently, when Patrolman Harvey approached the driver's side of the Chevelle, the driver fired one shot at him. Officer Harvey, for some unknown reason, never saw a muzzle flash, nor heard the weapon fire. And, even though the bullet went into his ankle, he never realized he'd been shot. I'm sure if he had known he would have blown the driver completely out of his socks. Harvey had a shotgun and if he had fired it at that close range there wouldn't have been much left of the driver.

I was upset that Officer Harvey had been shot, but I was also very happy it was such a minor wound. I knew he'd recover completely. But, the second thing that happened bothered me tremendously and I wasn't able to put it out of my mind so easily. Someone from the Deerfield Beach Police Department called our supervisors at F.L.P.D. and complained about us using excessive force during the apprehension of the two suspects from the Chevelle. Our sergeant and lieutenant immediately drove to the hospital to talk to Dave and I about these new allegations. We told them what had happened and they both seemed to be satisfied with our explanations. They told us they were going to meet with the Deerfield officer who complained, right there at the hospital. We exited the hospital and to our amazement up walked Deerfield Beach Sergeant Stupid, the guy who had broken my right hand. Was this the guy who had complained about US being brutal?

I really couldn't believe my eyes! This Deerfield Beach police sergeant had tried to do the Mexican hat dance on the suspect's back, and in the process had stomped on my right hand by mistake, now this no-balls idiot had the nerve to accuse Dave and I of excessive force. This burned me up and I could hardly control myself. For one thing, it just wasn't true! I may have felt like beating the scum bag to a pulp, but I didn't! And, if there was one thing I couldn't stand it was a hypocrite. Worse still was a hypocrite with a badge! I watched as my sergeant and lieutenant entered their vehicle and took note of the fact they put Sergeant Stupid right there in the front seat between them. After about fifteen minutes all three men exited the police vehicle. The Deerfield sergeant hurriedly walked over to his own vehicle, got in and then drove off into the darkness. We never saw, or heard from him, again!

Our two supervisors came over to where Dave and I were standing and informed us Sergeant Stupid had decided to withdraw his original complaint. It turned out he had been worried about a possible riot occurring as a result of the apprehension of the two suspects. Both subjects were black, which had nothing at all to do with the crimes they committed, or the way WE treated them afterwards. I'm not a racist, and I never have been! I can't speak for the other officers actions there at the scene of the stop, but I know Dave and I wouldn't have treated the suspects differently, no matter what color they were. To Dave and I the race of these two individuals wasn't even an issue. But, because the chase finally terminated in a lower income section of Deerfield Beach, and the suspects were black, the Deerfield sergeant was concerned the people in the area might riot. He never admitted this to our supervisors, but he apparently decided if there were allegations of police brutality, and then civil unrest in the area, he wanted F.L.P.D to get the blame.

As Dave and I left the emergency room with our two prisoners, and we headed back south to Fort Lauderdale, I was glad to leave the City of Deerfield Beach behind us! Even so, this exciting, yet violent, incident had still been a tremendous learning experience for me, and for that I was grateful. After all; it had been my first high-speed chase, the first time I was shot at, the first time I fired my own weapon in self-defense, the first time I was involved in an incident resulting in another police officer being wounded, the first time I was injured myself, and finally, the first time I was accused of police brutality. Yes, I learned a great deal from this incident and I knew I would never be the same person again. I also hoped that at least some, and maybe even all, of these very valuable lessons would remain with me forever.

2

PURGATORY

I had the broken bone in my right hand set and then several days after the Deerfield Beach chase the penicillin I received caused an almost totally incapacitating pain deep within my lower back. I wasn't even able to get out of bed to go to the doctor. The doctor had to come to me. I may have been one of the last living people in the United States who actually got a doctor to make a house call. He gave me a quick shot of cortisone and this seemed to do the trick. At least for the time being. The pain left my back and after a few more days I was finally able to get out of bed. My problems were far from being over, however. For some mysterious reason, which no doctor has ever been able to explain to me, the penicillin reaction now invaded my right knee. It ballooned up to the size of a small cantaloupe and the doctor had to use a rather large needle to drain it of excessive fluid. This wasn't a pleasant experience.

On a positive note though, one very nice thing did happen to me as a result of the Deerfield pursuit. My partner Dave and I were both named Police Officers of the Month for July 1968. This was something brand new and as far as I could determine Dave and I were the very first Fort Lauderdale Police Officers to receive this prestigious award from our local F.O.P. lodge. It's now a honored tradition and each and every month some deserving F.L.P.D. officer receives this award. But, Dave and I can truthfully say we were the first! That alone made me very proud!

During the next few years I changed doctors several times, experimented with gold shots and continued to have my right knee aspirated on a regular basis. Several things were disturbing. For one thing, my condition wasn't getting any better. In fact, it was getting worse! The overall time period between aspirations was becoming less and less, and for some new unknown reason my left knee now also began to create excessive fluid in the knee joint. I'd heard of so-called "sympathetic pain," but this was ridiculous! In the end, I was having both knees done and after just a few short days of relief I'd be in severe pain and in need of the procedure again. It became an intolerable situation! I couldn't do my work properly and I also knew there was a definite "officer safety" issue involved here. I was trying to keep my medical condition a secret, but it wasn't easy. I dreaded the thought that I might someday be the cause of one of my brother officers being seriously injured because of my inability to perform and back them up adequately. There was really only one final solution and that, of course, involved having surgery.

On May 4, 1971, almost three full years after my initial injury, I had my first knee operation. My doctor was a respected orthopedic surgeon named Hall. Doctor Hall was good and he even had several Miami Dolphin football players as clients. I felt a little bit better knowing I had one of the best cutting on me. Doctor Hall's original Pre-Op. diagnosis was Rheumatoid Synovitis. For some unknown reason, the penicillin had caused my right knee to produce excessive amounts of synovial fluid. This joint fluid lubricated the knee. Doctor Hall intended to perform a Synovectomy. In plain layman's terms, this procedure involved the removal of the entire synovial sac where this fluid was usually produced and stored. I asked him how would I be able to get along without it. Doctor Hall gently reassured me, "I won't promise you'll be totally cured, but I will promise you'll be better off than you are today." That was just fine with me because I knew I was a mess and I knew I couldn't go on like this any longer.

When they opened my right knee up approximately 1500 ccs. of yellow colored joint fluid suddenly came gushing out. This fluid contained numerous bits of cartilage which shouldn't have been there. Doctor Hall's Operating Room Record read: *"The interior of the knee joint was inspected and found to be markedly destroyed with erosion of the joint cartilage of both the femur and the tibia to the point that there was very little normal appearing joint cartilage left. Unfortunately the cruciate ligament had been eroded away. The medial meniscus was torn asunder in two and a portion of it slipped back between the femur and the tibia and yet the knee despite this was not locked. The lateral semilunar was atretic, torn, ragged and grayish and fribable in character. The synovium was thrown into great folds and there was at least two lbs. of dark, red, villous, proliferative, thick synovium throughout going way up into the suppapatellar pouch extending up into the thigh and measuring somewhere about ¾'s of an inch to an inch in thickness in some areas. It enveloped everything."*

Doctor Hall began a tedious dissection of the anterior synovium, and a posterior synovectomy was done through a separate incision behind the medial collateral ligament. Every bit of synovial tissue was removed from the lateral compartment of the joint. The patella ("kneecap") was inspected and its undersurface was found to also be devoid of cartilage. Instead, it was covered with pannus which had eroded away the entire joint surface. According to Doctor Hall, *"The pannus was scraped away until we got down to raw bleeding bone and then the knee joint was irrigated with copious amount of Neomycin-Bacitracin solution."*

After the surgery was over Doctor Hall informed my wife Pat that I had tolerated the complicated procedure very well, despite its magnitude. I still had to go through the pain and suffering of therapy but I was confident the worst was finally behind me. I was wrong! Even with extensive therapy my right knee still did not respond to treatment. It remained stiff and rigid and every time I tried to bend the knee joint, even a little bit, it was extremely painful. I had visions of going through the rest of my police career like Marshal Dillon's Chester on "Gunsmoke." Doctor Hall's new diagnosis and recommendation was anything but encouraging. He felt certain my right knee was now infected and he suggested a new operation. Reluctantly, I agreed. I really had no other choice!

I must admit that prior to this second operation, as I lay there alone in that hospital bed, in a private room because of the infection in my right knee, I did have some serious thoughts about losing my leg. These weren't very pleasant thoughts and without a doubt this had to be the lowest point in my life. I flirted with bouts of depression more than once and sometimes even wondered if I'd be able to go on. Looking back now on this terrible experience I fully realize how blessed I was to have a woman like Pat as my wife. Pat and I had been married the year after my injury. It was a simple ceremony; Pat and I, the Justice of the Peace, and the man's wife as a witness. Pat was unaware she was getting damaged goods but I don't think it would have made any difference even if she had known. I definitely made out like a bandit and I know I got the better part of the deal. Pat was the best thing that ever happened to me!

One month after my first surgery I had my second operation on my right knee. When they opened up the previous 15 inch long incision they observed a massive hematoma. I suppose I should be just as grateful for what Doctor Hall did not find, as well as what he did see. Although there was definitely some infection, it was not out of control. There was no pus, no gross inflammation, and most important of all, it was treatable. There also didn't appear to be any new damage as a result of my previous condition. It didn't look like I'd be losing my leg after all. It was wonderful to be alive!

Then, unexpectedly, something else happened that totally demoralized me. One evening shortly after my second operation one of Doctor Hall's associates came to my room. Doctor Hall was unavailable so Doctor Pike was making his rounds for him. After he briefly looked at my chart we began to talk. He knew I was a police officer and he started asking me questions about law enforcement in general. It was a subject I loved to talk about and I enthusiastically tried to answer his many questions. I told him how much I enjoyed police work and how I was looking forward to the day when I would be able to return to my work.

Doctor Pike looked directly at me and in a somber and serious voice stated, "You know Gary, you'll never be able to be a police officer again. At least not on the road, doing what you did before."

I was devastated! I couldn't believe what Doctor Pike had just said. Before I could recover from my shock however, he told me to have a nice evening and then he left the room.

Once again my wife Pat came to the rescue and I looked forward to her daily visits. Young children weren't usually allowed inside the hospital rooms so my wife and our two girls would stand in the parking lot and wave. The hospital was a huge multi-story complex and I didn't even know if they knew which room I was in, but they eagerly waved anyway. Just seeing this made me feel better. Pat was also a very resourceful woman and with the help of one of the senior nurses, who happened to be married to one of our police captains, she was able to smuggle me a pizza on a few special occasions. There's nothing like a pepperoni and mushroom pizza to lift your spirits! After all, you can only eat so much hospital food.

After a lengthy stay in the hospital I returned home and tried to put my life and career back together again. I was still just barely able to hobble around on crutches and at times this created some very embarrassing moments for me. One day my wife got brave and she left me home alone with our youngest daughter Natalie while she went grocery shopping. We had a new dog in the house and unfortunately he wasn't completely house broken. Before I could get to him, to let him out of the house, he decided to take a dump right there in the middle of the living room. Luckily, it was a small dog, so it was an equally small dump! Even on crutches I believe I would have been able to handle things if only my daughter Natalie hadn't picked that exact same moment to wake up from her nap. Now Natalie, bless her little heart, was still young enough that she wasn't yet completely potty trained. Seeing the dog squatting there must have given her all the inspiration she needed because she quickly pulled down her panties and then she also left her own small contribution on the living room rug.

As I clumsily charged toward the dog to stop him my wooden crutches almost came out from under me. The dog immediately stopped squatting and started to run away. When I changed direction to go after Natalie, the dog must have interpreted this as a signal it was okay for him to continue doing what he was doing. He stopped, squatted and started to poop again. The same thing happened when I hobbled toward Natalie; she stopped squatting, moved to a new location, and then when I turned my attention back to the dog, she'd take another dump on the rug. This is how it went for at least the next five minutes, Natalie and the dog taking turns pooping on the living room rug.

I have to assume God has a sense of humor because at this same exact moment my sergeant and another officer happened to stop by my house to see how I was making out. This was nice of them, but under the circumstances, I really wish they hadn't. They knocked at the front door but with all of the commotion that was going on inside the residence I didn't hear them. The front door was slightly ajar and I guess when they heard my yelling they decided to investigate. After all, they were cops! They opened the door and there I was; dazed, out of breath, unshaven and looking like a damn bum, standing in a living room full of shit! And, of course, both Natalie and the dog were nowhere in sight.

"Gary, did we catch you at a bad time?" the sergeant said, as his eyes looked past me into the living room.

"No sir, not at all," I quickly replied. Yeah, right! Here I was standing in the middle of the biggest pile of toxic waste I had ever encountered and I was telling my sergeant everything was hunky-dory. He must have thought I had gone insane!

I eventually explained what had happened and the sergeant, the other officer, and I, all had a good laugh. Well, at least I laughed! I'm not really sure they bought my story because the dog never did show himself. I suspect he knew he had done wrong and he wasn't going to come out of hiding for anything. And, because of the mess in the living room I didn't invite them in either. They both seemed very content to just stand there outside. I learned from the sergeant that his unexpected visit was more than just a social call, he also needed to know when I thought I'd be able to come back to work. I was still extremely troubled by what Doctor Pike had told me about my never being a police officer again, but overall I considered myself to be a positive individual and I realized he was just expressing his own opinion. Even so, I knew I still wasn't able to go back to work right then, and this included any "light duty" assignments the department may have had in mind for me. As much as I wanted to, I knew I couldn't.

Eventually I did come back however, and for a period of time I worked inside our Communications Section. Even though I enjoyed answering the phones, and dispatching now and then, I still could not wait to get back out on the streets. It's really kind of hard for me to explain what the actual attraction is. Hell, most police officers I know don't even fully understand what it is that draws them like some magic magnet to police work. Is it the action? Maybe. It might also be the unique nature of the work itself. No two days are ever the same. Some days may be boring and uneventful, but there's always that thought in the back of your mind that something big may happen at any given moment. Whatever it was, I knew I was a street cop, and that's where I belonged - on the streets! And, when I was finally assigned back to Patrol that was one of the happiest days of my life!

Most smart people know immediately when they've made a mistake. It may be hard for them to admit it, but they still know it just the same. Almost from the very beginning my right knee let me know that I had come back to the road to soon. I was working the evening shift in Fort Lauderdale's north beach area and this section of the city was very active most of the time. There seemed to be a constant wave of suspicious subjects to check out, reckless drivers to stop, tickets to write and back-ups to be made. But, day-by-day, getting in and out of my patrol car, began to take a heavy toll on my right knee. It started hurting me more and more and I soon realized I'd have to do something about this. Once again, I was faced with an almost intolerable situation.

I met with my lieutenant, who just happened to be my first sergeant when I joined F.L.P.D. five years earlier. I advised him of my medical problem and reluctantly requested a transfer back inside to Communications. He seemed very sympathetic to my plight and I think he understood the extreme pain I was in. This pain however, wasn't just in my right knee. No, it was much, much worse than that. I was also hurting inside! Doctor Pike's terrible words now came back to me and I wondered if he had been right all along. Maybe I never would be a cop again, at least the way I wanted to be. I just couldn't imagine my spending the rest of my police career answering the phones and dispatching on the radio. Don't get me wrong, there's absolutely nothing wrong with either of these jobs and both are a vital link in the overall picture. The men and women who do this important work in Communications deserve much more praise and recognition than they usually receive and I don't mean to demean their dedicated efforts. It's just that I was a street cop and once that taste gets into your mouth you're never ever the same again! Once again, my morale hit rock bottom.

I tried to make the best of my self-imposed purgatory in Communications. I say self-imposed because I had been the one to request this assignment, because I knew I wasn't able to physically cut it out on the road. I probably could have fooled my sergeants and the lieutenant for who knows how long, but at what cost to myself and my fellow officers? It just wasn't worth the risk! I decided I would do the best job I could and I'd make the most of a bad situation. I also decided I wasn't going to waste time feeling sorry for myself. This negative emotion accomplished nothing! I had been a police officer long enough to know that there were many other people in the world who were much worse off than I was. I had a beautiful and caring wife, two lovely little girls and the satisfaction of knowing that I belonged to one of the best police departments in the State of Florida. No matter what happened, no one could ever take those things away from me.

I stayed in Communications for a little over a full year and during that time my right knee seemed to become stronger and more flexible with each passing day. I continued with my therapy, both at home and at a local center not far from my doctor's office, and I began to see the proverbial light at the end of the tunnel. I also tried to maintain a positive attitude and I kept telling myself that I would someday eventually return to the road. This time however, I didn't intend to repeat the same mistake I had made before. I wasn't going to request reassignment back to Patrol until I was 100% certain my right knee was ready. This wait-and-see what happens kind of attitude also helped me develop a trait I had never paid much attention to before; Patience! Now, I patiently waited for the day when I would be able to return to the road.

My eventual return to the Patrol Division came at a good time for me. Fort Lauderdale P.D. was growing and some new and exciting things were happening and I definitely wanted to be part of these important changes. Unfortunately, in a great many ways the law enforcement profession is exactly like the military and your overall reputation among your peers and your superiors can often make or break you. If they think of you as a self-starter, motivated, dedicated and reliable, then you're probably on the fast track and you'll eventually do very well. But, if you happen to get a negative label pinned on you, for whatever reason, then you might as well forget about any of the more prestigious assignments that periodically come along. It really isn't fair, but that's just the way it's always been. In my mind, I couldn't imagine a more negative or distasteful thought than for my fellow officers to think of me as a has-been cripple. So, for the next several years I worked extremely hard trying once again to establish a meaningful name for myself.

I'd always had a secret desire to be a detective. There's no doubt in my mind that Sergeant Joe Friday and "Dragnet" were at least partially responsible for this. During my youth I was a great fan of Joe and I could almost recite from memory key portions of his classic, "What is A Cop?" which he did on one of the "Dragnet" episodes. I was especially drawn to his very eloquent description of the modern police detective: *"Four years in uniform and you'll have the ability, the experience and maybe the desire to be a detective. If you like to fly by the seat of your pants, this is where you belong. For every crime that's committed, you've got three million suspects to choose from. Most of the time you'll have few facts and a lot of hunches. You'll run down leads that dead-end on you. You'll work all-night stakeouts that could last a week. You'll do leg work until you're sure you've talked to everybody in California....* "

I was born in Fresno, attended grammar school in Oakland, and even lived outside smoggy Los Angeles for one year, so Joe Friday's impressive speech totally convinced me! I wanted to be a detective and some day I knew I would be!

Wanting to be something and then actually reaching that goal are two different things. My overall job performance since my return to the Patrol Division had been consistently above average and I was routinely rated "Outstanding" in many other important areas. I began to regain some of the confidence I had previously lost as a result of my medical problems with my right knee. I felt I had a pretty good reputation as a hard worker so I wasn't embarrassed at all when I requested a transfer to the Detective Division. The first time I did this I didn't get it, but I didn't let this bother me because a more senior officer received the nod, and I knew he deserved the reassignment just as much as I did, if not more.

The second time my request for transfer was turned down was a little harder to take. The final decision had come down to one other officer and me, and one detective sergeant had even told me I was the favorite. When the other officer was picked I couldn't understand why. I was senior to him and as far as I could determine my overall work performance was also better than his too. When I asked for the reason why I was told it was because he wrote a very good report. I have to say with all honesty, this explanation really didn't cut it. One of my strong points has always been my report writing skills and I knew this was just an excuse. I now began to have some more doubts about myself. Was I viewed as a "gimp," a cripple, is that why I wasn't chosen? I hoped that wasn't the real reason why!

3

1968 – 1974

During the late 1960's, and then into the early 70's, Fort Lauderdale, Florida, experienced a rising crime rate disproportionate to its population (150,000). Major crimes increased 13 times faster than the city's population did. Between 1968 and 1973 violent crimes in the *"Venice of America"* skyrocketed an astonishing 140 percent! Meanwhile, the city's population rose only 13 percent during this same tumultuous period. Because of alarming statistics like this the United States Department of Justice and the Bureau of Criminal Justice, Planning and Assistance declared Fort Lauderdale a high crime rate area. This action enabled the city to become eligible for federal funds. This was the era of the federal grant and Uncle Sam's dollars were in great demand. Many police officers, myself included, were able to eventually earn college degrees thanks to this federal money. Now, Fort Lauderdale P.D., like almost every other police agency in the United States, wanted its share of this extremely lucrative pie.

In mid-1973 Fort Lauderdale made application to the Law Enforcement Assistance Administration (LEAA) for federal funds for the creation of a specific crime control unit to combat the crimes of robbery, burglary and street level narcotics. LEAA Grant 73-22-06 was approved and Fort Lauderdale's Tactical Impact Unit, known locally as T.I.U., was eventually created. Originally slated to begin operations in December of 1973, T.I.U. did not actually begin working together as a unit until the following year. But, before T.I.U. even hit the streets of Fort Lauderdale in February of 1974, many hours of detailed planning went into the creation and role of this unique unit. The City of Fort Lauderdale had a very real problem with the violent crime of robbery and our upper management decided this would be T.I.U.'s number one objective. Burglary and street level narcotics would also be targeted at times, but these other crimes would only be secondary considerations. Detailed computer analysis of overall crime patterns showed exactly what areas of the city the unit should target and special maps were prepared which identified these specific areas of importance. The entire T.I.U. concept sounded very appealing to me and I quickly decided if I couldn't be a detective, then I definitely wanted to be a part of this brand new unit. Career-wise, and satisfaction-wise, this was one of the best decisions I would ever make. It was also a decision that almost cost me my life a few times!

F.L.P.D. already had the people on board to do the job so we didn't ask the federal government for any extra manpower as part of our grant application. The LEAA Grant was basically an equipment type grant and the federal money would pay for all of the new unit's vehicles, as well as the rest of the sophisticated equipment we intended to purchase. Some of this new equipment included; small Honda motorcycles for surveillance work, night vision scopes, 35mm cameras, an electronic tracking system called a "Bird Dog" and state of the art laser-guided .22 caliber machine guns. Most of these things weren't cheap, but they were all vitally important if F.L.P.D.'s new tactical unit was to be a success.

With robbery, and even more specifically armed robbery of small businesses, the stated number one target of T.I.U., a new thinking had to be established as far as police weaponry was concerned. Experience with robbery impact programs in other cities; such as New York, Detroit and Los Angeles, clearly showed the potential for deadly force confrontations. An analysis of these other programs revealed that the use of deadly force may be employed in up to 76% of robbery responses when officers arrive while the culprit is still at the scene of the crime. Fort Lauderdale was fortunate to have a progressive minded Chief of Police named Leo F. Callahan to head its 412-man police department. Chief Callahan and his staff realized the necessity of providing T.I.U.'s officers with adequate weapons that would give the advantage to the officer, and not to the offender. What was required was a weapon more potent than the standard .38 cal. police revolver, one that would be more accurate than a 12-gauge shotgun, a weapon that would effectively neutralize a culprit if that need should arise, but one that would do so with a minimum amount of risk to the general public as a whole. That weapon was the "American 180"!

Chief Callahan requested approval for F.L.P.D. to purchase six of these .22 cal. machine guns. In these days of civil unrest, cries of police brutality, and a huge assortment of other complaints and gripes against the police, this was really a gutsy request. After all, not many police agencies in the 70's could boast about having modern laser-sighted machine guns in their arsenals. In fact, I believe Fort Lauderdale P.D. became one of the very first in Florida, if not the first, to have the "American 180" in its inventory. I always respected Chief Callahan for having the courage to provide his officers with the best possible weapons available. Many other chiefs wouldn't have done so, and would have merely said, "Make do with what you already have."

During my early years at F.L.P.D. I worked for a number of different supervisors. They all had their own individual quirks, mannerisms and styles and no two supervisors were ever the same. Most were very capable officers and a pleasure to work for. A few however, were downright incompetent and probably wouldn't know a real bad guy if he came up and introduced himself to them! I'm glad to say this type of supervisor always seemed to be in the minority. When the names of the three new T.I.U. supervisors were finally announced; Lieutenant Bob Burns,

Sergeants Joe Gerwens and Dan Vaniman, I was pleasantly surprised! In my opinion, these men were the best damn supervisors in the entire Fort Lauderdale Police Department. I knew Lieutenant Burns and Sergeant Gerwens quite well and had previously worked for each of them. Sergeant Vaniman was a newer supervisor, but had a very good reputation among the troops. If I could have picked any three supervisors, I would have picked these men. From that moment on I knew I was going to be very happy in my new assignment in T.I.U.

Of the three new T.I.U. supervisors I knew Sergeant Joe Gerwens the best. He had been my sergeant in both Patrol and Communications and now this would be the third time we'd be working together. Joe was a tall, well-built and handsome individual, with strong but rugged features that left no doubt at all about who was in charge. If there is such a thing, then he seemed to be a natural as a police sergeant. He was all the positive things I thought a good sergeant should be. As Joe briefed the twelve of us that first night in February, when we were all together as a unit for the very first time, I was ecstatic! It was truly an electrifying experience and we were all very excited about what lay ahead of us. After all, we were embarking on a brand new mission and we'd be doing things in a totally new and different way. Well, at least it would be different for F.L.P.D.

Sergeant Gerwens told us we'd be working almost exclusively out of uniform, in a variety of unmarked vehicles, and using the various pieces of new equipment the department had purchased for T.I.U. We would also be shielded from the normal police responsibility of handling routine calls for service. Instead, T.I.U. would implement a wide variety of countermeasures, some overt, most covert, in an effort to successfully impact the crimes of robbery, burglary and street level narcotics. One of the other things Joe stressed that very first day was that we should not

31

consider ourselves to be the "elite" of Fort Lauderdale P.D. We were indeed fortunate to be the initial members of a totally new and unique unit, and this was exciting! Even though we were going to be able to do many things most of our brother officers couldn't, that still didn't make us elite. Lucky seemed to be a much better word. In theory, I suppose what Joe had to say made a whole lot of sense. Most of us just happened to be in the right place at the right time and I'm not really sure we were chosen for any special reason other than we were warm bodies that were available. We were all members of Fort Lauderdale's regular Tactical Patrol Unit and this made it easy for the brass to merely transfer us from one specialized unit to another. Even though we were told not to think of ourselves as the elite, I'm sure every one of us felt that we were still definitely the best of the best. If a man didn't feel that way, then he really had no business being in T.I.U. in the first place!

Sergeant Gerwens also told us one other thing; no matter how great an arrest might be, we should not expect any written commendations or awards. It wasn't that our sergeants and the lieutenant were hard-hearted, lazy or just didn't care. They truly felt that this was the way it should be. After all, part of T.I.U.'s mandate was to crack down on the violent crime of armed robbery, so if a T.I.U. officer made an in-progress robbery arrest, he was just doing his job. Their feeling was that officers should not be commended for merely doing the job expected of them. In the beginning, this seemed to make sense to us and none of us protested their decision. For one thing, it wouldn't have done any good! But, more importantly, we were all volunteers and we were extremely proud to be part of this brand new unit. Commendations and awards were the last things we were thinking about.

Our first few months in T.I.U. were a definite learning experience. At least they were for me. My new partner was a young officer named Michael Gillo. Mike, who was boyishly good-looking, had been an M.P. in the Air Force before joining F.L.P.D. He told me he had held a "Top Secret" security clearance and some of his important duties had even included guarding nuclear weapons. His youthful appearance helped to conceal this past however and Mike looked more like your typical college student in Fort Lauderdale for the yearly "Spring Break" ritual. He was also a very meticulous individual and I would eventually come to envy his organizational and planning abilities and skills. If Uncle Sam had trusted him enough to guard our nation's most powerful and destructive weapons, I guess he'd do okay taking care of Momma Jones' only son!

Besides getting acquainted with my new partner Mike, I also had to learn about all the new equipment our unit received as a direct result of the federal grant. I have to admit, my previous assignments in Patrol, Communications and the Jail didn't do anything at all to prepare me for my new role in T.I.U. I had no knowledge at all about VARDA Alarms, night vision scopes or even machine guns. I had to learn about each new piece of equipment from scratch, but I definitely wasn't alone. Very few of T.I.U.'s initial members, and this included our two sergeants and lieutenant, had a working knowledge or even an understanding of these things. Therefore, we all learned about them together.

Perhaps most important of all, we also had to learn modern surveillance techniques. Again, I had very little previous experience doing this kind of police work. It's hard to follow some turkey around, especially without him knowing it, when you're driving a big ole black and white marked unit. Most bad guys have a tendency to see you. So, most of this learning about stakeouts and surveillances was accomplished by good old American on-the-job training. We'd see a suspicious looking individual, in a car or maybe even on foot, and we'd follow him. The first few times we did this we got burnt right away. But, as the man says, "Practice makes perfect!" Eventually, after many, many failures, and an equal number of disappointments, we became quite proficient at what we did.

Because our number one target was armed robberies we always sat on area convenience stores from the time we went on duty at 7:00 p.m., until the stores closed which was usually right around 11:00 p.m. Most of our new VARDA Alarms didn't arrive as scheduled and we had to make do without them. In an effort to cover as many stores as possible, in the beginning our supervisors had many of us working solo. There were always one or two teams roaming around in their unmarked vehicles, just in case we needed them for a surveillance, but most stakeouts were initially carried out by individual T.I.U. officers. One man, one store, became the general rule. These initial one-man stakeouts sometimes required us to be a little bit innovative. In addition to a shortage of working VARDAs we also unfortunately were missing a few of our unmarked vehicles. The car dealership hadn't shipped them yet. Because of this some of us were forced to use T.I.U.'s small Honda motorcycles for transportation to and from stakeout locations. On more than one occasion I putt-putted down busy major thoroughfares with my gun, radio and binoculars secretly hidden beneath an old army fatigue jacket I liked to wear. At one particular store, in the south end of the city, I hid the motorcycle in some bushes across the street, and then I took up my location in a large ficus tree in someone's back yard. When the people in the house finally spotted me, the gentleman who owned the residence came out and demanded to know what the hell I was doing in his favorite tree. Even when I told him who I was, and showed him my badge and police I.D. card, he didn't believe me. Why should he? After all, I looked like a bum! But, when I showed him my gun, radio and binoculars, he said I could stay in the tree for as long as I wanted.

Not all cops are cut out for stakeout duty. Sitting on stores all by yourself, with no one else to talk to for hours at a time, can drive some guys almost insane. You have to be a very patient individual if you're going to be successful and for many cops patience just doesn't come that easy. Maybe it's because most of us are use to a more hectic pace. For cops hectic is almost a normal condition and sitting around doing nothing seems like blasphemy. When you're pushing a marked unit around a busy zone on an evening shift you're normally going from call, to call, to call. Many nights, if things run true to form, you're damn lucky if you even get a chance to eat. All these things come into play and that's why some good cops can never quite adjust to doing stakeout duty. Some of the cops who do adjust however, find little diversions to help them pass the time. Take Officer Ray for example. One night he also had solo duty at an area store without a VARDA Alarm and he decided it might be better if he could watch the store from within, rather than from outside. With the clerk's permission he entered the store's cooler and that's were he stayed for the next three hours. I'm not sure if the cold finally began to take its toll on him, or what. I suspect he was just getting bored and he decided he needed to do something different to liven things up. So, when one unsuspecting customer opened the cooler door and reached in for a can of beer, Officer Ray's hand suddenly appeared out of nowhere and handed him an ice cold Budweiser. The poor guy almost shit his pants!

I've always felt I was at least a semi-patient person although I'm sure my wife Pat would dispute this statement if she were given the opportunity. Maybe I should say I was usually patient at work, but at home there were definitely times when I was a lot less tolerant. Anyway, I normally didn't have a problem doing most stakeouts. No matter how long they lasted.

Okay Officer, It's Decision Time!

(Situation #3)

You are staking out a convenience store in the southwest section of the city. You're alone and the store, which is only moderately busy, doesn't close for another two hours. You're bored and tired. You decide to do one of the following:

What is your answer? (put an "X" in the space in front of your answer)

☐ _____ I would leave the store and drive around the neighboring residential area looking for potential bad guys.

☐ _____ I would take the laser-sighted machine gun and then I would put the little red dot (laser beam) on an unsuspecting individual who is leaving the store. You do this just for laughs and the individual is never in any real danger.

☐ _____ I would ask my supervisor for relief.

☐ _____ I decide to bite the proverbial bullet. No matter how I feel I will stick it out until the store closes.

An analysis of this situation appears at the end of the book

(Do not go there until you have finished reading this chapter)

I admit it! When I got bored I sometimes was guilty of minor indiscretions. And, like Officer Ray and most of the other original members of T.I.U., I sometimes looked for ways to make the time pass more quickly. The American 180 Machine Gun was a new toy for all of us and its sophisticated laser sighting system sometimes provided us with a good source of entertainment, although that clearly was not its intended function. Once, when a really bad looking dude entered the store I was watching, I eagerly waited for him to do his thing. But, when he casually exited the store after making a small purchase, I couldn't resist the totally irrational urge to try the laser out on this unsuspecting subject. From my hidden point of observation across the street from the store, which happened to be behind a gas station, I carefully sighted the American 180 onto the man's chest. I watched with childish delight as the laser's red beam appeared as a dancing red dot on his white colored shirt. It took the man a few moments before he even noticed the red dot, but when he did he immediately tried to brush it off his chest as if it were some strange species of exotic insect. Then, when he couldn't get rid of the pesky little red dot with just one hand, he used both. I wish I had a camera to capture that moment. There this guy was, standing alone in front of this convenience store, his arms flailing wildly against his chest, as he desperately tried to get the small red dot off his shirt.

The American 180's laser sighting device only had two obvious disadvantages. For one thing, it was heavy and just a little bit cumbersome. But the 180 itself was rather light and easy to control, and overall the two pieces of equipment seemed to be a perfect match for one another. The second drawback was a potential liability, however. If you kept the laser beam on target for an extended period of time, the recipient could easily see where the red dot originated from. It really wasn't that hard to follow the red beam back to its point of origin. This is why I turned the laser system off after only a few seconds. I didn't want the man in front of the store to know where the red dot had come from. He now stood there motionless, almost as if he were worried that if he moved, the mysterious red aberration might suddenly reappear.

In every man's life there are a few things he might do differently if he got the chance. Most of these things probably would involve important or truly momentous events, but I suspect I'm not alone in wanting to change even some trivial or insignificant things I'm not really that proud of. Targeting that one poor soul in front of the store would probably be on my list of things not to do, if I had it to do over again. At the time it seemed like just a harmless prank, meant only to amuse me. In my defense I have to say the man never was in any real danger. My weapon had been secured in such a way that even though it was pointed in his direction, it could not have fired. I'm absolutely certain of that! Also, he never knew that a weapon was involved and the only thing he saw was that annoying little red dot. But, even though no Florida laws were apparently violated, I did violate department policy and I'm sure my supervisors wouldn't have viewed this matter lightly. In fact, in hindsight, I know I probably would have been kicked out of T.I.U. if my supervisors had known about this childish prank.

Even though we became quite proficient at following bad guys around without them knowing it, for the most part, T.I.U.'s first few months of operation were relatively unspectacular. There had been a few in-progress robberies, and we had made some good arrests as a result. But there weren't the almost nightly shootouts with crazed armed robbers most of us had envisioned when we joined the new unit! While a few of us, like my partner Mike, had already witnessed their first robbery in-progress, most of us, like me, hadn't. I knew it was a fact that most veteran police officers go through entire twenty-year careers and never witness a robbery from start to finish. I hoped that by being a part of T.I.U., that wouldn't hold true for me too.

4

MAY 31, 1974

While I patiently waited for MY first robbery in-progress my partner Mike was about to chalk up yet another one! He was staking out one of the many convenience stores located on busy S.W. 27th Avenue, a north/south artery connecting Davie Boulevard to the south, with Broward Boulevard one mile to the north. A lone black male had been acting suspiciously in the area, and while we all sat on our own individual stores, he was being followed around by the T.I.U. mobile units and our department's "Police" airplane which quietly circled overhead, at about 500 feet.

Fort Lauderdale P.D. had had an Aviation Unit since late 1969. Two enterprising F.L.P.D. officers were working off-duty for a local radio station, flying a Cessna 150 and giving out traffic reports to drivers on their way to work. One day these imaginative officers brought along one of the department's old portable police radios, which weighed right around 25 hefty pounds. F.L.P.D. ground units happened to get involved in a high speed pursuit and the two airborne officers quickly took the initiative and reported what they saw from the air. This helped the ground units tremendously and the suspects were eventually apprehended. F.L.P.D.'s Aviation Unit was born!

Now, as these airborne cops reported each and every turn this new bad guy made with his vehicle, our mobile units were able to easily follow along behind him at a discreet and totally unobserved distance. I think all our heartbeats quickened a notch or two when the pilots reported the suspect had now parked his vehicle one block to the west of the store and he had turned off his lights. Mike was located directly across the street from the store and when the bad guy came walking from the west Mike had no trouble at all spotting him. He watched as the suspect crossed 27th Avenue and then entered the convenience store, which was empty except for the lone female clerk.

"He's at the counter now!" Mike quickly advised. The bad guy had been in the store for only a few seconds and it was very apparent he didn't intend to waste any time at all.

We all knew the original game plan by heart. It didn't make sense for one of us to try and stop a robbery that was already in progress and we had all been told beforehand that we wouldn't take bad guys down until AFTER they had left the business. This way we eliminated the possibility a clerk might be hurt, killed or maybe even taken hostage.

"Okay," Mike began again, "he just walked away from the counter back into the store. Looks like he's looking around the aisles for something."

Right about this time Sergeant Dan Vaniman advised over the radio that after the robbery was over the bad guy would be allowed to get back to his vehicle before any attempt was made to take him down. These instructions weren't that clear though, and Dan offered this information only after the pilots overhead specifically asked about this. Sergeants Vaniman and Gerwens, along with several other T.I.U. officers, were apparently waiting for him at his vehicle. And, they intended to take him into custody when he returned to his car which was parked one block due west of the store.

I don't know if Mike heard what Sergeant Vaniman said about letting the bad guy get back to his vehicle. If he did hear it, he didn't reply. I must admit, I myself was a little bit surprised to hear these instructions. Here Mike was, directly across the street from the store, and when the bad guy came out of the store, he would have to let him go. It just didn't seem right! Most cops don't like to let dirt bags go for any reason and I think I knew Mike well enough to know this probably bothered him at least a little. But, I also knew he could probably disobey the sergeant's orders and get away with it too - if he really wanted to. All he'd have to say was the bad guy saw him so he had to go ahead and act. Our supervisors might not totally buy this explanation but they really wouldn't be able to prove otherwise. I've known a few officers who, I'm sure, would have purposely disregarded the sergeant's instructions. The overall temptation for glory would have been just to great for them to resist and they would have tried to take the subject down all by themselves. I also knew that this type of reckless one-on-one confrontation most likely would have resulted in a deadly shootout. As I continued to listen to the police radio I briefly wondered if Mike was considering this risky option.

I heard part of Mike's next transmission, but I don't think any of our other tac (tactical) guys did.

"Okay, looks like he's doing it...." Mike radioed, just as Sergeant Vaniman called to another Yankee unit, telling him what specific position he wanted him to cover. Mike was accidentally covered for several very important seconds, but then Dan and the other tac units stopped talking, and Mike's next transmission came across crystal clear.

"....you want him to get to the car, or you want me to take him sarge?"

"I want him to go to the car. Keep us advised. Is it going down, or what?"

It was very apparent Dan Vaniman hadn't heard Mike's first transmission that it looked like the bad guy was "doing it."

"10-4, it's going down! Do you want me to let him get to the car, or do you want me to take him?"

Sergeant Vaniman's voice was now very firm. "Let the culprit get to the car!"

"10-4, okay," Mike answered back without any hesitation. "He's bringing the clerk to the back room, her arms are in the air! Okay, he's coming to the front door. He's opening the front door, now he's coming out. He's running across 27th Avenue at this time. He's just going across the road, running." Even though Mike sounded calm and very much in control these were obviously tense and stressful moments and I knew the adrenaline had to be pumping, just a little! You'd never know it by his voice though. As he described each new move the suspect made he almost sounded like a sports announcer giving the play-by-play of a major league ballgame. Hell, I've heard sports announcers get more excited than Mike did!

Okay Officer, It's Decision Time!

(Situation #4)

If you were in Mike's situation and you just witnessed the subject robbing the store, what decision would you make? Obviously, the correct thing to do would be to follow the sergeant's orders, and let the lone robber go by you. But, be honest, what would YOU really do?

What is your answer? (put an "X" in the space in front of your answer)

❑ _____ I would follow the sergeant's orders (and let the subject get back to his vehicle where he could be arrested by the other tactical officers).

❑ _____ I would disobey the sergeant's orders (and take the subject into custody myself; later, I would tell the sergeant that I had to act because the suspect saw me).

❑ _____ I don't know what I would do under these circumstances.

An analysis of this situation appears at the end of the book

(Do <u>not</u> go there until you have finished reading this chapter)

When the bad guy exited the store and then ran westbound across 27th Avenue Mike remained totally concealed in his hiding place and he let the subject pass him by, just like Sergeant Vaniman had told him to do. I'm sure this was a difficult thing for Mike to do and it required restraint and self-control. It also showed me several other very important things about my new partner. First of all, because Mike followed orders, and he did exactly what Dan had instructed, it became quite obvious to me that Mike was more than willing to be a team player. If the T.I.U. concept was to be a total success, then all twelve of us would have to work together as one big team. There really wasn't any place for someone who was only interested in individual glory and accolades. Now, at least in my eyes, Mike had just passed this test with flying colors.

Mike also showed that he wasn't just another trigger happy cop out to blast someone. Unfortunately, when some police officers are involved in life-and-death situations, and are forced to use their weapons, this is exactly how some of the media unfairly portrays these officers. No, Mike wasn't just another violent cop looking for a good excuse to shoot someone! If he were, he had the prefect excuse right there on 27th Avenue. He had a real bonafide bad guy coming right at him, with a gun still in his hand, and a bag of money in the other. And, Mike, following his sergeant's orders, let him run away!

When the suspect finally arrived at his own vehicle, Sergeants Vaniman and Gerwens, and a bunch of other T.I.U. Yankee units, easily took him into custody. I imagine the bad guy was really surprised and probably didn't know what the hell hit him. What hit him was F.L.P.D.'s Tactical Impact Unit! May 31st also ended our first full quarter of operations. In his Quarterly Report Sergeant Gerwens stated, "During this quarter, a total of 11 persons were apprehended in the act of committing 6 separate armed robberies of locations unit personnel had staked out. It is also noteworthy that during these arrests, although the culprits were all armed and had just committed a robbery, the apprehensions were made without a shot being fired or anyone being injured."

Amen to that!

5

JULY 17, 1974

"Lafayette Drugs" was located only a few blocks west of downtown Fort Lauderdale and it had been burglarized many times before. So, when the dispatcher advised all units of a silent listening alarm at the drugstore my partner Mike and I both knew it probably was not a malfunction. Mike and I weren't that far away so we advised the dispatcher we would be responding. The business was located on the southeast corner of the busy intersection at S.W. 7th Avenue and 2nd Street. The front faced 7th Avenue, and the north side 2nd Street, but there wasn't that much traffic during these early morning hours right after midnight. The east side of the single story structure was a solid wall but there was also a side door at the south side too. I advised the dispatcher that we would cover the southwest corner of the drugstore when all units moved in. That way we'd be responsible for both the main entrance facing 7th Avenue and the side door at the south side as well. And, as with all drugstore listening alarms, we'd also pay very special attention to the building's roof. I don't know why, I guess it was the demonic lure of drugs, but drugstore roof jobs seemed to be in vogue during the summer of '74.

When all units were finally in position, and it really didn't take that long, the dispatcher gave the word to "Move in!" Mike and I pulled into the empty parking lot directly in front of the closed business and immediately observed that the front entrance area of the store was apparently all secure. But, when our vehicle's headlights lit up the south side portion of the building, we saw something entirely different. At the side door, at the south end of the rectangular shaped building, there was usually a small light left on at all times. That light was now out! We could also just barely make out the shadowy shapes of two subjects hiding there in the darkness. Both subjects appeared to be white males and at first glance it looked like they were working on the side door. When they saw our lights they momentarily froze. We were driving an unmarked vehicle and I suspect the two subjects hesitated because they weren't sure if we were the police coming to get'em, or maybe we were just some dumb tourist using the parking lot for a turnaround. It didn't take them very long to figure things out however, and after a few more seconds they took off running eastbound.

Both males ran through the backyards located directly behind the drugstore and its adjacent property, and even though Mike and I immediately exited our vehicle and started after them, we weren't able to catch them. They disappeared into the night and we really didn't know where they had gone. I don't know why the marked unit covering the northeast corner of the business didn't see them as they ran east, but for some reason he didn't. A perimeter was quickly set up and after we searched a few backyards on our own we waited for K-9 to arrive. As additional marked units poured into the area I became even more confident we'd eventually find these two guys. Mike returned to the drugstore and verified there had indeed been an attempt B&E at the south side door. He also waited there for the callout to arrive.

The two culprits from the attempt B&E at "Lafayette Drugs" were more than likely contained within a two block square area. We were almost positive they were hiding somewhere between 2nd Street to the north, and the New River two blocks to the South; 6th Avenue to the west, and 5th Avenue to the east. I showed K-9 Officer Hodges the last place Mike and I had seen the two suspects and that's where he and his trusty partner Rex began their track. Almost immediately the dog seemed to pick up the scent. He started off in that same direction pulling along Hodges who had him on a long lead. Hodges had to almost fight to maintain control of his dog. Rex seemed to want these guys almost as much as we did. Maybe even more! I suspected he envisioned a tasty meal at the end of the track. As Hodges and Rex disappeared from my view, entering the overgrown brush to the east of 6th Avenue, I knew from that moment on the two suspects were doomed!

The entire area was saturated with marked units so I decided to take up a post that had not been assigned to anyone else. At first I positioned myself near the southwest corner of the perimeter, but then when a uniformed officer wanted to check out a possible abandoned vehicle that was located just north of me, I advised the dispatcher I would back him. I knew I was an extra body and I could help most by filling in the gaps and providing back-ups as needed. After we checked out that suspicious vehicle, which turned out not to be involved in any way in our caper, I ended up near the northwest corner of the perimeter. That's when I first made contact with Sergeant Randy Richardson, the supervisor-in-charge of the K-9 unit. He was on foot, and without his dog.

By almost every standard I knew K-9 Sergeant Richardson was considered a capable and competent police supervisor. I didn't care for his overall style of leadership however, which was much more autocratic than I preferred. To me, he almost seemed like a dictator and the K-9 unit was his own personal Latin American country he could dominate. He didn't allow any disobedience and he also didn't allow any discussion or dissension as well. I knew Sergeant Richardson quite well and before he had been promoted to the rank of sergeant he had been one of the officers I had ridden with when I was a brand new rookie. I never will forget the day he gave a young boy on a bicycle a Juvenile Citation for riding his bike without a light on it. The one strange thing that stuck out in my mind was the fact it was only four o'clock in the afternoon and the sun was still shining brightly. After he had finished with the boy he gave me his own personal philosophy about police work. "An arrest a day, and a ticket a day, keeps the sergeant away," he offered smugly. I must admit, I never heard him say anything at all about making good quality arrests, or about writing meaningful tickets, and this bothered me. No, it wasn't just his rigid Draconian style of leadership I resented, it was also his somewhat perverted attitude about what made a cop a good cop. For these reasons I usually tried to avoid Sergeant Richardson whenever possible. I had never had any problems with the man, like some other officers had, and avoiding him seemed to be the smart thing to do.

Not long after K-9 Officer Hodges and Rex disappeared into the brush midway between 2nd Street and 2nd Court, Hodges came across the police radio all excited and apparently out of breath. He advised he now had one of the suspects spotted and he and Rex were moving towards that subject to attempt an apprehension. Even though he never specifically requested help or additional assistance the urgent tone of his voice clearly gave that impression. Sergeant Richardson immediately started running in a southeasterly direction through the backyards, and I ran south on 6th Avenue and then east on 2nd Court. If the suspect managed to elude Officer Hodges and his dog, and made it down to 2nd Court, then I'd be in a perfect position to cut him off. Or, at least, that was what I planned.

As I continued to run eastbound along the sidewalk on the north side of 2nd Court, I observed several other officers east of me also running towards Hodges' last estimated location. I wasn't sure, but I suspected these other officers had probably abandoned their perimeter positions to the east at 5th Avenue. Just then, as I got midway between 6th and 5th Avenues, Sergeant Richardson came out from between two houses. He was still running at full speed. He observed me and then slowed down. He asked me something like,

"Who's covering the west side?" He would later say I responded with, "No one." This isn't entirely accurate. For one thing, I didn't know for sure which units had left their perimeter positions to go to the aid of Officer Hodges, and which units had stayed put. The only officer I was almost certain did not leave his position was my partner Mike, who was still back at the drugstore. My reply to Sergeant Richardson was more like, "I don't know, maybe no one."

Sergeant Richardson told me to go back "there" just in case the second suspect, who was still unaccounted for, doubled back and tried to escape somewhere along the 6th Avenue side of the perimeter. When Sergeant Richardson told me this I admit I hesitated for a couple of seconds. Unfortunately, the K-9 sergeant interpreted this as an apparent intent on my part to resist his order. Nothing could have been farther from the truth! I merely was going to ask him if I shouldn't continue on to Hodges' location for a possible identification, because Mike and I were the only two officers to actually see the suspects. I wondered if the sergeant knew this. Even if Hodges apprehended the first suspect he and Rex were tracking, without a positive I.D. from Mike or I, the most he could be charged with was Prowling, not attempt B&E which is what they were actually guilty of.

Sergeant Richardson didn't give me a chance to say any of this however, and he once again told me to go back "there." Even though I had no idea at all where "there" was, I knew he meant somewhere along the 6th Avenue side of the perimeter. I did not say a word and instead turned around and began walking back to my previous position near the southwest corner of the perimeter. Sergeant Richardson was a supervisor and I would do as he instructed. I have never been one to argue with a sergeant and I wasn't about to start tonight. Even though I suspected he didn't know about Mike and I seeing the two suspects, he was right to want the west side of the perimeter covered. He was a sergeant, and that was good enough for me.

I arrived back at the corner of S.W. 6th Avenue and 2nd Court and then another T.I.U. Yankee unit advised the dispatcher he had just seen a subject walking in a northeasterly direction between the houses, going north from New River towards 2nd Court. He thought this might possibly be the second culprit. Officer Hodges and Sergeant Richardson had already taken the first suspect into custody and now I didn't know if they'd be able to also go after this second subject too. I doubted it.

<u>Okay Officer, It's Decision Time!</u>

(Situation #5)

The second suspect might be headed your way. The first culprit has already been taken into custody by the K-9 officers and you're not sure they'll be able to successfully intercept and apprehend this second subject too. What do you do?

What is your answer? (put an "X" in the space in front of your answer)

❏ _____ The main objective is to catch the bad guy, if possible. So, you forget about the minor verbal altercation with the K-9 sergeant and you move eastward along the sidewalk.

❏ _____ Because of the verbal altercation with the K-9 sergeant you decide to play it safe, and <u>not</u> to move at all. You realize by doing this you probably won't be able to make contact with the second suspect.

❏ _____ You attempt to raise the K-9 sergeant on the radio, to ask his permission to move east along the sidewalk.

An analysis of this situation appears at the end of the book

(Do <u>not</u> go there until you have finished reading this chapter)

I slowly began walking back eastbound on 2nd Court because I wanted to be in a position from which I could intercept this second subject, if possible. This is when my luck really turned shitty! I never did see this second subject but I did have the privilege of encountering Sergeant Richardson once again. As he, Officer Hodges, and his dog Rex, and some other officers headed southbound across 2nd Court, in search of this second suspect, Sergeant Richardson and I again crossed paths. I was standing very near the same spot where I had been before. He gave me that famous stern look that was almost his trademark. Seeing me near the same spot where we had had our original altercation, he apparently assumed I had not gone back to "there" as he had ordered me to do. He was wrong, of course, in making this assumption! I had gone back to the area where I had previously posted myself, so there was no way at all I had disobeyed him.

Back at the drugstore, after both subjects had been safely apprehended, and were on their way to jail, Sergeant Richardson took me aside. First of all, I was definitely grateful he decided to talk with me in private rather than belittle and humiliate me in front of my peers. There were a few other supervisors I knew who firmly believed in this kind of bloodless public execution, but I'd always thought this was an extremely piss poor way to make a point with a subordinate. Secondly, I fully expected to get my ass chewed out by the K-9 sergeant, not so much because I felt I had really done anything wrong, but because I just knew that was Sergeant Richardson's style. In the past I'd been told by people in the know, that it was probably best not to argue with him, or even disagree. He supposedly took this type of response as a negative and he viewed it as an indication the person he was chewing on couldn't take constructive criticism. I decided I'd follow this advice and I'd throw myself at his feet and beg for mercy.

Sergeant Richardson asked me why I didn't stay at my "post" like he told me to. He also lectured me about K-9 dogs being able to recognize police uniforms, but because I was in plain clothes the dog probably wouldn't know who I was, and he could very easily mistake me for a bad guy if he was let loose and the handler wasn't around. This made sense to me and I told Sergeant Richardson, "You're right!" The reason I said this was not because I felt I had done wrong by leaving my "post," but I did feel that Sergeant Richardson was correct about an officer out of uniform standing a good chance of getting bit. Even though it was quite apparent the K-9 sergeant was irritated I must admit he never shouted at me, threatened me or did any of the other nasty things I knew he was capable of. It appeared to me he was at least partially satisfied with my answers so I merely repeated two or three more times, "You're right!" I suspected the previous advice I received, about not arguing with him, was good. It appeared Sergeant Richardson would be happy with my groveling and this would be the end of the matter.

Before our meeting ended I also volunteered the information that I originally tried to go to Officer Hodges aid because the tone of his voice sounded as if he needed help, and I didn't know if he were alone or had some other officers with him. In the past I've been told I sometimes don't know when to shut up, and I say much more than I have to, or should. Unfortunately, this turned out to be one of these times. I went on to tell Sergeant Richardson I forgot that with a K-9 dog as a partner Officer Hodges probably didn't need any help. I suspect now, looking back on this last comment, Sergeant Richardson probably thought I meant this as a sarcastic remark. This, however, was not the case. I've always had a very high regard for our K-9 dogs and I've always felt they are the best possible back-up any man could ever have. This is all I was trying to say and I wasn't trying to be sarcastic.

When our meeting finally ended Sergeant Richardson didn't give me a clue about what he intended to do next. I knew he'd probably contact one of the two T.I.U. sergeants and let them know about this incident at "Lafayette Drugs". I really didn't have a problem with this because I realized police department protocol almost required this. As a courtesy he needed to let my sergeants know what had happened. I could figure that much out! But, because our meeting had ended on an almost cordial note, and the K-9 sergeant said nothing at all about pursuing things any further, I really believed in my own mind that this matter was closed. How wrong I was!

The K-9 sergeant did eventually meet with my T.I.U. supervisors. He told them what had happened, but I'm sure he gave them his version of the incident, and not mine. In reality however, our two versions weren't that different. The problem was Sergeant Richardson assumed I'd disobeyed him, when I hadn't! He also assumed my comments during our meeting at the drugstore were sarcastic, and again they weren't meant to be! He ended his meeting with my sergeants by telling them he hadn't made up his mind if he would pursue this matter any further. I quickly had my answer though, because the very next day Sergeant Richardson submitted a typed two-page letter to the Major of our Operations Bureau. The letter described how my "manner was sarcastic" and my "initial attitude was insubordinate, defiant and finally direct disobedience." I have to say I was really shocked when I read the sergeant's letter for the very first time. In fact, I had to read it again a second time because I couldn't believe some of the things he had said. True, I could see how he might have viewed my comments at the drugstore as being sarcastic, but insubordination? Defiance? Direct disobedience? These words were all alien to me! I had never, in my previous 7½ years as a Fort Lauderdale Police Officer, ever knowingly disobeyed a direct order of a superior officer. It just wasn't in my nature to do something like that. So how could

Sergeant Richardson be so wrong? Maybe I should have tried to explain my actions after all, I finally concluded.

T.I.U. Sergeant Dan Vaniman was one of the newer bred of F.L.P.D. police officers. He was college educated, intelligent and very smart. Past experience had shown me that a college education didn't necessarily mean a man would also be smart and intelligent too, but in Dan Vaniman's case he definitely had all three! Like the other T.I.U. Sergeant Joe Gerwens, Dan looked and acted the part of a supervisor too. Two days after this incident at "Lafayette Drugs" Sergeant Vaniman responded in writing to Sergeant Richardson's letter. I was now torn between two very different emotions. I was sorry Sergeant Vaniman had to get involved in this matter at all because I knew he had much better things to do with his valuable time. Yet, I was also extremely grateful for the thorough and conscientious manner in which he handled his part of this complaint against me. Point by specific point, Dan described in detail each and every thing that happened that morning, and why. I knew it wasn't something he enjoyed, disputing a fellow sergeant's judgment, but Dan Vaniman was a fair and objective individual. If he didn't believe something was right, he'd say so! I was very thankful for that!

At the beginning of this mess I was concerned about how my sergeants would view me after this matter was finally concluded. I hoped it would be resolved in my favor, of course, but I still worried that Sergeant Richardson's accusations might give my sergeants reason to doubt me in the future. This was another good example of maybe winning the battle, but then losing the war! I didn't want that to happen. Sergeant Vaniman's letter of rebuttal was four pages long, and when I finally read it, I realized my concerns were apparently unnecessary. Dan's closing comments almost read like a letter of commendation. He said, "I have been associated with Officer Jones for over one and a half years as a supervisor and he is one of the most professional obedient officers I have ever seen in my six and a half years as a policeman. Officer Jones is exemplar in his attitude and his outlook of the police profession. The man has never been insubordinate to any order, even in the slightest manner, and he in fact volunteers in many situations many policemen would not. His work in terms of quantity and quality is of the highest caliber. It is felt by this sergeant that Officer Jones would not be insubordinate to any order and that he has the highest regard for his superior officers."

I appreciated the complimentary things Sergeant Vaniman had to say and it was nice to know he apparently had such faith in me. Dan concluded his letter with the statement, "The charge of insubordination has not been proved against Officer Jones and it is requested that this matter be cleared as soon as possible for the sake of all parties involved." I couldn't have agreed more!

==

Shortly after I submitted my own letter of rebuttal, and Sergeant Vaniman submitted his, Sergeant Richardson withdrew his complaint and I never heard anything else about this matter.

6

JULY 21, 1974

As bad as July had already been, on this horrible Sunday morning, just four short days after the "Lafayette Drugs" fiasco, things got about as bad as they could ever get! Dimitri Walter Ilyankoff; devoted husband, father and a 15-year veteran of the Fort Lauderdale Police Department, was gunned down while working the day shift in the extreme north end of the city. This area of town, which included many affluent neighborhoods, was normally very quiet and relatively crime free during day shift hours. But today, during a botched robbery attempt at a Red Lobster restaurant on U.S. Highway #1, forty-year old Officer Walter Ilyankoff would pay the ultimate price. Walter had taken a sacred oath to protect and serve the citizens of Fort Lauderdale and now he would become the first police officer in the department's history to be shot and killed in the line of duty.

We never will know what was going through Walter Ilyankoff's mind as he exited his patrol car and walked towards the still closed restaurant. He had been dispatched reference a robbery in-progress and even though he acknowledged the call, he still approached the business with his gun securely holstered, and only a harmless looking clipboard in his hand. I guess he thought the robbery was already over, or maybe even a false alarm, and he was only there to take the police report. If, in fact, this is what Walter thought, he was very, very wrong! Two suspects had already fled the scene but they left behind an associate who was armed and desperate. When Walter opened the restaurant's door this twenty-year old black male, Alvin Bernard Ford, coldly and deliberately shot him twice. Walter fell to the

58

ground. One bullet pierced a lung, the other had grazed his diaphragm.

A female restaurant employee witnessed what happened next. She was hiding in a utility closet and watched everything through the narrow wooden slats in the door. Walter's wounds were very serious, but he was still able to transmit over the police radio clipped to the lapel of his uniform shirt.

"Help, help, help, I've been shot," he moaned weakly. "Help...I've been shot. Help...."

I'm sure no one who was working that morning, and who heard Walter's pathetic plea for help, will ever forget it! Over the years a few of my friends, men who were working that tragic day, have told me they sometimes still hear Walter's voice in their dreams. Even those of us who heard the tape much later won't ever forget those awful words and the way Walter said them. I know I won't! They'll be a part of me until the day I die!

After Walter's plea for help there was a great deal of confusion and initially no one seemed to know for sure which unit had transmitted that awful message. Precious seconds were lost as everyone scrambled about and tried to figure out who it had been, but even if they had known immediately it's doubtful anyone could have reached Walter in time to help him. According to the female employee, Alvin Ford walked over to the police car and when he saw the keys were missing, he walked back to where Officer Ilyankoff lay prone in the restaurant's parking lot. "Man, where are your keys?" Ford demanded. Walter said he didn't know.

Alvin Ford stripped Officer Ilyankoff of his police radio, car keys and .38 cal. revolver. And then, like some savage wild animal in the jungle, he put the barrel of the gun behind Walter's right ear and fired a single bullet into the wounded officer's brain. This was a cold-blooded act born out of hatred and it showed Ford's total disregard for the sanctity of human life. It was also unnecessary because Walter's chest wounds had already rendered him totally incapable of mounting any overt action against anyone. Walter was no longer a threat to him, but Ford still executed him anyway. Alvin Ford, who happened to be a former state prison guard himself, at the Union Correctional Institution at Raiford, was now a cop killer!

After Officer Ilyankoff's brutal murder Alvin Ford fled the scene in Walter's patrol car. He abandoned Walter's cruiser several miles away from the restaurant and then drove north to Gainesville in his girlfriend's green VW. Twelve hours later Ford was arrested outside his girlfriend's home in Gainesville. Both of Ford's associates were also apprehended and all three were charged with the murder of Fort Lauderdale Police Officer Walter Ilyankoff. It's often said that almost every adult remembers exactly where they were, and what they were doing, when they heard the startling news of the assassination of President John F. Kennedy. I would venture to say the same might also be true about the killing of Officer Walter Ilyankoff, although obviously on a somewhat lesser scale. I'd bet money most members of F.L.P.D. in 1974, regardless of their rank or stature, more than likely remembers exactly what they were doing when they heard the awful news about Walter's violent death. And, if they don't remember, they should! Walter Ilyankoff was one of us, he was one of Fort Lauderdale's finest, and the least he deserves is that we never forget how and why he died!

My family and I were spending an enjoyable summer day at Snyder Park when I first heard the terrible news about the death of Walter Ilyankoff. This large and beautiful city park had an old fashioned swimming hole as its centerpiece and my wife Pat and I liked coming here more than we did going to Fort Lauderdale's famous beach. I was standing in knee deep water, about ten or fifteen feet away from the park's manmade beach, when I looked up and saw Sergeant Dan Vaniman standing there in the water not to far away from us. He was also there with his family but I hadn't seen him until now. We made some small talk for a few seconds and then he suddenly asked me if I'd heard what happened to Walter Ilyankoff. I said, "No." That's when he told me the gruesome details.

I don't really remember much more about what happened there at Snyder Park but I don't think we stayed very much longer. The total impact of what Dan had told me really didn't hit me until we got home. I may have even been in a mild state of shock, I don't know. Walter Ilyankoff and I had never really been that close. Besides being way senior to me, he always worked different shifts than I did and we just never seemed to be around each other that much. This isn't to say I didn't know and respect the man, because I did! Compared to most other Broward County police agencies, Fort Lauderdale P.D. was a large department, but we weren't so large we didn't know and care about one another. I sadly remembered my last actual conversation with Walter. He had a personal problem he wanted me to help him with and I told him I'd take care of it for him. This wasn't that big of a deal. It didn't involve anything illegal, immoral or unethical. If it had, Walter would never have asked me to do it. I'm quite sure of that! No, this was just one cop doing another cop, a brother officer, a favor. Walter's last words to me were, "Kids, they'll break your heart." He said "Thanks," and that's the last time I talked with him. Now, he was gone.

Once we were home from our day at Snyder Park I sat down on the bed and asked Pat, "Why did they have to kill him? He couldn't have hurt them. He was already shot!" Pat didn't answer. What could she say? I was hurting and there was nothing at all she could do about it. No one could. Now, for one of the few times in my police career I cried like a baby and I'm not ashamed to say that I did. A brother officer was gone, senselessly. And, even though I wanted to know why, I knew there weren't any real answers. After all, this was a part of the dangerous job we had all chosen and it was a hazard we all faced on a daily basis. The bullet that killed Walter Ilyankoff had all our names on it - but today it just happened to find Walter.

That night I prayed for Walter and his family. I also thanked God for the many blessings He had given me, even though I may not have always realized it, or acknowledged them, at the time. I knew tomorrow would be a new day, and hopefully it would be a better day too. Then, I suddenly remembered what tomorrow was. July 22nd was our wedding anniversary and Pat and I had now been married for five wonderful years. Yes indeed, God's powerful and positive message promising us continued hope is not always obvious to us, and we often have to search for it!

==

The 1970's was the deadliest decade in modern law enforcement history and a total of 2,182 police officers died in the line of duty. 1974 was the deadliest year, and 268 officers, including Fort Lauderdale Police Officer Dimitri Walter Ilyankoff, lost their lives.

*   *   *   *   *

Alvin Bernard Ford was convicted of 1st Degree Murder and sentenced to die in Florida's electric chair. He cheated "Old Sparky" several times though, and in 1991 he died in prison of natural causes.

7

AUGUST 8, 1974

The sometimes boring one-man stakeouts were mostly just a thing of the past now. Mike and I almost always rode together as a team and so did most of the other members of T.I.U. We still concentrated our total efforts along and adjacent to Davie Boulevard, a major east/west artery in the southwest section of the city. From U.S. Hwy. #441, which was the city's westernmost boundary, to I-95 two miles to the east, there were at least a dozen different convenience stores we needed to watch. This smorgasbord of inviting targets was every hold-up man's dream come true. But, it was also an equally good hunting ground for us too!

The tragic death of Officer Walter Ilyankoff just a few weeks ago continued to haunt all of us. Outwardly, I'm sure we probably didn't show it, but this brutally heinous crime still bothered us just the same. Yet, even the worst disasters usually produce some infinitesimal good. It might be hard to find, and you may have to really search for it, but it's usually hidden there somewhere. I like to think Walter's sacrifice wasn't in vain and that we all eventually learned some valuable lessons as a result. I, for one, vowed never again to take anyone, or anything, for granted. True, this was often easier said than done. Also, I'm not a naturally violent person, and I don't really enjoy seeing others suffer, even if they might deserve it. But, after Walter's death I reminded myself that if it ever came down to a case of "me" or "them," if I had anything at all to say about it, "me" would definitely be the winner! I cherished my wife and two daughters and wanted to go home to them at the end of each night's work. I wasn't about to let some filthy scum bag take them away from me that easily, simply because I wasn't mentally prepared to do what I might have to do someday. No, Walter's death wasn't totally in vain! It had made me mad, and it had also made me just a little bit harder than I'd been before. I suspect many other F.L.P.D. officers, in and out of T.I.U., probably came away from this gut wrenching experience with these very same feelings. Now, I almost felt sorry for the next stupid slob who tried taking on a Fort Lauderdale cop. I was pretty sure he'd probably get much, much more than he bargained for!

It didn't take T.I.U. very long to find a couple of simple minded idiots who were apparently more than willing to test my theory about what would happen to the next poor soul who tried to take on one of Fort Lauderdale's finest. On this clear Thursday evening, right around 10:00 p.m., T.I.U. Officer Alan Brown observed two black male subjects in an early 70's model two-door Ford Torino, which appeared to be a goldish brown color. They were acting suspiciously at a drive-thru milk store located in about the 3400 block of Davie Boulevard. The Torino pulled up to the east side of the building, where the clerk couldn't see the car, and the passenger got out. He was a slim built individual apparently in his teens. While the driver pulled their vehicle up to the north side of the store, as if to make a purchase, the passenger stayed hidden there at the east side of the building. Just then several other vehicles pulled in behind the suspect's Torino and the driver drove off leaving the passenger still there on foot at the east side. It didn't appear as if the driver bought anything at all.

The Torino headed west on Davie and the passenger started walking in an easterly direction away from the store. As this subject walked, the Yankee unit watching him observed him to place some kind of an object into his right rear pant's pocket. They speculated that this might have been some sort of a weapon. The Torino made a U-turn on Davie and came back eastbound and picked up the subject who had been out on foot. They made another U-turn and now they headed back westbound, going towards U.S. Hwy. #441. At #441 the subjects made a right turn and headed north. Even though they were no longer in Fort Lauderdale, we still followed them anyway. If we had dropped them completely they could have easily returned to the city once again and we would have never known it. Also, it seemed obvious to all of us these two losers were definitely going to do it, and we all wanted to be there when they did! For statistical reasons it might have been nice if they did it in Fort Lauderdale, but we could really give a shit less where they finally decided to do their thing, just as long as they did do it somewhere! So, we continued to follow them north into the nearby City of Lauderhill. I have to give our three T.I.U. supervisors credit for not getting paranoid and for not Monday morning quarterbacking themselves even before anything actually happened. I knew all three of them were working, in fact Sergeant Vaniman and Lieutenant Burns were riding together. We never heard a negative peep out of any of them. Some sergeants I've known would have told us to stop the surveillance the minute we hit the city limits. They wouldn't have wanted to take the responsibility for allowing us to work outside our own jurisdiction, because in reality, we had absolutely no police powers outside Fort Lauderdale. In the City of Lauderhill we were just ordinary private citizens. Yeah right, we were private citizens toting HANDGUNS, SHOTGUNS and MACHINE GUNS!

We watched the two subjects as they once again cased a drive-thru milk store located just south of a large mall in the City of Lauderhill. This mall was on U.S. Hwy. #441. Now that we were out of our own city and in another jurisdiction Sergeant Vaniman asked the dispatcher to have Lauderhill P.D. respond to the area. He asked that several marked units be in the general area but that they stay completely out of sight. He also requested an unmarked Lauderhill detective unit respond to their location so our two departments would have better communications, and wouldn't have to relay every bit of information through our dispatchers. In almost no time at all a Lauderhill P.D. detective arrived at their location and he got into the unmarked rental car containing Sergeant Vaniman and Lieutenant Burns.

The subjects drove around the area a little bit more and then parked their Ford Torino on the north side of yet another convenience store. They exited their vehicle, got something out of the trunk, and then instead of going to the store as we all expected, they disappeared into a large multi-story apartment complex located directly behind the business. The Lauderhill detective with Sergeant Vaniman and the lieutenant advised that most of the people living in that complex were elderly. It was now approximately 10:30 p.m.

In addition to all the T.I.U. Yankee units and Lauderhill officers waiting for the two subjects to return to their vehicle, our always dependable aerial unit was also overhead. Around 11:05 p.m. the subjects came running back to their vehicle. Our police plane "Aerial 1" saw them running and immediately alerted the rest of us on the ground. Mike and I were located across the street from their vehicle in the mall's northernmost parking lot and we also saw them when they came running back to their car. Sergeant Vaniman rightly decided it was time to find out what they'd been up to and he gave the order to "move in" and stop the subject's vehicle before they could leave the area. But, when we heard the excessive squealing of tires, Mike and I both knew it was too late for that now. The subjects were already in their vehicle and moving! They quickly headed back to the main highway and then southbound on #441. A marked Lauderhill patrol unit was right behind them.

At first it didn't seem as if they were actually trying to get away from the Lauderhill marked unit and I don't think in the very beginning they even realized the police had been there watching them. They apparently had done something wrong at the apartment complex and now, like most amateur crooks, they were just trying to get away from the scene of the crime as quickly as possible. It didn't take them very long to become aware of the police presence, however. When you have one or two marked units right on your ass, and another three or four unmarked units also tagging along, all with their lights and sirens on, it doesn't really take a rocket scientist to realize the cops have something more in mind than just a quick donut and a cup of coffee.

Mike and I raced along almost recklessly through the mall parking lot in a frantic effort to cut the suspect's vehicle off. As their Torino headed south on #441 at a high rate of speed, we also headed south but through the mall's northern lot. If we could get far enough ahead of them we'd be able to get out onto #441 in front of them, and then hopefully stop them, or at the very least slow them down a little. Mike was driving and this is what he was trying to do. I must admit I wasn't totally thrilled by this prospect. For one thing, it's not that much fun being the passenger in a vehicle involved in a high-speed pursuit. You have absolutely no control at all over the vehicle and you'd just better pray that the driver knows what the hell he's doing. It's a strange and helpless feeling and only a cop who's been through it can really understand what I mean. So, as we continued south through the mall's huge parking lot, at an extremely high speed, I was at least thankful for the late hour and therefore the scarcity of any parked vehicles. I also crossed my fingers!

I never thought it was a good idea to get in front of any bad guy you were chasing, either on purpose, or by accident. You never knew what he might do. You might only be chasing him because he just ran a red light, but for all you know he might be "Jack the Ripper," and he may have just killed someone. When you pull in front of him you give him the edge and an easier first shot if he decides to take it. This is another reason why I wasn't that happy about our trying to cut these guys off. But, in the end it really didn't matter, because the two suspects in the Torino were easily walking away from our own Ford Torino that Mike and I were in. I guess not all Torinos are created equal!

The suspects headed south with the Lauderhill marked unit right behind them and behind the Lauderhill car was a T.I.U. unmarked vehicle containing Officers Al Smith and Bill Stewart. Mike and I, after our aborted bid to cut the suspects off, had fallen in behind Smith and Stewart. Behind us were a few more Lauderhill marked units and one or two other cars that we had no idea at all who was in them. The first major intersection south of the mall was busy Sunrise Boulevard and another T.I.U. car waited for the suspects there. Officer George Long and his partner Matt Palmieri had come up from the south and they were joining our party just a little bit late.

Upon reaching the intersection at Sunrise Boulevard the suspect vehicle made a right turn and headed west. If the suspects had gone east on Sunrise they would have gone back towards Fort Lauderdale, but now they were headed into the City of Plantation, a large and pretty community located just south of Lauderhill. We were far enough back that I really couldn't tell if Long and Palmieri had forced them to make this turn by blocking the road, or if the suspects turned west just because they wanted to. But, turn they did.

Just as the suspects made their right turn we heard an unmistakable series of quick "pops" which we immediately recognized as gunfire. It sounded to us as if it had come from the suspect's Torino. Al Smith would later say in his report, "The passenger in the culprit vehicle turned around in his seat facing toward the Lauderhill P.D. unit and a single round was fired from the culprit vehicle. It was at this point that the Lauderhill P.D. unit returned fire."

I'm not sure, but I believe this Lauderhill unit may have been a two-man car, so the passenger is probably the one who shot back. Bill Stewart wasn't as sure as his partner about where the gunfire originated. He also heard the first shot but didn't know if it had come from the bad guys or the Lauderhill unit. Bill later described what happened next, as the suspects continued westbound from #441. "The gunfire continued at a fast rate and it sounded from the rapidity of the shots that the police unit was in a running gunfight with the culprit vehicle."

As the suspects drove up the long entrance ramp to actually get onto Sunrise Boulevard itself, the observer in "Aerial 1" broadcast their direction and location. The Lauderhill marked unit was still on their tail, with Smith and Stewart right behind him. Long and Palmieri were now behind them. Mike and I almost brought up the rear, but there were still several more cars behind us. Another voice suddenly came across the police radio and I recognized it immediately. It was Sergeant Vaniman. The Lauderhill detective with them had just received word from his own dispatcher that the two suspects had committed an Aggravated Assault on a female while they had been away from their vehicle and out of our view at the apartment complex. Sergeant Vaniman relayed this information to the rest of us.

At the next intersection, which was N.W. 47th Avenue, the suspect's Torino made a left turn and headed back southbound once again. On the south side of Sunrise Boulevard there was a large and deep drainage canal, and this canal ran all the way from U.S. Hwy. #441 where they had first turned westbound, to Florida's Turnpike about another half mile to the west. Now, they crossed over the concrete bridge spanning this canal, which happened to be the only crossover for miles. I'm not sure they knew that and I don't think they even knew where they were going. They were just trying their best to get away from the police posse who were right on their ass.

They were now headed south on 47th Avenue but this road quickly turned into 8th Street. Then they were traveling back eastbound again. 8th Street was very short and dead ended into N.W. 46th Avenue and the subjects had to choose between going right or left. A right turn would have taken them south into a large residential area and they probably would have had a much better chance of getting away from us. They chose left however, and this took them north on 46th Avenue, backs towards the 47th Avenue bridge that spanned the large ditch on the south side of Sunrise Boulevard. This turned out to be a very bad decision on their part. It took them back north into an area that was quickly being flooded with additional patrol units. This is why I don't believe they knew where they were, or where they were going. It turned out I was right. We later learned both subjects were from Dania, another smaller jurisdiction due south of Fort Lauderdale.

46th Avenue stopped at N.W. 9th Street and the only thing the suspects could do was turn left onto 9th and head back towards 47th Avenue and the bridge. They couldn't go north because the avenue stopped, and besides they had that damn drainage ditch in front of them to contend with. To the right of the entire 800 block of 46th Avenue was a very large and vacant field and if they had wanted to bail out of their vehicle this would be the perfect place for them to do it. I was sure they didn't have a clue that "Aerial 1" was overhead reporting their every move. If they tried to flee on foot into the field I didn't think they stood a chance of getting away from "the eye in the sky". But, they didn't know about the police plane so I was surprised when they didn't even try.

They made the left onto 9th Street and headed back towards the 47th Avenue bridge. This time though, the bridge was blocked and they quickly realized it was impossible to go back north over the bridge to Sunrise Boulevard. The intersection ahead was also at least partially blocked by another unmarked unit so the Torino's driver suddenly left 9th Street and drove up into a closed gas station located there on the southeast corner of the intersection. Sergeant Vaniman, Lieutenant Burns and the Lauderhill detective were right there and had seen the Torino coming back westbound on 9th Street towards them at a high rate of speed, with their lights off. They quickly exited their own vehicle and sought cover. As the suspects drove recklessly through the gas station property, one of the two culprits fired off one more shot at the Lauderhill detective who was out on foot. The detective fired one shot back at them.

At this point in the pursuit, because we were behind the lead units, Mike and I weren't really a factor. As the subject's vehicle began to cut through the closed gas station we had just made the left turn off of 46th Avenue onto 9th street, and we were now heading westbound. I would estimate we were about two-tenths of a mile behind the fleeing Torino. I looked over to my right across the wide canal to Sunrise Boulevard and observed another marked unit running Code III parallel to us. Most of my attention was focused on what was happening there in front of us and I really didn't notice which jurisdiction the car belonged to. I assumed it was Lauderhill or Plantation, or maybe even B.S.O. I'm sure the two suspects in the Torino also probably saw it and this was just one more reason why they again turned south, instead of north.

"Aerial 1" continued to routinely report on the chase's location and direction even though these updates weren't really necessary. Unfortunately however, we weren't getting as much current information from the ground units actually involved in the pursuit. No one advised that the suspects had fired a shot at the Lauderhill detective at the gas station and that he had fired back at them. In fact, I don't believe anyone ever advised "Shots Fired!" - at any time during the lengthy pursuit. True, we all eventually became aware of this fact, either by personally witnessing it, or by hearing the shots going off. But, to my knowledge, no one ever transmitted this information over the police radio.

These comments aren't meant to be critical, even though they may sound like they are. I know there were a combination of different circumstances that contributed to this apparent lack of important information being put out. For one thing, the lead car in the chase was a Lauderhill P.D. marked unit and none of us, with the exception of Sergeant Vaniman and Lieutenant Burns, had direct radio contact with him. Also, it's not that damn easy driving at excessive speeds, talking on the radio and then maybe shooting your weapon accurately and safely, all at the same time. I know, because I've tried to do this myself a few times. It's not easy! So, sometimes talking on the radio has to take a back seat, and this may mean some officers involved might not always get all the information they'd like to have. If that's the way it has to be, then so be it! No one ever said this damn job would be easy or that things would always work out perfectly like they should. This is why most police departments spend a great deal of money looking for officer candidates who are capable of thinking for themselves. Police administrators want people who can evaluate whatever information might be available, men and women who can think logically, and who can then make good sound decisions based on the facts they know to be true at the time. I believed Mike and I fit into this category and were capable of doing this.

The subjects had made one large complete circle; first south on 47th Avenue, east on 8th Street, north on 46th Avenue and then back west on 9th Street to 47th Avenue again. I guess I was a little slow to realize this fact, but Mike wasn't. Because he was driving he seemed to know exactly where we were at in relationship to the bad guy's Torino. I have to admit it though, when he suddenly braked and pulled our car over to the side of the road, I immediately thought that he'd lost his mind. As the police car right behind us shot by us like a rocket I looked over at Mike in disbelief. For the life of me I couldn't figure out what he was doing. I know I had a shocked look on my face and I said something like, "Mike, what the hell are you doing? They're getting away!"

But, Mike knew exactly what he was doing, he just didn't have time to explain his actions in detail. As he whipped a quick U-turn and now we headed back eastbound on 9th Street, in the direction we had just come from, he exclaimed confidently, "They're coming back around!"

I suddenly realized what he was thinking. The suspects were now headed back south on 47th Avenue again. They'd have to go back east on 8th Street to the dead end intersection at 46th Avenue. There, like before on their first time around the circle, they'd have to turn either right or left. If we could get to the T-shaped intersection before they did we might just be able to block it and the chase would then be over. Smart guy, this Mike, I thought to myself! I was sorry I ever doubted him.

After we made the U-turn it didn't take us very long to travel the short distance back to 46th Avenue. We made a quick right turn and headed south. The suspect's Torino was just arriving at 46th Avenue and it immediately became apparent to both Mike and I that we had failed in our efforts to beat them to the intersection. Now, I knew they'd look north and see us, and then they'd turn south into the residential area. But, to my amazement, they once again turned left and headed back north on 46th Avenue. As they made this left turn I observed muzzle-like flashes coming from the driver's side of the Torino. I also heard what sounded like another shot being fired. They were now coming right at us! I noticed the Torino was still being driven without any lights. I suspected they had seen the large open field along the east side of 46th Avenue during their first time around the circle route, and now I figured this time they were going to bail out for sure. Nothing else really made sense.

The Torino continued coming north at a high rate of speed and at any second I expected them to stop the vehicle and bail out. I mean, they had to see Mike and I coming southbound towards them! We still had our portable Kojak-type light on our roof, lighting up the night with brilliant flashes of blue. But they didn't seem to be slowing down at all. It almost appeared as if they were playing a deadly game of chicken with us and they intended to keep on coming until one of us pulled over to the side of the road. I knew it wouldn't be us though, and now I really doubted that they intended to stop too. Mike must have realized this at about the same time I did because just as I clicked off my shotgun's safety and started to lift the weapon away from my lap, he yelled out, "Shoot'em!"

I could see the Lauderhill marked unit directly behind the suspect's Torino. One of my worst fears was that I might miss the bad guy's vehicle entirely and maybe even hit the Lauderhill officer's car by mistake. I definitely didn't want that to happen! Shooting from a moving vehicle, at a moving vehicle, was always a very tricky and risky situation. Mike had already started to brake and we were now slowing down even if the bad guys weren't. I impatiently waited for our vehicle to come to a complete stop, and with each fraction of a second that passed the suspect's Torino got closer and closer. When we had slowed down enough for me to safely get out of our car I opened my door and jumped. I believe our vehicle may have still been moving forward when I did this but I can't really be certain of this. All my attention was focused on the suspect's Torino which was now getting dangerously nearer. There didn't seem to be any question about it, they apparently intended to ram us if we didn't get out of their way.

Okay Officer, It's Decision Time!

(Situation #6)

This is a situation where the use of deadly force would obviously be justified. The two suspects reportedly committed an Aggravated Assault (a felony) and they are now resisting arrest with violence (also a felony). Shots have been fired by them and now they also appear to be using their vehicle as a weapon too. It seems as if they now intend to ram you. Even though your partner has told you to "Shoot'em!" - this awesome decision still rests with you, and you alone. Assuming you have a clear shot, would you fire your weapon?

What is your answer? (put an "X" in the space in front of your answer)

❑ _____ Yes! I would fire my weapon.

❑ _____ No! I would not fire at this time.

An analysis of this situation appears at the end of the book

(Do <u>not</u> go there until you have finished reading this chapter)

I quickly raised my departmental issued 12-gauge shotgun to my right shoulder and began to take aim. I knew I didn't have much time left. The suspect's Torino was no more than four or five car lengths away from us now.

Okay Officer, It's Decision Time!

(Situation #7)

Okay, the decision has been made that you will fire your weapon, which in this case is a 12-gauge pump-action shotgun. But, what is your target? Do you aim at the driver of the approaching Torino, who seems intent on either ramming or running you down? Do you aim at the passenger, who is probably the one doing most of the shooting from their vehicle? Or, do you take aim at the Torino's tires and try to disable the vehicle and thus bring this chase to an immediate halt? What do you shoot at?

What is your answer? (put an "X" in the space in front of your answer)

❑ _____ I would fire at the vehicle's tires.

❑ _____ I would fire at the vehicle's driver.

❑ _____ I would fire at the vehicle's passenger.

An analysis of this situation appears at the end of the book

(Do <u>not</u> go there until you have finished reading this chapter)

I put the shotgun's front sights on the Torino's windshield right in line with where I knew the driver's head would be located. In the movies the hero cop always shoots at the bad guy's tire and when he hits it the tire explodes into a million pieces. Well, that's Hollywood, but in real life things don't happen that way! If there was one lesson I had learned during my early years as a cop, it's that you can't kill a car. Sure, you can fill it up with lead, but it will usually keep on going until you actually take out the driver. The driver should always be the target, not the car itself. So, I wouldn't be taking any wasted shots at the vehicle's tires. That was for damn sure! If I had to use deadly force to protect Mike and I, I'd be aiming for the driver. It was as simple as that.

I didn't waste valuable time breathing in, holding my breath, or doing any of that other junk they always talk about at the range. I squeezed the trigger firmly and then the shotgun suddenly discharged. This first round was OO buck. Each OO buck round contained nine .33 caliber balls and this was more than enough to take the driver's head off. But, I had been in such a hurry to fire I apparently hadn't taken into account the Torino's forward movement. I aimed for the windshield but when the nine metal pellets reached their target an instant later the Torino had moved forward enough that they instead impacted on the post separating the windshield from the vehicle's front door. The blast blew a nice big hole into the door post. A few pieces of shrapnel, or maybe it was even just a stray pellet or two, entered the passenger compartment and hit the driver in the head. Even though he wasn't seriously wounded I guess he finally decided this was as good a time as any for him to say "Uncle!" – and he laid down prone across the front seat of his vehicle.

After I fired that first shot though, I had no way at all to know if I actually hit the driver. True, I no longer saw the bastard sitting up in the vehicle, but was he down because he was taking cover, or was he really hit? And, if I did hit him then how badly was he wounded? I quickly ejected the spent casing from the shotgun and racked a new round of OO buck into the weapon. As I did this I also moved towards the rear trunk area of our own vehicle. This was the same direction the suspect's vehicle was still going, although much slower now. By this time Mike had also exited our vehicle and he was standing in the middle of the street midway between both cars. The suspect's Torino continued to roll ahead slowly and now it was directly abreast of our car. Mike was so close to both vehicles he could have easily reached into either one and touched the steering wheel if he wanted to. He had his S&W 9mm automatic in his hand and then he pointed the weapon into the interior of the suspect's Torino and opened fire.

I lost track of the total number of rounds that Mike fired but it sounded as if he emptied his weapon. He had a Model 39 just like I had and I knew the weapon could carry one round ready in the chamber, and another eight in the magazine. I thought he fired all of them. Later, in his police report, Mike said he "fired seven quick shots" as the suspect's vehicle moved past him, almost hitting him as it went by. Sergeant Vaniman's report, which was completed as part of his supervisory responsibilities, mentioned that Mike fired a total of eight 9mm rounds. No matter how many rounds he fired, whether it was seven, or was it eight, I was quite sure he had probably hit the driver a number of times. I couldn't see how he could miss, not with him standing there by the driver's door, shooting straight down into the vehicle through the open window. His weapon was no more than three or four feet away from the suspect, and I was quite certain that Mike had taken him out.

When the suspect's Torino finally rolled to a complete stop, two things immediately happened; there was a great deal of confusion, and suddenly all hell broke loose! Some of this confusion obviously resulted from the belief the suspects were still shooting at us. Even with their vehicle now stopped, some civilian witnesses, as well as a few of the officers present, thought at least one more shot had been fired from inside the suspect's Torino.

Al Smith exited his unmarked car and was standing somewhere directly behind the Torino when he thought he witnessed another shot being fired from inside the suspect's now stopped vehicle. He was carrying a departmental issued shotgun and he "opened fire putting two rounds of OO buckshot through the back window of the vehicle." The Torino's rear window was completely blown out by these shotgun blasts. When Bill Stewart exited their vehicle he also witnessed another possible shot being fired by the suspects. He was carrying a small .38 caliber snub-nose revolver and he quickly fired off five rounds into the suspect's vehicle.

I was still partially concealed behind the trunk area of our vehicle when I heard the rapid-fire succession of more shots off to my right. I didn't know who it was at the time, but this was Smith and Stewart firing their weapons. I'd have to also say there seemed to be many more shots fired than just the ones eventually accounted for. I suspect a few more officers probably fired their weapons but then never admitted to it later. I don't think this was because they were worried about getting into trouble, because if ever a situation called for deadly force, this was it! No, they probably just didn't want to do the additional paperwork routinely required anytime an officer fires his weapon.

Even though I thought Mike more than likely finished off the driver, after I initially got a piece of him with my shotgun, I was still very much concerned about the passenger in the Torino. I suddenly sensed something go by me and immediately felt that this was another shot directed at me from the interior of the vehicle. Things were happening so damn fast it was hard to say what happened when. All I know is I still couldn't see either the driver or the passenger and I felt at least one of them was firing at me while they were crouched down and hidden in their seats. I quickly fired off three more rounds of OO buck through the driver's door open window. If I couldn't see my target, hopefully some of the buckshot would ricochet off the inside portion of the passenger's door and down into the interior of the passenger compartment itself. Some of these pellets should find their mark. After the three rounds of OO buck I fired off the last remaining round in my shotgun. This was a rifle slug and I tried to put it where it'd do the most good, into the engine of the Torino. I didn't want them to be able to drive off, just in case they might be thinking about doing this. One slug in the right place in the Ford's motor would make sure they wouldn't be able to.

After I emptied my shotgun I quickly put it down on the pavement and then I drew my own 9mm automatic. I started to move forward just a little towards the Torino but then I heard what sounded like yet another shot being fired from somewhere within the suspect's vehicle. I also felt something strike the little finger of my left hand and my immediate reaction was I'd been shot at and hit. My little finger had a very minor cut on it and it was also bleeding just a little. If I had been shot I knew my wound, if you could even call it that, wasn't serious. But, I wasn't about to just stand there and let the suspects have another whack at me. I quickly fired off three rounds from my 9mm automatic. Once again, I couldn't see what I was shooting at, I just hoped the bullets would ricochet around the interior of the vehicle and eventually strike a deserving target. I still heard more firing off to my right and although I didn't actually see any other officers, because all of my attention was focused straight ahead, I knew I wasn't alone.

Someone off to the right began yelling, "Cease fire! Hold your fire!" I'm not really sure who this was. I didn't know if this person might be a supervisor, or just another officer. I hesitated a second or two, wondering if he might know something the rest of us didn't. I also speculated that this individual, whoever he might be, probably just came up on the scene and saw all of us firing at what looked like an empty vehicle. He may have thought that everyone in the Torino was already dead, or he may have thought they somehow managed to get out of the car and had escaped. I thought about both of these possibilities and although I seriously doubted that they had been able to escape from the Torino without us knowing it, I realized they might indeed already be dead. After all, it wasn't as if we hadn't done our best to accommodate these two bad guys. Taking on any cop was always a very risky proposition, but in light of Walter Ilyankoff's brutal murder just a few weeks earlier, for these two clowns their actions against us had almost been downright suicidal! So, yes, maybe they were dead. And, yes, it was definitely time to find out.

I had been standing alongside the right rear area of our vehicle and the trunk portion provided me with a certain amount of cover. During most of this exchange of gunfire the trunk area had been between me and the driver's side of the bad guy's vehicle. Now however, something very strange had taken place. Even though I hadn't moved my position all that much while I was firing, the rear of our vehicle was no longer there in front of me. Mike was still out on foot and our car had apparently moved forward all by itself. I didn't even realize this until after the shooting had finally stopped. I later learned that when Mike originally exited our vehicle to shoot at the Torino's driver, he either failed to put it all the way into "Park," or for some unknown reason "Park" never fully engaged. This caused our vehicle to eventually roll forward.

I never witnessed this mighty act myself but Mike later told me that when our car started moving forward Bill Stewart tried to stop it all by himself, with just his brute strength. This would have been after he fired off his five shots at the suspect's vehicle. When Stewart saw our unattended vehicle heading his way he boldly got in front of it and in a valiant attempt even Hercules would be proud of he tried to hold our car back. He put himself into a spread eagle frisk-like position, with the palms of both of his hands up against the front of the hood of the runaway vehicle. His feet were firmly planted on the pavement and spread wide apart and he looked more like a prisoner being searched, than a cop! Mike said our car seemed to be winning this battle of strength and slowly but surely it pushed Stewart back. I don't know if he finally just gave up, or what, but our car did eventually roll all the way forward until it struck the unmarked unit Stewart and Smith had been operating.

Many of us began to yell for the two subjects to exit their vehicle. I still couldn't see either one of them and I thought they were both more than likely already dead. Or, at the very least, seriously wounded and therefore unable to comply with our orders. I was just a little bit startled when the driver's door began to slowly open. I couldn't see it from my own position at the driver's side of the Torino but the passenger's door also began to open slowly. Then, like a couple of sneaky serpents, they both slithered their way out of the vehicle and onto the ground. One second they were hidden deep within their own vehicle and the next second they were laying there prone in the dirt. That's how fast they got out. I guessed each decided it was now best if they didn't piss us off more than they already had. I'm sure that's why they slithered out of the Torino on their bellies, like snakes, instead of getting out and standing up like men!

The driver was handcuffed almost immediately but now the unruly passenger apparently changed his mind and decided he didn't want to be taken into custody after all. There were more than enough officers with the driver so I went around to the passenger side of the Torino and assisted in securing this little misfit. He was definitely outnumbered and I can't figure out why he suddenly decided to resist.

There was no way at all for him to win! You might think he probably got the shit beat out of him, but you'd be wrong! He didn't! We only used the force necessary to subdue this worthless creep, and nothing more!

When we looked at the subjects more closely we found that both of them had only very minor wounds. I suspected the driver's wound, which seemed to be just a graze, occurred back when I first fired my shotgun. Considering the fact I was trying my best to take his head off, I would have to say he was a very lucky young man! The passenger also had a minor wound to the head, most probably the result of a ricochet when all that angry lead had been flying around the interior of their vehicle. Again, a very lucky individual! I couldn't believe my eyes! I mean, we fired off more bullets than they did during the "Gunfight at the O.K. Corral," yet these two bad guys still managed to walk away alive. I'm sure Wyatt Earp rolled over in his grave.

Al Smith eventually detailed the damage to the suspect's Torino in his report. "In looking over the culprit vehicle the undersigned counted a total of 20 bullet holes in the body of the vehicle. Five of these were in the rear of the vehicle and the remainder along the left side. The rear window had been blown out by the shotgun blast from Smith's weapon, also the rear left passenger's window had been partly broken out. Also, the left rear tire was flat."

The only damage Smith failed to mention was the newly remodeled door post I had hit with that first round of OO buck from my shotgun. "Unbelievable," I thought to myself! If that had been me in that vehicle, or some other innocent soul, it would have been all over! We'd be dead! I never will understand how these two cretins managed to escape without any serious injuries. I guess it just wasn't their time to go!

We gave these guys some first aid at the scene and then shipped both of their asses off to the nearest hospital which happened to be in Plantation. We were later told that they both tried to escape from the hospital but that Plantation P.D. was right there and prevented them from doing this. Meanwhile, at the scene, we began the important task of protecting and collecting valuable evidence. George Long, who happened to be our unit's unofficial photographic expert, retrieved the 35mm camera he almost always carried, and he began taking crime scene photos of the vehicle and the scene. One thing that was immediately distressing to all of us was our failure to locate the suspect's weapon in, or around, the Torino. We all knew that shots had been fired, so where the hell was the damn gun! We couldn't find it!

I know some people might be skeptical and may even wonder if there really was a gun at all, or did we just make it up to cover our butts. But, the simple truth still remains that there were a number of civilians, who had been out on foot, who also witnessed the suspects firing out of their vehicle. It's my understanding that at least four different people heard shots being fired, and two even said the suspects fired at the marked Lauderhill P.D. unit chasing them. One witness, who happened to be an armed security guard at a large apartment complex there in the 800 block of 46th Avenue, even said the Torino's driver fired one round at him as they drove by. This guard drew his own six-shot revolver and pointed it towards the suspect's vehicle but then he observed a small boy in his way so he holstered his gun without firing a shot. I never personally met with this security guard and I think Al Smith is the one who eventually located and interviewed him. I admit, when I heard the guard's story it immediately sounded kind of fishy to me. They fired a shot at him as they drove by? Okay. A small boy got in his way and he couldn't return fire? Yeah, right! It sounded to me like our security guard was a frustrated cop in disguise and he had exaggerated just a wee bit. He'd have one hell of a story to tell his fellow guards, and maybe even his boss, that was for damn sure! But, I didn't want to completely discount what the guard had to say, because you never really know. As unlikely as his story sounded, it might just be true after all. Just like that damn phantom gun we couldn't locate.

Not being able to find the suspect's gun was bad enough but I also received another bit of news that was almost even more disturbing to me personally. After the shooting had stopped and the two subjects were finally taken into custody, this is when we learned that another civilian had been caught right in the middle of our stop of the Torino. When the suspects headed north on 46th Avenue that last time, and Mike and I headed south towards them, a small 1972 red colored VW was right there in front of them. This VW was being operated by a twenty-year old female. I never even saw this other vehicle! All my attention, and my emotions, were focused on the suspect's Torino. And, as I prepared to take that first shot, I apparently blocked everything else out of my mind. I'd heard of "tunnel-vision" before but never in my wildest dreams had I ever experienced something like this. There had been another vehicle, right there in front of me, and I never even saw it! I couldn't believe it!

The girl in the red VW had seen the approaching blue lights behind her so she started to pull over to the right side of the road to let these police cars pass. She must not have been in south Florida for very long because no one else ever seems to pull over when they see blue or red lights behind them. Anyway, after I fired off that first round, and it hit the Torino's driver's side door post, the suspect's vehicle slowed and then ran into the rear of this girl's now stopped VW. Then, that's when all hell broke loose! I have to say it again, because it seems so incredible, but I never saw this VW, not even after I got out of our own car and began firing at the two suspects still inside of their vehicle. All my attention was concentrated straight ahead and the only thing I was looking at was the interior of the Torino. That red VW could have been a World War II-era Sherman Tank and I still probably wouldn't have seen it!

The girl in the VW heard all of the shooting, of course, and she did the smart thing and she laid down flat across her front seat. Thank God, she wasn't hit by any of our rounds! I think she was probably safe from all of my fire though, because except for that first shotgun round I fired, all the rest of my shots were due east, directly at the Torino. At the time of the shooting I remember being pleasantly surprised by the fantastic line of fire that fate had presented to me. Directly behind the now stationary Torino was that very large and vacant field, the one I thought the suspects wanted to bail out in. So, even if any of my fire missed the Torino, it would have ended up in the dirt and the muck of the field. I couldn't have asked for a better backdrop for my fire.

The rest of the police fire however, which came from the south where Smith, Stewart and most of the other officers were located, was an entirely different matter. All these officers had been shooting to the north towards the rear of the Torino so any stray rounds that missed the suspect's vehicle could have easily found their way to the girl's VW. But, when we inspected her vehicle later we found only one possible bullet hole in her car's left rear fender. I wasn't sure I believed in miracles but if there is such a thing, then this young girl's brief encounter with, and her eventual escape from the dreaded Angel of Death, was truly a miracle!

I don't know when exactly our supervisors arrived at the scene of the stop but I'm almost certain they got there while the shooting was still in progress. One of the first things they mentioned to me was my failure to seek adequate cover even when it became apparent that we were being fired upon by the occupants of the Torino. They saw me standing there in the middle of the street blasting away at the Torino, apparently totally unconcerned about my own exposed vulnerability and safety. I knew they weren't being overall critical and they did have a valid point. Also, I fully understood the spirit in which they offered this constructive criticism. I really didn't have the heart to tell them the truth, but finally said, "Sergeant, I was behind cover. But then our vehicle rolled away all by itself and left me in the middle of the street alone."

They both looked at each other, smiled, shook their heads in apparent disbelief and then turned and walked away. I knew they believed me though, because no one would ever make up such a stupid excuse like that!

There are several different reasons why I'll always remember this one specific Thursday. In addition to being the date of our first T.I.U. shootout, there was another reason which was even more significant. I've always been a history buff of sorts, as well as an avid reader and follower of current events. I think it's important to know what's going on in the world so I like to read the newspaper every day and watch the news on television whenever possible. After the "Watergate" scandal became hot news back in June of 1972, President Richard Nixon's own knowledge and possible involvement became suspect. I'd voted for Richard Nixon in '72, but not in '68, so I was very much interested to learn if all these rumors and innuendoes were really true. These historic events eventually culminated during the first chaotic week of August. Thomas Jefferson reportedly once said, "Few politicians die, and none resign." This may have been true back in Tom's day, but no longer. On Thursday night, August 8, 1974, the same exact night as our violent encounter with the two suspects in the Torino, President Richard Nixon appeared on nationwide television and solemnly announced to the world, "I shall resign the presidency effective at noon tomorrow." Vice-President Gerald Ford, appointed to that office after Spiro T. Agnew resigned in disgrace in October of '73, would become our nation's 38th President.

No, I'd definitely remember this damn night for a long, long time! How could I ever forget it? History had been made; in our nation's capitol, by a fallen president; and in south Florida by the proud men of Fort Lauderdale P.D.'s Tactical Impact Unit! But, fate had a few more surprises in store for us, and somewhere in the not so distant future the men of T.I.U. would become a small part of President Gerald Ford's own personal history, and he would become a part of ours. It wouldn't happen for another year and a half, and it wouldn't be a truly historic event reported around the world, but it would indeed happen and T.I.U. would be there!

==

The original report of an Aggravated Assault had been incorrect. The two suspects had really committed a burglary, then raped and robbed a 72-year old female.

*   *   *   *   *

I eventually determined that the minor "wound" to my little finger had been caused by some flying glass from the suspect's vehicle. Mike was also hit by flying glass.

8

SEPTEMBER 15, 1974

I'm not really sure who spotted them first. It might have been Mike, or it could have been me. I don't know. What I do know is he and I seemed to work in almost perfect harmony and most of the time we'd spot suspicious activity at exactly the same moment. I don't know how we did it, but it happened quite often.

"See that?" I asked, as our unmarked vehicle passed by the *Little Giant* store located on the south side of busy Davie Boulevard. The small rectangular building seemed to be made entirely of brick and the north side of the store, which faced onto Davie, was a solid brick wall. So was the south side too. There were two drive-up lanes on the east and west sides of the building and the business catered almost exclusively to a clientele in vehicles.

"I see them," Mike answered back. The light colored Camaro slowly headed southbound away from Davie Boulevard, right alongside the westside of the store. They went down to the next cross street, about one block away, made a U-turn and headed back northbound toward Davie. Both of these subjects seemed to be watching the store very closely.

The night clerk at the *Little Giant* was a robust individual named Bob. On face value he looked like he could easily take care of himself during most normal situations. He wasn't mean or nasty but his large size seemed to say, "Don't mess with me!" We all knew none of this would matter during an actual hold up, however. Even a boy, with a gun in his hand, could be very dangerous. Bob wasn't a fool though, and we knew he wouldn't do anything stupid. In fact, we were quite certain during a robbery Bob would do exactly what the bad guy wanted him to do. What we didn't know however, was whether or not he'd go ahead and activate the store's VARDA Alarm while a robbery was still in progress, or would he do the smart thing, and the safe thing, and wait for the bad guy to leave before he went ahead and tripped the silent alarm. That was the one big question still left unanswered!

Most silent alarms go directly to an alarm company or some other similar monitoring facility. This information about a robbery in-progress is then relayed to the appropriate police agency. If the alarm company does this right away there's always the slim chance the police might just arrive in time to catch the bad guy in the act. But, if the alarm company delays making this important notification, for any reason at all, you can almost bet next month's paycheck the bad guy will be long gone by the time the first marked unit arrives at the scene. The *Little Giant* was equipped with one of our unit's new VARDA Alarms. These sophisticated alarms completely negated the need for an alarm company to be involved. As soon as the VARDA Alarm was activated a tape recorded message announced a robbery in-progress over the tactical channel on our hand held police radios. This gave us a definite edge over the bad guys. Now, when we responded to one of these alarms, we knew for sure the bad guy was still there, or that he had just left seconds before.

The initial VARDA Alarms T.I.U. set up in area con-venience stores unfortunately needed to be activated manually. The store clerks were all given little hand held devices so small they could even be concealed in the palm of their hand. These devices looked very much like small garage door openers. The clerks were told to keep these triggering devices in their pant's pocket and if a robbery did occur we asked them to press the button while the robbery was still in progress. They could do this by simply pressing their hand against the outside of the pant's pocket, and if they weren't to obvious about this, the bad guy shouldn't even notice this. In theory, this was all well and good. In the real world though, it wasn't that simple!

Most store clerks politely listened to our sales pitch and a few bold souls even promised that they would definitely activate their alarms while the bad guy was still there. But, we knew that asking someone to trigger a silent hold-up alarm, especially while they were staring down the barrel of a gun, was just a bit much to expect from the average American store clerk. To do so would require some real guts and we really didn't feel that most of them would follow through on their promises. After all, the money being stolen at gunpoint wasn't theirs, so why should they needlessly risk their lives? There was also one more consideration some of the clerks were obviously concerned about. They didn't want to press the alarm button and have us roll up while a robbery was still in progress because they knew they might get caught dead in the middle of a shootout between us and the bad guy. So, when we made unannounced spot inspections at the various VARDA locations we weren't that surprised when we observed many of the triggering devices laying in plain view on the counters near the store's cash register. We knew these clerks wouldn't press their VARDA Alarm triggers until after a robbery was over. These clerks intended to play it safe. And, although we were all a little disappointed, I think most of us really couldn't blame them. In fact, under similar circumstances, and if we weren't cops, we might even do the same thing.

Bob at the *Little Giant* seemed to be different from the other clerks. Whenever we came by his store to check on the VARDA he always had the trigger device on his person. Sometimes he'd put it in his shirt pocket, but most of the time he had it in his pant's pocket like we suggested. Bob listened to us and he paid attention to what we had to say. Once or twice he even asked if he could practice setting off the VARDA, by touching the trigger button through his pants, just to see if it would in fact work! It did! Of all the clerks who had VARDA Alarms in their stores, Bob was the one I would have bet on. I was sure he would trigger the alarm while a robbery was still in progress and I think Mike shared this feeling too. As the Camaro headed back towards the *Little Giant* I knew it wouldn't be long before we would finally find out for sure.

I happened to be driving and that automatically made Mike the radioman. We usually flip-flopped these duties every other night. The driver of the Camaro was going real slow and it was extremely hard to stay with them without being to obvious. Mike got on the radio and asked for any other T.I.U. Yankee unit in the Davie Boulevard area to assist us. Al Smith, and his partner Andrew Colorado, advised they were about a half mile away. They were at Davie and State Road #7 (#441), which was Fort Lauderdale's westernmost boundary in the southwest section of the city.

"Okay, start coming up to Davie and 35, by the *Little Giant*," Mike advised them. "We've got two black males in a black over lime green Camaro, it's about a '70 I guess, something like that, it's got wide tires. They've been driving by the store here, looking real good!"

"10-4," Smith quickly responded.

Mike continued. "Alright, right now they're pulling up in front of the *Little Giant*. This is about the second time they've been by it. Going real slow, approaching Davie Boulevard. Looks like they're gonna be headed east when they do make the turn."

At about this time we heard another voice on the radio softly advise, "Don't scare'em off." Mike and I both recognized the voice immediately. It was our lieutenant, Bob Burns.

We managed to get the Camaro's tag number before they pulled into an apartment complex parking lot directly across the street from the *Little Giant*.

"I don't think they belong there though," Mike advised the other T.I.U. units.

"Okay Mike, you take the car and we'll cover the store," Smith replied.

"They're going real slow through the Lisbon Manor Apartments' parking lot! They're just eyeing the heck out of that store! Where you at now?"

Smith and Colorado were only a couple of blocks away.

"Keep coming on Davie, we'll take the store," Mike advised. "They've seen us twice. So, keep coming up! They should be pulling out of the Lisbon Manor lot any second!"

But, instead of pulling out of the complex parking lot the subjects backed their vehicle into a parking space at the east end of the lot. This was about as far away from the store as they could get. The *Little Giant* was located closer to the west end of the large parking lot.

Smith asked again about who would cover the car and who would cover the store.

"Okay, we're parked in that field, we can see the car real good," Mike advised them. There was a large vacant field across the street from the eastern portion of the apartment complex and we had an excellent view of the Camaro and its two occupants.

Smith quickly responded back. "10-4, we'll try to get up on the store then."

"10-4, they're out of the car now, and they're walking through the parking lot."

Another solo Yankee unit was also in the area and he began to watch two other stores immediately to the west of the *Little Giant*, just in case the subjects from the Camaro decided to meander down that way. This was Officer James Dawson, Yankee-60.

"They're still walking through the parking lot west," Mike began to advise. "One's wearing a white t-shirt, and one's wearing a rust or orange colored t-shirt."

While Mike was talking to our T.I.U. Yankee units on the tactical channel I asked the dispatcher to advise all marked units to stay out of the area. She broadcast this message almost immediately. "KTU-206 to all units, all channels. Per Yankee-56, stay out of the area 3200 to 3300 block Davie. All marked units stay out of the area, 3200 to 3300 block Davie. 2110 hours."

The overwhelming majority of patrol officers usually tried their best to cooperate with us and I really can't think of even one example when an officer purposely entered an area after being told not to. Most officers realized we were working something important and we wouldn't ask them to stay out of an area unless we had a very good reason. Unfortunately, we couldn't always say the same for some of the district supervisors. I remember one specific patrol lieutenant who seemed to take it personally whenever we would ask his officers to stay out of an area. One time he even got on the radio and hotly demanded, "Who are they to tell my people they have to stay out of an area? If we want to go there, we will!" There was the usual amount of anonymous clicking on the radio after the lieutenant's brief outburst, but even though he had almost told his officers to defy us, we still didn't see any marked units in the area until after we were done. I guess, I'm glad to say, the lieutenant's officers had better sense than he did!

"You still got'em Mike?" Smith inquired.

"Yeah, they're stopped right by the pool area there, and they're talking to a subject over there, but they're looking all around."

We were still located on the south side of Davie, looking north across the boulevard. In addition to the traffic on Davie itself there were also numerous vehicles parked in the apartment complex lot. Because of this we had a little bit of trouble keeping an eye on the two subjects so Mike decided to get out on foot. I advised Smith and Colorado of this change. "Yankee-56 to 62. They're out of our sight again. Looks like they might be walking across the street to the *Little Giant*. Mike's gonna be out on foot walking up there and advise us."

"10-4," Smith replied. "Okay we're south of the store, about two houses, on the west side."

Yankee-60, Officer Dawson, advised us he was in position as well. He was about two blocks to the west.

"Okay, they're walking up to the store now!" I advised over the radio. I know my voice sounded excited, because I was! I didn't know it at the time but someone else tried to transmit at the same time as I did but for some unknown reason my transmission luckily covered them. "Jim, why don't you head over here and stop at their car," I continued. "It's at the extreme east end of the parking lot, by that entrance there."

"You want me to go down and cover the car?" Officer Dawson asked back.

Again, I didn't know it when I transmitted but several other officers also tried to talk when I did. "Yeah, why don't you go ahead, they're at the *Little Giant* now!"

"10-4," Dawson replied, "I'll head down there."

He never made it!

Mike and I were still due east of the store. So when the two subjects slowly walked up to the west side of the business we temporarily lost sight of them. We did have an excellent view of Bob the clerk, however. We had already pulled away from our previous position in the vacant field and now we were stopped in an open gas station located east of the store itself. The only thing between the gas station and Bob's store was a small empty parking lot for several other closed businesses. We could easily see into the store through an open sliding glass type door. Bob was standing there facing the cash register and his back was to the cooler behind him. We could also see the other open doorway to his left. We couldn't have asked for a better location. It was perfect!

The two subjects suddenly appeared there at the open doorway on Bob's left, at the opposite side of the building. Even though we could see them, they were still on the other side of the store and it was a little bit difficult to make out exactly what they were doing. There were also several things between us and the two subjects that partially blocked our view; such as the store's cash register, advertisement posters on the sliding doors, and yes, even big Bob himself! But, our view of Bob continued to be totally unobstructed. Even though we couldn't see all the actions of the two suspects, we were in an ideal location to observe Bob's reaction, if there was one. We were sure we'd know from his actions whether or not the two guys made a purchase, or if they went all the way and held him up. I still wondered if he'd press that VARDA trigger when the time actually came.

Even though I fully expected something like this to happen I was still a little surprised when Bob the clerk suddenly threw both his arms into the air high above his head. I mean, one second Bob was there all alone, with the two suspects out of sight; then they suddenly appeared and before you could even say, "Well shit, it's a hold-up!" - Bob was reaching for the ceiling! It happened just that fast! I didn't hear any VARDA however, but there was absolutely no doubt at all in my mind these two guys were committing a robbery. Unless Bob was reaching for a pack of cigarettes, that he maybe kept hidden in the store's ceiling, no other conclusion seemed even remotely plausible. Bob told us later that the subjects asked him for a $.60 pack of Kools and as he rang up the sale the taller of the two, a cocky kid named Roman, drew a small caliber, short barrel, blue steel revolver from his pocket. The second subject Lorenzo quickly removed the cash from the register. When Bob raised his hands into the air the two subjects told him to put them back down. Now I remembered my previous belief that I would have bet money that Bob would hit the VARDA during an actual robbery. I guess my intuition about Bob had been all wrong.

Okay Officer, It's Decision Time!

(Situation #8)

Even though Bob the clerk did <u>not</u> activate the silent hold-up alarm (the VARDA), as you thought he would, you are still 100% certain a robbery is in progress at his convenience store. What do you do next?

What is your answer? (put an "X" in the space in front of your answer)

❏ _____ I would wait for the two subjects to leave the store before I did anything. I wouldn't want to create a possible hostage type situation by moving in to soon.

❏ _____ Most robberies are over in less than one minute, so I would immediately advise all our units to "Move in!"

❏ _____ I would want the suspects to get back to their vehicle in the parking lot across the street, and then we could take them down there at their car.

An analysis of this situation appears at the end of the book

(Do <u>not</u> go there until you have finished reading this chapter)

"Okay, it's a 41!" I declared loudly over the police radio. A "41" was F.L.P.D. code for a robbery. "The guy's got his hands up! Okay, we're gonna move in on foot! Jim, get across the street on the parking lot!"

Several more units tried to talk but for whatever reason none of these other transmissions were understandable. I'm not really sure what Smith and Colorado saw from the west, in fact, I didn't even know for sure exactly where they were located. They may have also witnessed the robbery going down and tried to advise this over the radio, but got covered. I just didn't know. But, I did know that Mike and I were seeing something most ordinary street cops never get to see. We were watching an actual robbery in progress. Mike had seen a few before, of course, including the one when he had been all alone at that store on S.W. 27th Avenue. But this was my first experience being present at a real live robbery and I have to admit it was truly thrilling! It was almost like being on a Hollywood film stage and watching actors making a movie, except there wasn't anything make believe about what was happening there in front of us! This was definitely the real thing!

"It's a 41!" I repeated. "Let's move in!"

From start to finish the average robbery usually takes no more than one full minute to commit. From that first awful moment when a bad guy tells the victim to "Give it up, or else!" – until the time he flees the scene, no more than one minute usually elapses. The *Little Giant* robbery on Davie fit this stereotype perfectly. I had just barely gotten out of our car, and advised the other Yankee units of the robbery, and then it was suddenly over. One second the two bad guys were standing there with Bob, who had his hands in the air, demanding that he turn over the money to them, and then a moment later Bob was all by himself again, and they were gone!

Mike and I had no way at all of knowing what was happening there on the far west side of the store. We knew this was where the two subjects were located yet neither one of us could see this side of the building. We also knew Smith and Colorado were somewhere nearby and I truly expected to hear the magic sounds of gunfire any second now. But, just in case the suspects managed to elude our two guys on the opposite side of the building, I told myself I needed to be ready to expect the unexpected. Any second now Mike and I might be face to face with one, or maybe even both, of the suspects. Before I could really do much heavy thinking on this subject however, one lone suspect suddenly appeared at the far northwest corner of the store. This was the boy named Lorenzo. He seemed to be running at full speed away from the open doorway where he had been just moments before. He was running in a straight line north towards Davie Boulevard but heavy vehicular traffic prevented him from being able to immediately cross the street. The suspect turned right and now ran eastbound along the sidewalk located between Davie and the north brick wall of the store. He was now running towards Mike and I.

My first reaction upon seeing this guy was to wonder where his partner in crime was. I quickly scanned the area right behind him but I didn't see a second subject anywhere. There was no gunfire from the west side of the store so I assumed that Smith and Colorado had already taken the second suspect into custody. If not, then I knew they were either chasing him down, or fighting him! Either way, they were on their own, because Mike and I now had to deal with this suspect in front of us. As we both moved towards him we kept a good distance between us. If this guy was armed and decided to shoot it out, he might get one of us, but he wouldn't get both of us! I was sure of this!

I don't think he saw us right away, but when he did he again tried to cross Davie Boulevard. I'm not even sure he initially recognized Mike and I as being police officers, but there's no doubt about the fact he definitely saw the guns we were carrying. I had my Smith & Wesson 9mm automatic,

Model 39, in my right hand, and it was pointed directly at his head. He had to see it! I didn't see what Mike was doing but I was also sure he had the suspect in his sights too. Mike happened to be toting a nasty-looking shotgun. Whether this kid knew we were the police, or if he just thought we might be a couple of "do-gooders" really didn't matter. He wanted to get away from us whoever we were, and that's why he tried to cross Davie again. But, the traffic on Davie still seemed to be unusually heavy and he quickly gave up any more thought of trying to do this.

As he continued to run straight ahead directly at me I looked very hard at his hands but I didn't see any sign of a weapon. In his right hand he held a brown paper bag which I quickly assumed contained the so-called "fruits of the crime," but his other hand appeared to be completely empty. I began yelling for him to drop the bag and to put both of his hands into the air. At stressful times like this pure adrenaline seems to take over and you walk a very thin line; between being in complete control, and almost being out of control. Being out of control in pressure filled situations like these might sound bad, but it really doesn't have to be. This is when your basic instincts take over and you react almost spontaneously and without even thinking. Hopefully, you'll do things the way you've always been trained to do them, and if your training has been good, you'll usually do the right thing.

All my attention was now focused on that one individual directly there in front of me. Mike and I had moved close enough to the store that we were no longer on the gas station property. We were standing in the middle of the empty parking lot located between the store and the station. The lone suspect had also entered this lot and now there was only about fifteen or twenty feet separating us. As he ran he continued to hold onto the brown paper bag and he didn't put his hands in the air as we had ordered him to do. It suddenly dawned on me that he could easily have a small handgun in the paper bag and because of his apparent unwillingness to discard it, he now became a definite threat to both Mike and I.

<u>Okay Officer, It's Decision Time!</u>

(Situation #9)

You are convinced this lone suspect has just robbed the store and now you are face-to-face with him, and he doesn't seem ready to surrender. You've ordered him to drop the paper bag he's holding, but he hasn't done this either. You know there could easily be a handgun hidden inside the paper bag. What should you do next?

What is your answer? (put an "X" in the space in front of your answer)

❑ _____ I would retreat backwards away from the advancing suspect.

❑ _____ I would give him one more chance to surrender.

❑ _____ I would fire a warning shot in the air.

❑ _____ Because I believe he may have a gun in the paper bag, I would shoot the suspect.

An analysis of this situation appears at the end of the book

(Do <u>not</u> go there until you have finished reading this chapter)

If this suspect had made one wrong move, that I might have interpreted as a hostile act, I was ready to blast him! My finger was on the trigger and I was ready! But, one of the things that definitely saved this young man's life was the fact I just didn't see a gun anywhere. In addition to looking at the suspect's hands, I also looked at his eyes too. I immediately saw something that made me almost feel sorry for him. I saw fear in his eyes and it was very, very obvious. I'm sure he was terrified. He was probably convinced he was about to die. I also suspect he was just beginning to realize his luck had run out. He'd been caught, and if he didn't want to die for sure, he'd better give up. He dropped the paper bag to the pavement. I held my fire.

A few moments after the subject dropped the paper bag the police radio suddenly began transmitting. "Armed Robbery in-progress! Varda 8, Varda 8...." Bob the clerk had finally triggered the store's VARDA. He hit it immediately after the two subjects had left his store. It had taken several more seconds for the VARDA to activate itself and then transmit the taped message. As the VARDA continued to transmit, "Varda 8, Varda 8," the subject obediently dropped down to the pavement. We ordered him to lay down flat on his stomach, but he failed to do this. Most cops know that a bad guy laid out prone is always easier to control and this was why we wanted to put this guy into this position. Experienced crooks all seem to know this too and when they're caught they usually assume this position without too much coaxing. To resist usually meant we had to use force, or as some might call it, "a little friendly persuasion." Most bad guys who have been around the block a few times know this, so they normally did what we told them the very first time. But, this kid must have been a real amateur because he just sat down on his butt as if he was going to have a box lunch at a church picnic. Sorry kid, this isn't gonna be no picnic tonight!

Mike and I immediately started to move towards him, to forcibly put him down onto his stomach. But, then we heard the sounds of an approaching vehicle. We turned and observed Officer Dawson's unmarked vehicle headed eastbound on Davie at a high rate of speed. He was coming from the west where he had been positioned. Just before the robbery occurred I asked Jim to cover the suspect's vehicle in the apartment complex parking lot, but before he could get there the robbery went down. Now, Jim was hauling ass trying to get to us as fast as possible. He obviously wasn't aware the robbery was over, or that our bad guy was already in custody. Well, almost in custody!

When Jim Dawson arrived at the parking lot entrance he made a hard right turn and drove into the lot. Problem was he was still going way to fast. He may have also misjudged his overall speed and the distance needed for him to slow his vehicle down, and then stop it. I don't really believe Jim purposely intended to run our culprit down, but that's exactly what it looked like. Here was this poor soul, who couldn't even pull off a simple robbery without getting caught, and now this crazy driver from hell was aiming right for him! Our subject may not have even realized Jim was a police officer and probably thought that Jim was just another typical south Florida driver. Anyway, when he saw Jim's car coming towards him, he tried to scoot out of the way. He was smart enough to know he'd better not stand up if he knew what was good for him, but his survival instincts still told him he had to move, and move quick! Seeing him do the duck walk in high gear was a sight I'll never forget. It was priceless! He was moving his arms and legs as fast as he could, but his butt never ever left the pavement! It was one of those rare moments in law enforcement that makes all your other sacrifices seem almost worthwhile. Almost! When this little scene was finally over, and our bad guy was in custody, I was surprised to find he hadn't worn a hole in the seat of his pants.

Smith and Colorado had taken the first suspect into custody immediately after the robbery occurred. This had been the boy named Roman. When we advised over the radio that the robbery was going down both of the officers rushed towards the store. They got there at the west side of the store just as the subject Roman was exiting. As luck would have it, he still had his back to them. I say luck, because he also had a small caliber revolver in his right hand. If he had come face to face with our two guys, with a gun still in his hand, I'm pretty sure he probably would have been shot. So, this 16-year old punk was indeed lucky! When Smith and Colorado yelled for him to drop the gun he immediately stopped and threw the gun into the air, almost as if it had suddenly become red hot. They put him up against the wall of the building but for some stupid reason he tried to turn and get away from them. This resistance brought about a very predictable response; Colorado took the butt of his shotgun and hit the subject in the stomach, and in doing so broke the wooden stock of the shotgun. There was no further resistance from this guy!

Like Mike and I, Smith and Colorado had been able to successfully take their guy down without firing a single shot. I think there's a very important point that needs to be made here! Police officers are no different than anyone else. We have emotions, and we have feelings. And, when we're threatened we also can experience fear too! Any criminal can be violent, but a person who commits a robbery, especially with a weapon, can be the most dangerous and unpredictable felon of all. Officer Walter Ilyankoff's murder showed just how true this is! So, anytime we could take a robbery suspect into custody without having to use deadly force, I think we accomplished a great deal. I've never thought of myself as being judge, jury and executioner. That awesome task rightly belongs to someone else! But, if I have to, I will kill to defend myself and others! The two young culprits from the *Little Giant* robbery were still alive and well because the members of T.I.U. were all true professionals. We weren't blood thirsty killers and we didn't shoot if we didn't have to! That's the important statement these two robbery arrests made.

When we finally inspected the contents of the brown paper bag the subject Lorenzo had had in his possession, we learned what some foolish kids are apparently willing to risk their lives for. There were only coins in the bag; $17.20 to be precise, and this was all in quarters, except for two lonely dimes. Lorenzo also had another $59.00 stuffed into his left front pant's pocket. It was very obvious he had been in a hurry. One of the one dollar bills he had stolen was sticking almost all the way out of his pocket and he probably would have lost it before he reached their getaway vehicle, if we hadn't stopped him when we did.

==

Lorenzo, who had been unarmed during the robbery, received one (1) year in the Broward County Jail, and five (5) years probation.

* * * * *

The armed subject Roman, who said he found the .22 caliber handgun he used, in some woods near a park, didn't get off so lightly. After being Adjudicated Guilty, he received five (5) years at the Florida State Prison.

* * * * *

Under Florida's current, and stricter sentencing guidelines, the subject Roman would have been facing much more time. Under Florida's 10-20-LIFE, a felon who uses a gun to commit a crime, like an armed robbery, would face at least 10 years in the state prison.

9

JAY SMILEY

Jay Smiley was a young assistant state attorney with the Broward County State Attorney's Office. He worked in the S.A.O.'s Case Filing Division so most of us in T.I.U. were well acquainted with him. He was the main guy we usually saw when we tried to file one of our felony cases, and we saw him frequently. I don't think it's a secret that many veteran police officers dislike, or at the very least distrust, most of the lawyers they come into contact with. I'm sure that feeling is probably mutual too. But, in our eyes, Jay was one of the good guys. He was on our side, fighting alongside us in his own special way, trying to rid society of the filthy scum that was out there preying on the innocent and the helpless. You'll never get rich being an honest cop! The same can be said for being a prosecutor. Jay would never make the big bucks a high priced defense attorney could easily command. But, at least he'd always be able to sleep at night!

I don't know what made Jay decide to pursue a career as an attorney but I sensed there was a police officer hiding somewhere inside his body. Therefore, it didn't surprise me at all when he asked Mike and I if he could ride with us one night. We immediately said, "Yes!" We normally didn't want anyone riding with us, but Jay was different. Besides having someone to show off for, it wouldn't hurt for him to see what we were actually up against. He had to file many of our cases and most of the time there wasn't a problem. But, there had been a few times when Jay had been on the fence and he was having a difficult time deciding whether or not a particular case should be filed. If he rode with us he might get a different insight into the real world of police work. We concluded it couldn't hurt, it could only help!

Most of the night that Jay rode with us was boring and uneventful. That's the way it always seemed to be when you had an observer riding with you. Nothing at all ever seemed to happen! I had my own special theory about this phenomenon. Most observers seemed to bring about a definite lack of action. So, why not put observers in every Fort Lauderdale Police car, then there wouldn't be anymore crime! Yeah, right! It was frustrating, though. We wanted to show Jay exactly how we worked. We wanted him to see how we performed under pressure. We wanted him to see us at our best. But, unfortunately for us, lady luck wasn't cooperating tonight! I guess we should have considered ourselves lucky, though. But like fools, who didn't know how good they had it, Mike and I continued to dig and dig, until we came up with something! That something eventually turned into a real piece of shit!

The car and the people in it appeared suspicious and our sixth sense told us we should check them out. We tried stopping them inside the city but before we knew it they had continued westbound into the county. They eventually pulled into an open McDonald's located just a few blocks west of the city limits. Maybe they were having a "Big Mac Attack" I thought to myself. The people in the car spoke very little English and to my untrained ear they sounded like Haitians. It was extremely hard getting them to understand even the basics. "Driver's license? Registration?" These questions weren't that hard! We began to suspect the subjects were probably illegal aliens and when we started asking them for their immigration papers and green cards, their understanding of the English language suddenly became non-existent!

One of the first marked units to arrive as a back-up was driven by Fort Lauderdale Police Officer MacKinley Smith.

This black patrolman was an ex-Marine, and a Vietnam Vet. I didn't know much about Officer Smith but it was very obvious he kept himself in good physical condition. I'd also heard from others that he didn't mind getting into a scrap now and then, and he didn't take shit from anyone! He was just your typical ex-Marine! To be quite honest though, I was extremely happy to have him here with us. By his mere presence alone I hoped we'd be able to prevent any problems from developing. Unfortunately however, this isn't what happened. One of the subjects we were questioning suddenly bolted and took off running in a westbound direction.

After I overcame my initial shock I started off in pursuit of this guy even though I knew there wasn't one chance in a million I'd be able to catch him. He had too much of a head start and with my bum knee slowing me down I knew I'd catch a cold before I'd catch him! I sensed there was someone else running alongside me to my right and when I glanced over in that direction I saw it was our observer Jay Smiley. "Good boy, Jay!" I thought to myself. The cop hidden inside of him had finally been able to escape! He had a smile on his face and I knew he was really enjoying this shit. As I struggled to merely keep pace with Jay I suddenly realized how much I wasn't enjoying this shit! The bad guy had run all the way to the end of the block and now he cut to the south towards the street behind the McDonald's. There were quite a few two-story apartment buildings located on the north side of this other street and a high chain link fence separated McDonald's and the apartment buildings. The fleeing suspect apparently was trying to get to the other side of this fence which ran the entire length of the block. I suspected he hoped he'd be able to lose us at the apartment buildings.

I'm not really sure what Mike did during all of this but I think he stayed with the remaining suspects we had stopped. After all, someone had to stay with them and their vehicle.

At first I thought that Officer Smith had also stayed with them too, but then he suddenly passed me. He was running at full speed and he made Jay and I look like we were almost standing still. It was embarrassing! I mean, I was huffing and puffing, and almost ready to pass out, and here comes super cop right by me! Now I knew I definitely wasn't gonna catch this bad guy, but it began to appear as if Officer Smith might! He was fast enough, that was for damn sure!

The fleeing suspect reached the end of the fence and then he cut back to the east. He was now running behind the apartment buildings and for the time being we could still see him. I knew he'd cut back south between the buildings the first chance he had and then he'd be gone. Officer Smith had also turned the corner at the end of the fence and now he too was running eastbound behind the apartments. Even though MacKinley seemed to be steadily gaining on the subject I still wasn't sure he'd be able to catch him before he got to a point where he could cut back south between the buildings.

Okay Officer, It's Decision Time!

(Situation #10)

The fleeing subject seems to be getting away and you're not sure if Officer Smith will be able to catch him before he turns south and disappears into the nearby apartment buildings. What should you do next?

What is your answer? (put an "X" in the space in front of your answer)

❑ _____ I know I can't catch the suspect, and Officer Smith is still way ahead of me, so I stop running and return to the suspect's vehicle where my partner is waiting.

❑ _____ I would continue to chase after the suspect, and Officer Smith who is behind him, but I would do nothing else at this time.

❑ _____ I would fire a warning shot in the air (to warn the subject that he should stop).

❑ _____ Fearing the subject could be armed, and this would make him a definite threat to anyone else he encounters, I would shoot him.

An analysis of this situation appears at the end of the book

(Do not go there until you have finished reading this chapter)

Suddenly, to my horror, I heard the distinctive sound of one single shot being fired. My first reaction was to think that the fleeing subject had just fired a weapon. That, of course, was the logical thing to assume. But, in all honesty, I couldn't see how he could have done this. I still had a fairly good view of the suspect as he continued to run at full speed. He had his back to Officer Smith and he was still running away from him. I never did see him turn around. It seemed unlikely he would fire a gun over his shoulder as he ran, without first taking aim. But, this job taught me long ago that anything's possible! If something was humanly possible, then somewhere there'd be a bad guy who would do it if he got the chance. So, I didn't totally discount this scenario completely.

I didn't have much time to think about all of this, however. A split second after I heard the shot Officer Smith suddenly collapsed and he fell to the ground. It was almost as if he had been cut down in mid-stride. One second he was running at full speed and gaining on the fleeing individual, then the next instant he was down on the ground. "My God!" I thought to myself. "The bastard shot him!" I already had my own gun out and immediately thought about shooting back at this guy but then before I could take aim and pull the trigger he disappeared from my view. Just as I had feared he reached an open area between two of the buildings and cut back south towards the street. As I turned the corner at the fence I observed Jay there right beside me. He had his own gun out and it looked like a small snub-nose revolver. I was impressed! Jay hadn't given up either.

It took Jay and I a few more seconds to reach Officer Smith. He was laying there on the ground apparently semi-conscious and obviously in a great deal of pain. I immediately called for an ambulance and then began to examine him. I was looking for a bullet wound but I couldn't fine one. Mac could barely speak but when I asked him if he'd been shot he indicated he hadn't. At first, I was totally baffled and I couldn't figure out what had happened. But then, we eventually determined he had tripped over a telephone pole guide wire. The backyard area of these apartment buildings was extremely dark and as MacKinley chased after the suspect he apparently never even saw the thin wire there in front of him. He hit it and went flying. The bad guy either saw the wire and somehow avoided it, or had been just plain lucky and missed it. Officer Smith however, wasn't so fortunate. The shock to his body when he hit that wire was like being struck by a lightening bolt. Extreme pain shot through ever inch of his body and he momentarily lost consciousness.

Now I had a new and even bigger problem to worry about. If the bad guy we were chasing didn't shoot at Officer Smith, then who the hell fired that one shot? "A sniper?" I asked myself. I began to wonder about this possibility when I suddenly realized there was one other explanation right there in front of me. I turned and looked at our observer Jay. He no longer had that shit-eating grin on his face and now he even looked just a little bit concerned. When no one else was around to hear us he quietly advised me he had been the one who had fired. My initial reaction can best be described as total bewilderment! Jay and I had been running side by side and we had both witnessed the same set of circumstances. As far as I could tell there was absolutely no justification at all for the use of deadly force. So, why had Jay fired? I decided I'd give him the benefit of the doubt. Maybe he saw something I didn't and this was why he felt the need to fire. Maybe?

"Gary, let me ask you something," Jay began somewhat meekly. "My firing that shot, was that justified?"
"Shit!" I thought to myself. This guy was an assistant state attorney! He filed felony cases every day! Now, he was asking me, a puny little police officer, if his actions were justified. Damn, if he had to ask, they weren't! I suspected he already knew that though. I tried to think of a diplomatic

way of saying what I wanted to say, but there really wasn't one.

"Jay, according to our use of force policy we weren't able to fire our weapons. We didn't know what specific crime the suspect may have committed, and as far as we could determine the subject wasn't an immediate threat to us, or any other people in the area. We can't just shoot at someone because they're running away from us. We might want to, but we can't."

"I see," he responded softly. He seemed to be a little depressed. I knew exactly what he was feeling though, because I'd been in Jay's position a few times myself. You get totally caught up in the intense fever of the moment and your adrenal glands begin to do much of your thinking for you. Again, if you've been properly trained your basic instincts usually won't let you down. But, if you're a novice like Jay, who's had very limited street experience, if any, it's very easy for you to do the wrong thing at the wrong time. Then, afterwards, you keep asking yourself, "Why the hell did I do that?" But, it's too late and you have to bite the bullet and live with your mistake. Hopefully, it's not a serious mishap and you will learn and grow from the experience, even if you still do feel like a damn fool! Hopefully!

I think it's safe to assume all law enforcement agencies require their officers to file some sort of a report whenever they fire their weapons. Fort Lauderdale P.D. has such a regulation and I suspect the Broward County State Attorney's Office also wants to be made aware of the use of deadly force by any of their personnel. This was Jay Smiley's responsibility, to contact his own supervisor and advise them of this incident. To be quite honest though, I don't really know if he ever did this. It wasn't my job to check up on him. I assume he knew his own agency's rules and regulations and he'd do the right thing.

After this incident was over Mike and I agreed to go back to our original practice of discouraging observers from riding with us. Besides causing what I liked to call "the lack of action phenomenon," they were generally more trouble than they were worth. As our buddy Jay dramatically showed us, they could be unpredictable and dangerous too!

===

Officer MacKinley Smith recovered fully and he eventually went on to become Fort Lauderdale P.D.'s first African American Captain.

10

PEE WEE

Some police officers are born with an almost natural ability to sniff out suspicious activity no matter where it may be found. They seem to stumble on one good grab after another. I think I can truthfully say that at times I've been blessed, or maybe even cursed, with this same mysterious affliction. I don't know what it is and it's not even something you can teach to someone else. It's just there and I really can't explain it. Most of the time I've been extremely happy with these unexpected surprises. Fate, and the sometimes fickle Gods of War and Police Work, have been very good to me! But, there have been a few occasions, when I've been off-duty for example, when I'd have been content if Fate would have just forgotten Badge #149 completely!

I really liked and respected Sergeant Dan Vaniman. He and I seemed to have a lot in common and even though he was one of my T.I.U. supervisors I still felt we could be close friends. My wife Pat and his wife also seemed to be compatible and our two daughters Kathy and Natalie were approximately the same age as his little girl. Kathy, our oldest was seven, and Natalie was almost five. So, on one particular Saturday, when a new Walt Disney movie was playing at a local theater in nearby Plantation, Sergeant Vaniman and I agreed to meet there with our families. We'd all go to the show together. Unfortunately, one of my major faults has always been procrastination. I am a sinner and I sometimes put off till tomorrow what should be done today. Because I'm a procrastinator I'm often late for appointments, parties, and yes, sometimes even the movies. This bad habit drives my wife crazy! This Saturday though I promised I'd be good and I made a special vow that we'd get to the theater on time!

The theater was located midway between our home and the Fort Lauderdale Police Station. I needed to pick up something important at the P.D. and since we had plenty of time before we were scheduled to meet Dan and his family, this short detour didn't seem to be unreasonable. As we headed eastbound on Broward Boulevard, and we were still in the county, my cop's eyes continued to scan our immediate surroundings. I know I should have turned off my own personal "alert mode" but I just couldn't help myself. When your job involves you looking for suspicious persons and activity it's very hard to turn off all your senses completely. If there was a toggle switch on my forehead I could have flipped it "off," but there wasn't one! So, even though I tried my hardest to focus entirely on my driving, and nothing more, I still found myself watching the various people, places and vehicles that were all around us.

The beat up old sedan caught my eye immediately. It was located on one of the many side streets leading away from the main thoroughfare Broward Boulevard. This particular street led into a residential area. It wasn't something an ordinary civilian might have even noticed or sensed, but it was something I definitely felt inside. I don't know how I knew it, but I was certain the dark colored car and its occupants didn't belong in the area. They were all wrong! I made a right turn and headed towards the suspicious vehicle which was about one full block south of Broward. My wife Pat didn't say anything at all but I could still hear her sigh just the same. I knew she was thinking, "Well, here we go again!"

The subject's vehicle was stopped by the side of the road right in front of a residence. There weren't any cars in the driveway and it appeared as if no one was home. One person was still in the vehicle in the driver's seat and another individual was out on foot up near the front of the single story house. This second subject appeared to be walking away from the side of the residence and I could see that he carried a round metal hubcap in his right hand. My first impression was that the hubcap had somehow come off one of the vehicle's wheels and this individual got out of the car to retrieve it. Then my suspicious nature suddenly kicked in and I realized that's exactly what these two guys wanted people to think! But, things weren't always as they appeared. I looked a little closer at the subject with the hubcap.

"Pee Wee!" I exclaimed out loud. Mike and I had arrested Pee Wee five weeks earlier.

"No daddy, I don't have to go pee pee," little Natalie answered back from the rear seat of our car.

"Are we still going to the movies?" Kathy asked, as my wife studied me silently. I'm sure she couldn't figure out what I was doing, or why.

"Yes honey, we are," I promised. "But, daddy has something to do first."

Pee Wee was a residential burglar but he wasn't proud and he would do almost anything for a quick and easy buck. His previous arrest had been the result of a good tip from one of our informants and when we busted Pee Wee at his apartment in the southwest section of the city, we caught him cold. We found several traceable items inside his apartment and eventually charged Pee Wee with Possession of Stolen Property. To make a long story short; the case filing prosecutor at the Broward County S.A.O., who was not our buddy Jay Smiley, wasn't that pleased with our overall Probable Cause. He decided not to file formal criminal charges against Pee Wee and he was released. Maybe we should have invited him to ride with us one night, like Jay did, but instead we appealed this somewhat ludicrous decision to his S.A.O. supervisor. After much discussion, debate and a little badgering too, they finally agreed with us that our initial charges had indeed been good. Warrants were issued for Mr. Pee Wee, who of course was now no longer available for comment. Mike and I searched for him in vain but the elusive little thief seemed to disappear completely. Until now, that is! And, as I watched him climb into his own vehicle, and throw the dirty hubcap into the back seat, I knew he was up to his old tricks.

The two suspects immediately left the residential area driving north the one block to Broward Boulevard. I know Pee Wee didn't recognize me as a police officer. He never got that good a look at me. But, I'm quite sure he noticed my vehicle. He probably thought we were the family that lived at the house he had been walking around. I suspect that's why they elected to leave the area in such a hurry. When they saw that I was trying to follow them, they sped up just a little bit more.

Okay Officer, It's Decision Time!

(Situation #11)

The subject Pee Wee is a known residential burglar and now you've seen him prowling around a residence he apparently does not live at. You also know there are active felony warrants for the subject. Even though your wife and kids are with you in your vehicle, you'd still like to arrest him, if possible. You do have your hand held police radio with you. What do you do?

What is your answer? (put an "X" in the space in front of your answer)

❑ _____ I radio the dispatcher and give her the vehicle's description, location, direction and why I want it stopped (to arrest the subject Pee Wee). I then let the vehicle go and I would <u>not</u> attempt to follow it.

❑ _____ I would try to follow the vehicle as long as I could, giving the dispatcher updates about its location and direction.

An analysis of this situation appears at the end of the book

(Do <u>not</u> go there until you have finished reading this chapter)

My intention, of course, was not to get into a high speed pursuit with the suspects. That would be insane! I had my family with me and I'd never do anything that would endanger any of their lives. They meant to much to me! But, the cop in me couldn't let go of the suspects that easily. I knew there were active warrants for Pee Wee and I wanted to get him, bad! So, I disregarded that little inner voice inside my head that told me, "Let him go! You'll get him another day. It's just not worth the risk!"

Pee Wee and his cohort continued east on Broward Boulevard. I wouldn't say they were driving recklessly but they were traveling much faster than the posted speed limit allowed. They were also weaving in and out of the two lanes of other eastbound traffic. Their driving may not have been totally reckless, but it definitely was careless! If their driving was careless, then mine had to be too! But I failed to recognize this fact at the time and I fooled myself with cocky and confident thoughts about my being totally in control of this situation. That's bullshit! When you're chasing another vehicle, no matter how fast you may be going, you're never totally in control. You might think you are, but you're not! My daughters didn't mind though and they seemed to be having a blast. After all, having daddy "drive crazy" was even better than going to the movies!

As I continued to tag along several blocks behind them I used my hand held radio to advise the dispatcher what I had. I requested a marked unit stop the vehicle and take Pee Wee into custody. I heard several units respond affirmatively but I wasn't really sure they'd be able to intercept Pee Wee and his friend before I ended up losing them. After all, there were some limits to what I was prepared to do, and I definitely wouldn't exceed them. The suspect's vehicle made a few more turns in an obvious attempt to lose the pests behind them and then eventually headed north away from Broward Boulevard. They were now on N.W. 27th Avenue and in a section of the county that wasn't the best.

There were a few isolated streets in this area I hesitated driving on even when I was in a marked unit and in full police uniform. Now, being in plain clothes and having my family with me, if the suspects drove down any of these streets I definitely would let them go. I may be crazy for chasing after them, but I wasn't stupid too!

The suspect's vehicle slowed down a little and I believe they thought they finally lost me. Whoever I was! Just then two F.L.P.D. marked units suddenly appeared in my rear view mirror. I quickly directed them to the suspect's vehicle which was still several cars in front of me and then watched intently as they tried to pull the two subjects over. I halfway expected them to flee, but they didn't. They pulled over to the right side of the road and waited for the uniformed officers to approach them. The two subjects were taken from their vehicle at gunpoint. None of us were about to take either one of them for granted. In addition to arresting Pee Wee for the outstanding felony warrants, we also found him in possession of a substantial amount of narcotics paraphernalia. This was also a felony charge.

When suspects are arrested and searched they're usually put in a standard "frisk" position up against the patrol car, with their hands on either the hood or the trunk of the police vehicle. One habit most cops seem to have is they put all of a suspect's property onto the hood or the trunk. They'll empty a suspect's pockets and then throw all the property they find onto their vehicle. Obviously, this would not include weapons. Our F.L.P.D. guys, who were like most other officers in this regard, systematically and thoroughly searched our bad guy Pee Wee. All the narcotics paraphernalia and other personal property they found they tossed onto the hood of their patrol car. When they were finally finished they put Pee Wee into the caged-in back seat area of their vehicle.

My daughters continued to watch this real life drama in front of them. They seemed to be fascinated. My wife Pat exited our car and quietly stood there by the passenger side of our vehicle. A few nosy pedestrians wandered by and one even asked Pat what was happening. She wisely said she didn't know. Even though I was sure Pat was keeping a watchful eye on our two girls, who were still seated in the back seat of our car, I remained close by near the front of my vehicle. I figured the uniformed officers had the situation under control and I didn't need to be there with them. Just then, I heard some shouting and observed one lone individual running away from the side of one of the patrol units. Several uniformed officers were chasing after him and yelling for him to "Stop!" My first thought was that Pee Wee, or maybe even the other subject who had been with him, had somehow managed to escape. I was wrong!

A few adventurous souls in this world seem to tempt fate on almost a daily basis and it's as if they can't help themselves. They do wild and crazy things; unbelievable things the rest of us sane people would never even think about doing. I'm not talking about someone who goes skydiving without a thoroughly tested parachute, or someone who goes swimming in a pool full of hungry killer sharks who haven't eaten for a week, although both would definitely make my "top ten" list of the things I never intend to do! I'm talking about the people who take real chances and do stupid things which are dangerous and hazardous to their health! You know, things like intentionally trying to piss off a police officer! Or, my personal favorite, when some idiot purposely tries to make a fool out of you. I know there are some people out there in Fantasyland who probably admire these individuals and would say they have a "real set of balls." Others, and I proudly include myself in this category, think these cavalier fellows are foolish and more than likely completely brain dead too! I guess it's all in your point of view.

The male subject the uniformed officers were chasing apparently was one of these adventurous types who liked to live life totally on the edge. After the officers had finished with Pee Wee and his friend, and both were safely secured in the backs of the police vehicles, this brainless refugee from society decided he'd be smart and he'd sneak up and steal all of Pee Wee's dope. The narcotics paraphernalia on the hood of the police vehicle wasn't the only "dope" involved in this bizarre affair. As I watched the officers chase the subject down I wondered what made a man so damn stupid! Are some of these nuts just born this way, or do they really have to work at it? I suspected this guy had toked one to many marijuana cigarettes for his own good. Now, he was being charged with one count of Theft of Evidence, a felony. "Dope" seemed to be a very appropriate word!

I explained my situation to the uniformed guys and they were more than happy to take care of the booking process for me. Pee Wee's arrest wasn't that complicated because he was being booked reference the outstanding warrants. His friend the driver was going to jail for Reckless Driving and it didn't take me very long to write out the citation and then he was on his way too. The third subject, the "dope" stealer, was just a little more complicated because there was some evidence involved. I've never been one to pawn off an arrest's paperwork on another officer, even if they were more than willing to take it. It didn't seem right to me, and I didn't like to do it. But, today's incident was a little different. Besides being off-duty, I still had my family with me. And, for my daughter's sake, and my sake too I suppose, I still hoped we'd be able to make it to the theater on time. So, I was very grateful when the uniformed officers volunteered to take care of everything for me. I knew I owed them, big time!

When we arrived at the movie theater in Plantation we didn't see Dan or his family anywhere outside the building. We purchased our tickets, bought some popcorn and sodas and hurried inside. Dan, along with his wife and daughter, was already there. The movie was just about to start. We made it! Dan asked me what had delayed us and I began to tell him about Pee Wee's arrest and the rest of what had happened. He smiled and shook his head from side to side. I knew he thought I was a good cop and he'd told me before that he admired my apparent ability to come up with good grabs on a regular basis. Now however, I wondered if he thought I was a bit of a fool too. That's exactly how I felt. I couldn't believe I'd put the lives of my family in danger as I had. No asshole's arrest was ever worth the price of their safety. I knew this, yet I still went after Pee Wee anyway. I promised myself this would never happen again!

I know I had matured quite a bit since I first pinned on F.L.P.D.'s Badge #149, back in early 1967. I knew this and I was very proud of this fact too! But, this one incident involving Pee Wee and my family suddenly made me realize I still had a very long way to go. I'd always wanted to be the best damn cop Fort Lauderdale P.D. ever had. I knew I wasn't there yet! On the negative side; my right knee still hurt me at times, but the pain was usually bearable and I was able to do my job without anyone knowing about it. For the most part, this even included my partner Mike. On a positive note though; my stats were almost always among the best, and the overall quality of my work was generally well above average. But, I knew if I really wanted to excel and be the best, I needed to develop the all-important trait of self-discipline. There were lots of bad guys out there in the world and no matter how hard I tried, I couldn't get'em all! I needed to remember that the next time I thought about taking an unnecessary risk. Some risks were necessary and they were just a part of the job. Some risks, like taking chances with my family's welfare, definitely weren't!

===

Unfortunately, Sergeant Dan Vaniman resigned from F.L.P.D. and he became an Agent with the U.S. Secret Service. Fort Lauderdale's loss was definitely their gain!

11

NOVEMBER 24, 1974

Even though Officer Walter Ilyankoff had been killed on a Sunday that grotesque offense against mankind was still the rare exception rather than the general rule. Thank God, most Sundays in Fort Lauderdale were usually quiet and peaceful and there never seemed to be that much real action on the Sabbath. I guess even bad guys needed a day of rest now and then. There wasn't any rest for Mike and I, however. On many Sundays we'd be prowling the city's streets hunting the different species of two-legged vermin that liked to strike our citizens without warning. This Sunday was no different. It was right around 2130 hours when we passed by the convenience store located at Davie Boulevard and 31st Avenue. Except for the clerk the store appeared to be empty. I noticed a new 1974 red colored Camaro backed up to the west side of the building. Two well dressed black males slowly walked towards the front of the store. "Hmmm," I thought to myself, "this looks promising!"

Even though these two guys appeared very calm, cool and casual, they also fit the armed robber's general profile too. For example: there wasn't a single car in front of the store, yet they had parked at the side of the building where the clerk couldn't see their vehicle. They also backed in, again apparently so no one else would be able to see their tag. "Yeah, they're up to no good!" I thought to myself, as we took up a new position north of the store, and to the west. We couldn't see what was happening inside the store but we still had an excellent view of the suspect's sporty red Camaro. If they came running back to their vehicle, or if the store's VARDA Alarm suddenly went off while they were still inside, either one of these things would be a pretty good indicator a robbery had probably just taken place. As we anxiously waited for the subjects to return to their vehicle we requested help from any other T.I.U. Yankee units in the area. Officer Robert Zuccaro and his partner Bill Stewart responded.

Before this other Yankee unit could arrive in the area however, the two subjects exited the store and came walking back to their vehicle. Since they were walking, and not running, and since there was no VARDA going off, Mike and I were both quite sure nothing had happened inside the store. Even so, we elected to follow them anyway. Their suspicious activities at this store had perked my interest, but there was also another reason why I wanted to follow them. This red Camaro fit the basic description of another vehicle used in a reported robbery up in the northeast section of the city, at a well known hotel on U.S. Highway #1. This robbery occurred about a half hour before we observed these two guys down here on Davie Boulevard. There was always the possibility these might just be the culprits from that other offense so I wanted to follow them a little more to see what they did - if anything!

The Camaro headed north on 31st Avenue and then west on Broward Boulevard into the county. We passed the McDonald's where Assistant S.A.O. Jay Smiley and Officer MacKinley Smith first became acquainted and then we passed the street where I saw Pee Wee out on foot doing his phony "I-need-to-get-my-hubcap" routine. These two guys in the Camaro seemed to know all the good spots! We continued west on Broward until State Road #7, then they once again headed northbound. Now we were in Plantation, headed towards the City of Lauderhill. "This sounds familiar," I thought to myself, as I remembered the two subjects in the Torino who refused to be killed, from back in

August. They also took us to Lauderhill and that extremely violent affair eventually ended with shots being fired!

At one point during our drive north on State Road #7 we managed to get close enough to the Camaro to get the vehicle's license plate number and then we ran the tag through teletype. We hoped the registration would be on file and we'd be able to at least find out where the vehicle belonged. If we could learn the subject's home address we might have a clue to where they were headed. But, when the registration check finally came back we learned the vehicle was a rental and the only address we were given was the car agency. We doubted there'd be anyone there at 9:30 p.m. on a Sunday, who'd be able to give us any information about the people who rented this vehicle, so we continued to follow it as it finally entered the City of Lauderhill.

In about the 1500 block of North State Road #7 the Camaro made a left turn and entered a mall parking lot. The subjects drove westward through the large lot until they reached the mall itself, then they turned south and drove alongside the entire length of the huge building. The street bordering the south side of the mall lot was N.W. 12th Street. The subjects eventually headed west on 12th and as they did they seemed to pay extra special attention to a drive-thru milk store located opposite the mall lot, on the south side of the street. Now my heart really began to pound excitedly. This was the same milk store the two subjects in the Torino had cased and we all knew how that caper eventually turned out!

"It's almost like déjà vu," I mentioned to Mike as I looked down at our vehicle's odometer. From Davie and 31st Avenue where we first observed these two guys, to the milk store here in Lauderhill, was approximately 3½ miles. His only response was a confident grin.

The Camaro made the first right turn after the mall and entered the residential area immediately in back of it. The subjects then made a few more quick turns and we eventually lost sight of them completely. We looked for them in vain but when we couldn't locate them again we advised Stewart and his partner they were no longer needed. They could head back to Fort Lauderdale. We also decided to return to our own city but by way of the drive-thru milk store on N.W. 12th Street, just in case the subjects in the Camaro had gone back there while we searched for them. Mike and I entered the mall lot at the extreme north end 16th Street entrance and we drove south towards 12th Street alongside the mall building, like the suspects had done earlier. Just prior to our actually reaching 12th Street however, we once again observed the suspect's red Camaro. It was parked in the middle of the mall's southernmost lot, midway between a large department store to the north, and the drive-thru milk store to the south. We had guessed right! They had come back!

We observed two male subjects outside the rental vehicle. These were the same two individuals we first saw down on Davie Boulevard. The driver was walking away from the rear of the Camaro back towards the driver's side. The passenger was bending down at the rear as if doing something with the tag. The trunk of the vehicle was open. The passenger eventually rose to a standing position, closed the trunk and then walked back around to the passenger's side and got in. Once again, Stewart and his partner were asked to respond to our area. They advised they weren't that far away and they'd be with us very soon. We probably should have waited for them to arrive in the area before we moved, but we were in the middle of the mall lot ourselves and worried that the suspects might spot us. So, Mike and I tried to take up a new and better position and while we were doing this the subject's Camaro drove off without our knowledge.

We knew they had to be somewhere in the immediate area however, because they seemed very interested in the drive-thru milk store located there on the south side of 12th Street. Stewart and his partner Zuccaro arrived in the area and they quickly observed the suspect's vehicle. The two bad guys had pulled their Camaro out of the huge mall parking lot across 12th Street to the south side where the milk store was located. The store faced both 12th Street to the north and 41st Terrace to the west. East and south of the store was a large "L" shaped building surrounding it on these two sides. Stewart and Zuccaro were across 12th Street in the mall lot. In fact, they were almost in the same exact location where the Camaro and the two suspects had been parked, when we first saw them again and the passenger had been doing something with the vehicle's tag. Now, our two guys could look straight south across 12th Street and easily see the suspect's vehicle as it slowly proceeded southbound along the eastern side of the "L" shaped building. When the Camaro finally reached the far corner, where the two "I" wings came together to form an "L", the vehicle made a right turn and disappeared from their view. The Camaro never came out at the 41st Terrace side however, so we were fairly certain they stopped somewhere along the south side of the "L" shaped building. Either that, or they had been able to slip away again! Damn, I hoped not!

Mike and I also pulled in alongside one of the buildings on the south side of 12th Street, but we were located a half block to the east of where the suspect's Camero had last been seen. We quickly drove to the far corner of the building but stopped just short of making a right turn to go behind it, as the suspects had done. A long alleyway ran in an east/west direction behind all these closed businesses. This alley was parallel to N.W. 12th Street, and it ran all the way from 41st Terrace, to State Road #7. We were almost sure the suspect's Camaro was stopped in this alley somewhere behind the "L" shaped building west of us. As we exited our unmarked vehicle to take a look I heard Officer Zuccaro advise the dispatcher to let Lauderhill P.D. know we were in their area and that a possible robbery was about to occur at our location. He also asked that one of their unmarked units respond as soon as possible. It was now 2153 hours.

We carefully peeked around the corner of the building we were at and looked westward down the long wide alley. There it was! Just as we had thought the suspect's fancy red Camaro was stopped there in the dark alley, right behind the "L" shaped building! Its lights were off and it appeared to be unoccupied. Two male subjects quickly walked away from the front of the car, which was facing west towards 41st Terrace. We were certain these were the same two subjects from the vehicle and it appeared they were indeed headed for the drive-thru milk store on 12th Street. When they rounded the building's far corner we lost sight of them completely but this really didn't matter because we knew Stewart and his partner Zuccaro were in position to pick them up. They did!

I've said it before, and it's definitely true - Mike and I were the perfect T.I.U. team! But, if there was one major difference between Mike and I it would have to be his willingness to take some extra chances I might not normally take myself. I guess you could say I was a little bit more conservative than he was. Don't get me wrong though, I don't mean this as a negative comment. Let's face it, some police officers can be to damn conservative! So, I'm not saying Mike's aggressiveness in some situations was all wrong, and that my cautiousness was all right, or even vice versa. What I am saying is that Mike and I sometimes had different thoughts about what was the best way to do certain things, but there never was any conflict or argument when we had a real difference of opinion.

Okay Officer, It's Decision Time!

(Situation #12)

It appears the two subjects from the Camaro intend to do a robbery at the drive-thru milk store. They've parked their vehicle in an alley, which is out of sight of the store's clerk, and now they appear to be walking towards the business. You and your partner are located in the same alley, but about one block to the east of the now unoccupied Camaro. What do you do next?

What is your answer? (put an "X" in the space in front of your answer)

❑ _____ We wait. Officer Stewart and his partner are in a position to see if the two subjects rob the store, and we wait to hear what they advise.

❑ _____ We move down the alley towards the suspect's unoccupied vehicle. If a robbery does occur, we will be in a better position to confront and apprehend the suspects when they return to their car.

An analysis of this situation appears at the end of the book

(Do not go there until you have finished reading this chapter)

I was surprised when Mike suddenly grabbed the American 180 laser sighted machine gun and trotted off down the alley. I hadn't expected this. I mean, there wasn't any real conversation beforehand, or exchange of ideas and opinions about what we should do next. Immediately after the two bad guys were out of our view completely Mike just picked up the .22 caliber machine gun and started off in the direction of the suspect's vehicle. I grabbed my own departmental 12-gauge pump shotgun and followed along behind him. As we both silently maneuvered our way down the dark alley, carefully hugging the shadows of each building we passed, I nervously wondered what would happen when we finally reached the Camaro itself.

There were several reasons why I might not have wanted to immediately approach the suspect's vehicle, as Mike obviously intended for us to do. First of all, everything seemed to indicate the two subjects intended to commit a robbery at the milk store, but what happened if they decided not to? What if they suddenly got cold feet, got scared off, or merely decided to drive around the block one more time? Then, when they got back to their vehicle, they'd find us there waiting for them. We'd be committed and have to act. Moving up to their vehicle was definitely the bold and adventurous thing to do, but under the circumstances I wondered if it was also the smartest. Being Mr. Conservative, as I am, I probably would have preferred to wait back at our own vehicle and see what they did when they got to the store. If it was indeed a robbery then Stewart and Zuccaro would tell us. True, the suspects would have time to get back to their vehicle and drive off but we'd be in a perfect position to follow them. If we handled things just right we might even be able to take them down without a high speed pursuit. And, if no robbery took place at all, we wouldn't have needlessly blown our surveillance and we'd be able to follow them some more if we wanted to.

Some people might call Mike impulsive, reckless or maybe even downright dangerous. Bullshit! Still others might say I was less than courageous, for even thinking about staying put back at our own vehicle. Again, that's just bullshit! The difference in our styles had nothing at all to do with his being adventurous or brave, or with me lacking courage. Mike and I had both proven ourselves many times before and we didn't need to prove anything to anyone now, including each other. I respected Mike tremendously and I hoped that feeling was mutual!

Stewart and Zuccaro watched as both subjects approached the east side of the milk store. The passenger, later identified as Carlton Johnson, age 24, entered the store first. Wallace Tompkins, the driver, who was also 24, entered right behind Johnson. Now, with both men totally inside the business, Stewart and Zuccaro also lost the eye. The female clerk didn't pay much attention to their overall descriptions but she couldn't miss the "big black handgun" the subject Wallace Tompkins was pointing at her. Stewart and Zuccaro couldn't see this, of course, but we all assumed something exactly like this was happening. True to form, the robbery took less than one full minute and at 2156 hours both subjects backed their way out of the business. Johnson backed out of the east door first, and then came Tompkins. Stewart and Zuccaro observed that Tompkins appeared to be holding a gun in his right hand and after he was completely out of the store he tucked it away underneath the tan colored windbreaker he was wearing. Both subjects now took off running southbound towards the area where they had left their vehicle. Zuccaro immediately advised the dispatcher the robbery had just gone down!

Mike and I were just arriving near the rear of the suspect's parked Camaro when we heard Zuccaro's transmission about the robbery. If I'd had the time to really think about it I probably would have congratulated Mike for being so right! This time his aggressiveness apparently paid off. According to Zuccaro the two bad guys robbed the store and now they were on their way back to their vehicle. And, thanks to Mike's boldness, we'd be there waiting for them! I didn't have the time to do any heavy thinking though, because as soon as Zuccaro's transmission ended, we almost immediately observed the two suspects rounding the far corner of the "L" shaped building. They were both running as fast as they could and they were headed straight for the Camaro. When we first saw them they seemed to be about twenty to thirty feet away from the front of their car. We were about fifty feet away, but we were nearer the Camaro's rear and not the front. Now, Mike and I also began running towards the suspect's stationary vehicle. We desperately wanted to get there before the two suspects did so we could stop them before they had a chance to drive away. The race was on!

Even though Mike and I were running straight ahead towards the two suspects and their vehicle we still took a few precious moments to survey exactly what was happening there in front of us. I don't believe either one of us rushed ahead blindly or carelessly. I know I didn't! These guys were armed and they had just committed a robbery and I wasn't about to take them for granted. I don't think Mike did either! So, we moved ahead cautiously, but as fast as we could. I know this seems to be a contradiction of terms, but this is the best way to describe what happened. Unfortunately, the two suspects managed to reach their waiting vehicle before we did.

The driver Tompkins entered the Camaro first. Almost immediately the vehicle's brake lights and backup lights came on. This happened so damn fast it actually surprised me. Tompkins didn't waste any time at all getting his vehicle going. It almost seemed as if they may have left the Camaro's motor running, either that or they left the keys in the ignition so they could start it right up. There was no fumbling around looking for the car keys, that was obvious!

As Tompkins did his thing behind the wheel, the passenger Johnson quickly entered the right side of the vehicle. Mike and I moved even closer to the rear of the Camaro. Now, for the first time I loudly shouted out a warning, "Halt! Police Officers!" To be quite honest, at this point in time I didn't really know if the two suspects even realized Mike and I were there. And, because we were both in plainclothes, even if they had seen us, they may not have known we were police officers. This is why that first verbal warning was so damn important. We wanted to give these two clowns every opportunity to surrender peacefully. If they decided not to, and if they chose to resist, then at least we'd be able to say we tried!

Carlton Johnson was entirely in the vehicle now and the passenger's door was completely shut. I could still see one of Johnson's arms though, and even part of his shoulder as he leaned halfway out the open window. I didn't see his head but I did observe a medium sized black object in his outstretched hand. It appeared to be some sort of a handgun. But, before I could even react, I observed a muzzle-like flash coming from the passenger's side of the Camaro. I also heard what I knew was the report of a weapon being fired. The bastard was shooting at me! Mike was off to my right, and although he couldn't see the suspect's vehicle from his present location, because the car was still hidden around the corner of the building, he also heard the shot that Johnson fired. Stewart from his own vantage point on the north side of 12th Street heard it too.

At almost the same exact moment that Johnson fired the red Camaro began backing up at a high rate of speed. The extreme gravity of my situation immediately became obvious to me; the passenger had just tried to shoot me, and now the driver was trying to finish the job by running me over! These guys were bad news and apparently meant business! Even though it appeared I was about to be run over the first actual thought that came into my mind was really kind of stupid. I wondered why this asshole was backing up when he could have easily avoided a confrontation with us by merely going straight ahead. If he had gone forward down the alley towards 41st Terrace he could have avoided Mike and I completely. Now however, he apparently had decided to challenge us instead.

Okay Officer, It's Decision Time!

(Situation #13)

This is another one of those violent situations where the use of deadly force is definitely justified. The passenger has fired a shot at you, and now the driver is backing their Camaro up at a high rate of speed, apparently trying to run you down. This seems to be intentional because they could have gone forward and avoided a confrontation entirely. What do you do? Would you fire your weapon?

What is your answer? (put an "X" in the space in front of your answer)

❑ _____Yes! I would fire my weapon.

❑ _____ No! I would not fire at this time.

An analysis of this situation appears at the end of the book

(Do <u>not</u> go there until you have finished reading this chapter)

I don't know why I even bothered to do it, but as I raised the shotgun up to my right shoulder I loudly yelled out one last verbal warning to the subjects in the Camaro. "Halt! Police!" Under the circumstances, yelling these two words seemed a little foolish and maybe even a bit ridiculous. These two guys were trying their best to kill Mike and I! Could anyone in their right mind really believe mere words were going to make these bastards stop? I didn't think so! I guess I shouted this last warning because that's what my training and my past experiences had taught me to do. The words came automatically. There wasn't any thinking beforehand, in fact, there wasn't any time to do any thinking at all! The Camaro still backed up recklessly and now it was getting dangerously close. So, even though I may have yelled out this one final warning, I was getting ready to fire! These were the only thoughts that really mattered now! My right index finger caressed the shotgun's safety to make sure it was off and then I firmly put my forefinger on the trigger.

I would estimate the Camaro was about fifteen or twenty feet away from me when I fired the first round of OO Buck. The rear of the vehicle was racing straight towards me and I tried to aim at the Camaro's rear windshield. I had two different targets to choose from; the passenger Johnson who had already shot at us, and the driver Tompkins who was trying to run us down. Again, there wasn't time to think about what I should do, I just instinctively aimed the shotgun at the driver's side of the passenger compartment and fired. His current actions seemed to be the most threatening to me. I'm sure an equally good argument could have been made that I should have directed my fire at the passenger. I wasn't really certain about exactly where the pattern of shotgun pellets hit, because immediately after I fired I had to jump to my right to avoid being run over. When I jumped I had to take my eyes off the suspect's vehicle but I did hear the pellets striking the car's metal body. What a beautiful sound! I knew I'd hit something!

At this same specific moment, when I was jumping out of the way of the speeding Camaro, I wasn't exactly sure where Mike was located, or what he was doing. I knew he was somewhere off to my right though and I suspected he also had to dive for cover or be run over by the suspect's vehicle. This is exactly what happened! Mike didn't actually see the Camaro until it backed around the corner of the building and came right at us! He saw me fire my shotgun and then we both had to dive to our right to avoid being hit. The Camaro missed Mike completely but it gently sideswiped my outstretched left leg as it went by. I felt the vehicle's metal body casually graze my leg. There was some minor pain and discomfort later but as I hobbled off to the right of the Camaro, nothing seemed to be broken.

The suspect's vehicle backed up a few more feet and then suddenly slowed and seemed to come to a complete stop. At first glance it may have looked like the suspects were giving up, but I knew this wasn't the case, and I'm sure Mike knew this too. To us, the reasons why they did this were very obvious; the driver wanted to change direction and now go forward! Before he could shift gears though he had to bring the Camaro to a complete stop. Mike and I were now standing right next to the passenger's door and we were almost so close we could have reached down and tapped Johnson on the shoulder, if we had wanted to! At this precise moment in time, because of our awkward and totally exposed position, Mike and I became our most vulnerable!

When we looked into the vehicle through the open passenger's window Mike and I observed the subject Johnson bending over in his seat and doing something with his right arm and hand. In my mind, even though I couldn't prove it at the time, I was totally convinced the subject Johnson was getting ready to shoot at us again. This time, with us standing out in the open, the chances seemed better than 50-50 that he'd probably hit at least one of us. Once again, my eyes were no longer on my partner Mike. They

141

were riveted on the Camaro and its two occupants. I jacked a new round of OO Buck into the shotgun's chamber and fired! The suspect's vehicle remained stopped for only a split second and then it headed forward away from us.

<u>Okay Officer, It's Decision Time!</u>

(Situation #14)

The suspect's vehicle is now going away from you. The Camaro's passenger has <u>not</u> fired any more shots at you and the likelihood that you will be run over also seems to be more remote now. With the vehicle headed away from you, and your partner, it seems you are now out of immediate danger. Do you continue to fire at the suspect's still fleeing vehicle, or do you stop?

What is your answer? (put an "X" in the space in front of your answer)

❑ _____ Yes! I would continue to shoot at the two suspects in the still fleeing vehicle.

❑ _____ No! Because they are headed away from me, I would hold my fire.

An analysis of this situation appears at the end of the book

(Do <u>not</u> go there until you have finished reading this chapter)

I jacked a fresh round into the barrel. Once again, I fired! I know there are some who will ask why I continued to fire even when the subjects were now going away from us. That's a fair question, but the answer should be obvious! Though they now posed less of a threat to Mike and I they were still a very real threat to any other police officers they might encounter. If they were willing to take us on as they did, then what would happen the next time a police officer tried to stop them? No, they might be going away from us, but they were still potentially very dangerous and we needed to stop them one way or the other!

"Blaaaaaaaaaat!" I really hadn't expected it, so this weird sound startled me when I first heard it. But, even though the sound surprised me, I recognized it immediately! "It" was the unique sound of the American 180 Machine Gun Mike carried. I really shouldn't have been surprised, though. I mean, what the hell did I think Mike was going to do with the damn thing? This wasn't "show and tell" at school and I knew he wasn't gonna just let the bastards in the Camaro look at it. I knew damn well Mike intended to use it if things turned shitty, so the high-pitched metallic-like grinding sound shouldn't have surprised me at all.

I noticed the distinctive red dot of the laser beam a split second after Mike opened fire. It first appeared on the passenger's side of the vehicle's rear windshield. I watched in awe as the red dot slowly moved across the entire length of the back windshield towards the driver's side of the vehicle. As it moved, it seemed to viciously slice away at the window itself and broken pieces of shattered glass flew off in all directions. It almost seemed as if someone had planted dozens of small explosive charges in the windshield itself and now these mini-charges were being detonated one at a time in very rapid succession. But, I knew it wasn't the red dot that was systematically dissecting the windshield, piece by devastating piece. It was the awesome fusillade of .22 cal. rounds the American 180 was spitting out, at an almost incredible 29.6 rounds per second. I've never seen such total and absolute destruction from one single weapon. In a horrible and terrifying way, it was truly impressive!

As Mike continued to maneuver the little red dot towards the driver I realized my own attempt to blow out the Camaro's back windshield had failed. I had tried to aim my first shotgun blast right at the rear window, but when I witnessed the ultimate destructiveness of Mike's American 180, I knew for sure I had missed the back windshield completely. It had still been there, or it was until Mike started taking it apart with the 180. I later learned the pellets from my first initial blast most likely impacted somewhere on the Camaro's trunk. There were several different patterns there on the trunk and one even partially destroyed the vehicle's trunk ornament. I was quite sure I could take credit for that particular prize! I'm sure the vehicle's excessive backwards speed and my desperate need to jump out of the way were both contributing factors in my missing the rear windshield with that first shot. As I now prepared to fire a fourth and final round of OO Buck at the escaping vehicle and suspects, I still couldn't help but marvel at the deadly precision of the American 180. Mike was like a skilled surgeon doing a very delicate procedure during an operation, and the American 180 was his scalpel! This time though, I wasn't quite sure the patients would survive the operation!

With all the shots being fired, and with all the lead filling the air, I never even noticed the sudden arrival of Stewart and his partner Zuccaro. After the robbery went down and the two suspects started back towards their waiting vehicle, Stewart and Zuccaro immediately crossed 12th Street so they could back us up. Zuccaro was driving their vehicle and I'm not really sure what he may have seen or heard. But, I know at least Stewart heard that first shot fired by the suspect Johnson. And, they both apparently witnessed the Camaro coming around the corner of the building backwards, at a high rate of speed. They watched as Mike and I jumped out of the path of the vehicle to avoid being run over.

Stewart quickly exited their vehicle and aimed his own departmental shotgun at the passenger's side of the Camaro. I was also ready to fire my fourth round of OO Buck into the fleeing vehicle. What happened next isn't totally clear. I don't know if I fired first, or if Stewart did. But, we did both fire! Two more deadly patterns of OO Buck, eighteen .33 caliber balls in all, savagely slammed into the suspect's vehicle. Still, it continued to move away from us. Mike's American 180 continued its strange sounding report, "Blaaaaaaaaaat!" In fact, from the moment Mike first fired, until now, the eerie noise had not let up. It seemed like almost an eternity, but only several seconds had actually passed. It's true what they say about how things sometimes seem to happen in slow motion when you're involved in life and death struggles. It had only been seconds since Mike opened fired, yet it seemed a lifetime!

After momentarily blasting part of the driver's side of the Camaro, Mike started moving the red dot back towards the passenger. Mike had already fired approximately forty .22 caliber rounds when the American 180 suddenly jammed. The suspect's vehicle turned to the left now and quickly headed eastbound down the long alley towards State Road #7. As the Camaro sped away Stewart fired one more last round of OO Buck. He aimed for the open rear windshield area of the vehicle. Thanks to Mike, the windshield itself was no longer there! But, as I watched the vehicle speed away, I couldn't believe my eyes. We poured so much lead into the Camaro I couldn't see how the two occupants escaped injury! Yet, they somehow still managed to drive away. With all of this lead in their vehicle I would have thought it would have to stop just because it weighed so damn much! It was unbelievable!

My attention was still focused on the departing Camaro so I really didn't notice Officer Zuccaro or his vehicle. Mike, of course, was still out on foot and lugging around the now useless American 180. Stewart, with his shotgun, was also there. But, what I failed to notice was the fact Zuccaro apparently never exited his own vehicle at any time during the brief but wild encounter with the suspect's and their Camaro. He never fired a shot and he apparently never even tried to! There are those who say Zuccaro froze, that he was almost in a state of shock because of what he saw there in front of him. They say he stayed there in his vehicle, with both his hands tightly clutching the steering wheel, unable or unwilling to do anything else. I'm sure some uncompassionate souls might even label him a coward. I think that title is a little harsh! Zuccaro was not a coward! He just wasn't cut out to be a tactical officer. He was a very nice guy, who had a great gift for gab, and he could tell wonderful stories. But, he didn't have the basic instincts you needed to survive in the often violent world of urban warfare. And, make no mistake about it, this was a damn war we were in! It was the good guys versus the bad guys!

"Go after them!" Mike finally yelled to Stewart, who was standing there by the open passenger's door of his vehicle. I guess we were all momentarily mesmerized just a little by the Camaro's unexpected departure. I'm sure none of us ever imagined they'd be able to get away from us, but they did! Stewart jumped into their car and Zuccaro started off in pursuit of the suspects and their vehicle. I expected to see them hauling ass down the alley, going for all they were worth as they chased after the Camaro. But, to my surprise, and I'm sure Mike's too, Zuccaro drove off rather casually, almost as if he had nowhere in particular to go. Then, as he headed eastbound down the alley towards State Road #7, he picked up his speed just a little, but he still wasn't driving as fast or as hard as he should have been. Needless to say, Zuccaro and Stewart quickly lost sight of the suspect's damaged vehicle. It was last seen going south on State Road #7, a scalded dog with its tail on fire!

The dispatcher was advised the Camaro had been lost and she immediately put out a B.O.L.O. for the vehicle and its two fugitive occupants. In addition to Armed Robbery charges, we also wanted both subjects for Attempted Murder! As additional marked and unmarked units flooded into the area, Mike ran to the drive-thru milk store to check on the welfare of the lone female clerk. He arrived just in time to see her running away from her own store, headed off in the general direction of another nearby convenience store. Her store had no phone in it so she was on her way to the other store so she could call the "Police" to report the robbery. "Not necessary," Mike told her. "The 'Police' are already here!"

One of the many F.L.P.D. units actively searching for the two suspects and their vehicle was a patrol lieutenant named John Hill. Shortly after Stewart and Zuccaro lost the Camaro Lieutenant Hill located it nearly two full miles away from the scene of the savage shootout in Lauderhill. It was sitting in the middle of an elementary school parking lot. This school, located in an unincorporated area northwest of Fort Lauderdale, was about midway between Davie and 31st Avenue, where we first picked them up, and the drive-thru milk store they robbed. The vehicle seemed unoccupied, but Lieutenant Hill wisely elected to wait until he had adequate backup with him. Within seconds a two-man reserve unit arrived and this is when Lieutenant Hill first approached the suspect's vehicle. He found it wasn't unoccupied after all!

Lieutenant Hill observed the passenger Johnson still seated inside the bullet riddled Camaro. At least 36 bullet holes were at the rear trunk area and along the right side of the vehicle. Johnson was slumped forward, his motionless head hanging over the vehicle's center console. This is why Lt. Hill didn't see him until he actually approached the vehicle itself. The suspect had been shot a number of times and he didn't appear to be breathing. The lieutenant correctly concluded he was dead. At a deposition later a young defense attorney would ask him how he knew he had found the right vehicle. Lieutenant Hill believed in saying things the way they were, so in his normal straight forward kind of style he casually responded, "It was the only car I saw that looked like Swiss cheese, that had a fucking dead guy in it!" I'm told the attorney asked no more questions after that!

The driver of the Camaro was nowhere to be found. There was a considerable amount of blood on the driver's seat, along with a few fresh drops of blood on the pavement, approximately five feet away from the driver's door, so it appeared he had also been hit by some of our fire. When Lt. Hill finally broadcast the news that one suspect was still in the vehicle dead, I have to admit I did not experience any positive, or even negative feelings. I wasn't bubbling over with joy because one of us; Mike, Stewart or I, had been able to kill someone! But, I wasn't overcome with feelings of remorse or guilt, either! I know it sounds cold and hardhearted to say, but this was just something that happened. We hadn't planned to take the suspect's life away from him, and it had been his decision, along with Tompkins' choice, to resist! Killing Johnson, however unfortunate, was just the price of doing business! And, I wasn't going to let it get to me! After all the pros and cons are added up, and then tossed aside, the only real thing that matters was the fact we were all alive and well, and that no innocent civilians were hurt too. Mike, Stewart, Zuccaro and I, would all go home to our families tonight. I wasn't proud we had to kill another human being, even though he had forced us to do it. But, I wasn't ashamed either!

When I first learned the news that we had killed at least one of the two suspects in the Camaro my initial reaction was to feel I had probably hit him with some of the pellets from my four rounds of OO Buck I fired. But, nothing could have been farther from the truth! When the medical examiner came to the school and examined the subject Johnson for the very first time he discovered that Johnson had been hit by at least 10 different .22 caliber bullets. All these rounds impacted in the suspect's back and according to the M.E. all were apparently fired into the Camaro through the rear windshield which had been totally destroyed by Mike's fire. This cursory examination at the scene was just a little bit off, though. At the autopsy the very next day the M.E. found that Johnson was hit 12 times, with 10 of these rounds hitting him in the back, and 2 in the back of the head on the right side. 9 bullets were removed from Johnson's body, along with partial fragments of 3 more. All were .22 calibers.

Some truly important things in this life are worth dying for! And, others definitely aren't! I'm sure each man's list of the things most dear to him would be different though, and what I might consider important and worthwhile, another man might not. There are a few things I think we'd all agree on, however. For example: most people in the military are extremely dedicated individuals, or they wouldn't be there in the first place. I imagine many of these modern day patriots would say dying for our country would be a noble sacrifice they'd be willing to make, if fate ever called upon them to do so. A mother's love and protective instincts for her child might be another good example. There are many documented cases where mothers willingly gave up their own lives to save the lives of their children when they were being threatened. I'm sure there are many more examples, but I can't believe Carlton Johnson's reasons would make anybody's list! I know they wouldn't be on mine! Carlton Johnson; ex-con, robber and wanna-be cop killer, died for one of the stupidest reasons of all - he died trying to keep some property that didn't even belong to him in the first place! When the M.E. examined Johnson, there in that red Camaro at the elementary school, he found a brand new unopened pack of Kool cigarettes clutched tightly in the suspect's left hand. A pack of Kools - that's not worth dying for!

After the Camaro was located, with Johnson's body inside it, the manhunt for the fugitive driver who was still at large immediately intensified. From the amount of blood on the driver's seat, as well as the fresh drops outside the car on the pavement, it seemed a pretty good bet he'd been wounded. But, how bad? That was still the million dollar question. From the look of Johnson's fatal wounds I suspected we might just find the second bastard dead in a field somewhere. No such luck though. A thorough search of the surrounding area turned up nothing and to our dismay that also included the weapon used by the two subjects during the robbery, and by Johnson when he fired that first shot at us. Once again, the damn gun was missing! Bad guys who liked Kools, and missing guns in Lauderhill, these two things were becoming annoyingly common!

Tracking down the elusive driver really wasn't that hard, but it was time consuming. One of our midnight shift detectives eventually made contact with someone from the car rental agency. When the detective explained why we urgently needed the rental information the agency manager quickly agreed to meet him there at the closed business. The detective learned the Camaro was rented on November 21st, just three days before the Lauderhill robbery. It was rented to a U.S. Postal employee named Wallace Tompkins. Mr. Tompkins' own car was in a local dealership body shop being worked on and that well-known business had recommended him to the rental agency. That recommendation, along with a fifty dollar deposit, and Tompkins drove off in a brand new sporty red Camaro. The vehicle, originally due back November 23rd, hadn't been returned on time, so it was now technically an overdue rental. The most interesting piece of information we learned from the rental contract was that Tompkins lived in an apartment complex on N.W. 43rd Terrace, right behind the mall in Lauderhill. 43rd Terrace was the same exact location where we first lost the subjects and their vehicle, prior to finding them again just before the robbery. Surprise! Surprise!

We didn't learn about this until much later but Tompkins' girlfriend reported the Camaro stolen several hours after the robbery and shootout in Lauderhill. She apparently drove the vehicle to a local Elks Lodge in our city and parked it there right around 8:15 p.m. She went inside. Her sneaky boyfriend Wallace Tompkins came by and took the Camaro without telling her. He really didn't steal it though, because he had been the one who rented it in the first place. He and his buddy Johnson did their wild thing at the drive-thru milk store in Lauderhill, and as they say, the rest is history! Tompkins' girlfriend didn't know about any of this and when she came out of the club a little after midnight, Cinderella's little red carriage was gone! So, she did what any good girlfriend would do, she called the police to report her boyfriend's car stolen. She was sure he was gonna be pissed! An F.L.P.D. marked unit responded and took the report. While they were there with the girl she called home and even spoke with the subject Tompkins. The officers had wanted to know where the vehicle's paperwork was and he said it was in the glove compartment. The officers didn't realize the supposedly stolen Camaro was the same one as the one shot up in the City of Lauderhill. After making sure the girl had a way to get home the officers resumed their normal patrol activities.

After he abandoned the shot up Camaro, with Johnson's corpse still inside it, Wallace Tompkins stole a bicycle and pedaled his way home to his apartment in Lauderhill. This was about a two-mile trip. Considering the fact he had been wounded this must have been a very painful experience indeed! Tompkins was home when his girlfriend called to tell him his rental vehicle had been stolen from outside the Elks Lodge. She told him the "Police" were there taking a report and I'm sure he must have felt relieved. He probably assumed we'd think the car thieves were the suspects responsible for the Lauderhill robbery and he must have felt he was home free. Tompkins should have given us more credit though because we did eventually put everything together. Lauderhill P.D., along with several of our T.I.U. guys, hit the address given to us by the car rental agency. Wallace Tompkins was there inside the apartment. I wasn't there at the subject's apartment but I was told Tompkins initially said that he had no knowledge at all of any robbery. And, he didn't even know his rental car was stolen until his girlfriend called him and told him so. He probably felt he was doing a pretty good job snowing these dumb cops, that is until one of them suddenly slapped him sharply on the back as if to say, "Okay fellow, we'll see you later!" When Tompkins doubled over in pain and fell to the floor in agony I suspect he finally realized he really hadn't fooled anyone after all. Tompkins had been hit several times in the back and the officer just happened to slap him in the right spot. It's truly amazing what a few well placed .22 caliber bullets will do. Lauderhill P.D. arrested Tompkins. He was told he was being charged with Robbery, Attempted Murder and Third Degree Felony Murder. Whenever someone dies during the commission of a felony, even if that someone happens to be a bad guy, that's Felony Murder. After Tompkins was read his rights he admitted his own part in the Lauderhill caper. It was right around 1:45 a.m.

Tompkins' girlfriend wasn't charged, even though she had given him some first aid for his wounds. The officers at the apartment apparently were convinced she knew nothing at all about the robbery beforehand, and she didn't even know how he had been injured. I suspect she had her own suspicions though! Although the officers at the suspect's apartment recovered a bloody pillow case and some bandages, they didn't find the weapon involved. It was still missing! Damn!

12

THE FIRST YEAR ENDS

After this last deadly encounter in the City of Lauderhill several important things happened. First of all, we were advised the Broward County Medical Examiner wanted us to meet with him at the morgue and he wanted us to bring the American 180 with us. Even though the message we were given said we could come by the morgue at our own convenience all sorts of wild thoughts began to race through our minds. The M.E. that wanted to see us was not the same one who had been out at the school the night of the shooting. That was an assistant M.E. The one who wanted to see us was the main man at the morgue. He had also been the one to do the autopsy on Carlton Johnson the day after the shooting and I couldn't help but wonder, "Was this guy trying to build some sort of criminal case against us?" Maybe he wanted to inspect the laser-sighted machine gun to see if our version of the incident was plausible.

Mike and I were both just a little bit nervous as we pulled up to the front of the morgue. I'd been there before on other cases and I never really felt that comfortable walking through these large glass doors. This time however, I felt a sense of dread. These feelings were funny and I really couldn't explain them because I knew we hadn't done anything wrong. The armed robbery at the Lauderhill convenience store, and then the subsequent killing of Carlton Johnson, had been a good shooting. We did what we had to do and given the same exact circumstances again I'm sure I'd do the same things I did that fateful night. So I wondered, why this feeling of apprehension? Sadly, the answer I finally came up with was that deep down in my heart I really didn't totally trust the system I was a part of. I knew that being right wasn't always enough.

As we quietly entered the front doors Mike carried the long brown case which contained the American 180. We left the machine gun inside the case because we didn't want to give the unsuspecting receptionist a coronary. We asked for the doctor and she told us to have a seat in the waiting area while she went to go get him. Only a few minutes passed before she returned with the M.E. following along right behind her. Doctor Abdul Farouk was a well known certified pathologist skilled in forensic pathology and he had even written several reference books on the subject. He was an expert in his field and for some unknown reason just knowing this made me that much more nervous and uneasy.

Doctor Farouk was originally from the Middle East and although his English was adequate his speech left no doubt about his true nationality. "Good!" he exclaimed loudly, his accent making the word sound like "Wood," with a "G" at the beginning. "I see you brought it with you! Please, may I see it?"

Even though we had some difficulty understanding a few of his words, his eyes told us exactly what he wanted to see. He was staring at the long brown case and when Mike put it down to open it, I glanced over at the doctor and noticed he was smiling.

"Here it is," Mike said proudly as he removed the light-weight machine gun from its case.

"Ah, beautiful!" Doctor Farouk remarked. He really did seem to be enjoying himself.

"Do you want to hold it?" I asked, as Mike showed him how the round ammunition drum rested on the top of the weapon.

"Yes! Yes, I would!" the M.E. responded enthusiastically. Then he added, "You know, I'm doing a new reference book and I needed some material about machine gun wounds and what they do to the human body. This is just perfect! Perfect!"

It didn't take very long for Doctor Farouk's comments to register. Mike and I looked at each other and we both began to laugh but Doctor Farouk was so engrossed in his inspection of the American 180 he never even noticed our unusual reaction. Our worst fears and nightmares, that Doctor Farouk had some sinister and evil motive for wanting to meet with us, and see the American 180, had been totally groundless. He wanted material for his new book, and nothing more! I have to admit that in addition to being slightly amused by the whole affair I was also just a little bit angry with myself. After all, I once again had allowed myself to become almost paranoid, even though I knew we hadn't done anything wrong.

Being a Fort Lauderdale cop was often hard enough and I definitely didn't need to imagine things that weren't true. Paranoia was a disease that had destroyed many a good cop and I'd always vowed it wouldn't happen to me. After this meeting with the M.E. I once again made this same promise to myself. I didn't know what the future might bring. Someday, I might even get shot or stabbed by some bad guy, but I definitely didn't intend to drive myself crazy with negative thoughts which were only counterproductive. The meeting with Doctor Farouk had taught me a valuable lesson.

It didn't take long for my resolve to be tested once again. Because we had shot and killed someone the entire incident had to be investigated by the Broward County Grand Jury. That was the law and it really didn't upset me because I fully realized this was the price of doing business. And, I knew that if I wasn't willing to play by the rules then I had no business being a cop. No, having to appear in front of the Grand Jury really didn't bother me. Again, I knew we had acted properly and I was also confident the people on the

Jury would come to that very same conclusion. After all, why wouldn't they? Fort Lauderdale, like many other large and progressive police departments around the country, had our own legal advisor. This attorney worked only for us and he reviewed a multitude of law enforcement related issues. This, of course, included his reviewing all police shootings which resulted in a death. So, it really wasn't unusual that Mr. Languine reviewed the death of bad guy Carlton Johnson. It was s.o.p., and like the upcoming Grand Jury, we expected it. What we didn't expect however, was Mr. Languine's opinion that Mike might have some possible problems because he used a machine gun during the shooting. Mr. Languine's hypothesis was simple; Mike and I were Fort Lauderdale Police Officers, but in the City of Lauderhill we were acting as private citizens, and we had no police powers at all. Any private citizen could have taken action as we had and it would have been entirely legal. Mr. Languine pointed out however, that in most cases it was illegal for private citizens to possess machine guns, let alone use one to kill someone. He speculated that Mike might just have a slight problem with the Feds because of this. How in the hell do you have a "slight problem" with the Feds, I wondered. Even from my own limited police experience it seemed that whenever the Feds became involved in anything, it usually turned into a larger than normal pile of shit!

Mr. Languine wasn't sure if this issue would come up during the grand jury probe of the shooting. He said he doubted it would but he cautioned us that we might want to rethink our previous decision to voluntarily appear before the grand jury as we had planned to do. Once again, that debilitating feeling called paranoia began to invade my mind. Maybe we shouldn't appear before the grand jury, I thought. I suddenly remembered my experience at the M.E.'s office and I got very mad at myself. "This is asinine!" I said out loud. It was obvious Mike agreed with this assessment entirely. Mike, Stewart, Zuccaro and I did eventually appear before the Broward County Grand Jury. Once again, my worst fears never even came close to materializing. The people on the jury were warm and caring and it was also obvious to me that most, if not all of them, seemed to be at least a little bit sympathetic to what a police officer had to sometimes endure. Most of their questions were about T.I.U. and the incident, but one individual wanted to know more about the American 180 itself. Unlike Doctor Farouk, I'm sure he wasn't writing a book, and he was just curious.

The Feds never expressed even the slightest interest in the Lauderhill incident and I learned yet another valuable lesson, this time about police department legal advisors and the shitty advice they sometimes dole out! Contrary to Mr. Languine's belief we might receive some negative reaction, F.L.P.D. got quite a bit of positive media attention instead. The Christmas holiday season was fast approaching and it was now a prime time for robberies. Almost every year robberies increased during November and December. I guess even robbers have to buy Christmas presents too! Then, after the holidays were over, the number of robberies usually declined dramatically. This year was definitely different, however. The day after the killing of Carlton Johnson the front page of the *Fort Lauderdale News* boldly reported in big black type: "Holdup Suspect Killed In Shootout" – "Laser-Aimed Gun Riddles Car." Below the informative article itself was a detailed picture of the suspect's battered red Camaro with Johnson's lifeless body still partially visible there in the passenger seat. The caption beneath the picture said it all: "Suspect's body is slumped in car riddled by shotguns and laser-sighted machine gun."

After Carlton Johnson's death, and the subsequent stories in the press about this event, robberies in the city didn't increase as they usually did – they decreased! Some skeptics might say this was merely coincidental but if you asked any member of T.I.U. I know they'd tell you differently. We were all totally convinced that robbers, in addition to maybe buying presents at Christmas time, if they weren't out stealing them instead, also read the papers too! Now they knew what that damn little red dot meant and they'd go somewhere else to do their Christmas shopping!

1974 was now drawing to a close and even though Carlton Johnson was dead and his accomplice Wallace Tompkins was safely behind bars awaiting trial, T.I.U.'s second deadly encounter in the City of Lauderhill still produced a few more unexpected surprises. One of these new developments involved Lauderhill's Chief of Police. Almost immediately after the robbery and shooting we began to hear "rumors" the Lauderhill chief might be upset with Fort Lauderdale P.D. because we had come into his city without being invited. Someone, and I don't even remember who it was, even suggested we had made Lauderhill's chief look bad. After all, it wasn't his own people who caught Johnson and Tompkins in the act, it was Fort Lauderdale's T.I.U.! I know this sort of narrow-minded thinking sounds totally absurd, and it is. Unfortunately though, many high ranking law enforcement managers continue to embrace this parochial kind of philosophy.

Lauderhill's Chief of Police was a professional cop and we quickly learned there was absolutely no truth at all to this "rumor" about him being upset. His philosophy was very simple; bad guys belonged in jail and he didn't give a damn about who put them there. He was my kind of chief! Later, when he was asked about his reaction to T.I.U. operating within his city, he supposedly replied that he thought we had done a damn good piece of police work. He also reportedly said we could come and work for him anytime we wanted. I appreciated the offer because you never knew for sure what the future might hold. Today we might be heroes, but tomorrow we could easily be on the shit list and unemployed. Being a police officer was something like riding a roller coaster at an amusement park. After every up, there usually was a down! And, just when you thought the ride was over, and nothing else could happen to you, there'd be another twist or turn to endure. But, in the end, you'd almost always find yourself back on solid ground once again - assuming you survived the ride itself! That's what it was like to be a cop!

For a long time, even before the 2nd Lauderhill Shootout, our F.L.P.D. brass had been trying their best to convince Broward County's Sheriff we needed countywide police powers. Surveillances regularly took us outside our own city limits and as Lauderhill had shown twice there was always the potential we'd become involved in a police action in a surrounding jurisdiction. Lauderhill showed exactly what could happen! Our legal advisor's warning about us being just private citizens in these O.J. situations unfortunately was very true. If we intended to operate in neighboring municipalities, outside our own city limits, we definitely needed to be sworn in as B.S.O. deputies. The problem was most sheriffs were very reluctant to relinquish any of their powers and to deputize all the members of T.I.U. meant doing exactly that. The current sheriff, Eugene Stevens, would have at least a dozen new deputies running around his county and he would have absolutely no control over them at all. It was a situation most county sheriffs definitely would avoid, if possible. The sheriff of Broward County was no exception to this unwritten rule. Again, selfish parochialism sometimes became even more important than mutual cooperation and teamwork.

The 2nd Lauderhill shootout, and all the positive media attention that went along with it, suddenly seemed to change all of this. A deal was finally struck between the sheriff and F.L.P.D. and we were told we would now be deputized. Even though we were eventually sworn in as Broward County deputies, and received I.D. cards to prove it, we weren't given the gold star that usually went along with the job. If we wanted one we'd have to go out and buy our own. I don't know if this failure to give us badges was merely an oversight, a budgetary consideration, or what. I suspect there was still some resistance to our being deputized within the upper management ranks at the sheriff's department and this was probably someone's way of protesting the decision one last time. Being deputies was an honor afforded to very few city police officers. It just didn't happen! So, most of us in T.I.U. went out and bought our own badges. We wanted that gold star! You might say it was an ego thing, and maybe you'd be right. I don't know. I do know one thing though; it was a visible symbol that we were indeed among the elite of F.L.P.D.

At about this same time we also began to rethink our supervisor's original philosophy about not giving commendations to T.I.U. officers because we were merely doing our job. True, if we were dispatched to a robbery in-progress call, or even if we responded to a VARDA Alarm and made an arrest, I think we all pretty much agreed that no commendation was warranted. But, if one of us happened to spot some suspicious subjects and then followed them until they finally did commit a robbery, as many members of T.I.U. had done during the past several months, then we all felt these types of self-initiated activity definitely deserved some sort of official recognition. I think we were all pleasantly surprised by the response we received from our supervisors. They listened to us and seemed to be sincerely interested in what we had to say. They didn't promise us things would definitely change but they did promise they would reevaluate their original position. Police bureaucracy is very much like the military's no questions asked mentality and I must admit this willingness to listen to mere subordinates was very refreshing. Unfortunately, it didn't always happen that way.

T.I.U.'s impressive exploits throughout most of 1974, and then the beginning of 1975, helped establish us as one of Florida's premier tactical and/or surveillance type units. During T.I.U.'s first thirteen months, from February 1, 1974 to March 10, 1975, the entire unit made a total of 500 arrests.

161

That's not bad for only six two-man teams! A large percentage of these arrests were for felony type charges. Mike and I were proud of T.I.U.'s accomplishments. We were also equally proud of our own contribution as well. Of the 500 bad guys, and gals, T.I.U. arrested, Mike and I apprehended 143 of them, or about 28% of the total. And, approximately 45% of our arrests were for felonies. Armed robbers were still T.I.U.'s number one target, so we were especially happy with the overall success we'd had in this one specific area. Mike and I arrested 20 subjects for armed robbery; well, really 19, because Carlton Johnson foolishly decided to forgo the formal booking process! Overall, 75% of our robbery arrests occurred while the crime was still in progress, or immediately afterwards. Yes, Mike and I had had a very productive first year. And, we enthusiastically looked forward to more of the same for the rest of 1975!

Mike and I were pleasantly surprised when we learned our supervisors had recommended us for a commendation. I say surprised because even though our supervisors told us they would rethink their original philosophy about not giving out commendations, up until now no one in T.I.U. had received one for anything. There had been many, many good arrests, but no commendations. The 2nd Lauderhill shootout, which resulted in the killing of bad guy Carlton Johnson, was the perfect example. In most other large police departments around the country that type of self-initiated police action would have been "Officer of the Month" material; and, maybe even worthy of "Officer of the Year" consideration. Mike and I got nothing! And, what frosted us even more was the fact that the F.L.P.D. officer who eventually did get "Officer of the Year" got it because he shot at an armed robber who pointed a shotgun at him, but then he missed the damn bad guy entirely! Oh, he was able to shoot his own police vehicle though! Life isn't always fair!

The Bureau Level Commendation we received, dated March 24, 1975, was written by Captain Warren Braddock. As commendations went it was short and to the point: "I wish to express my appreciation and commendation for a job well done. Your alertness and attention to duty has resulted in many arrests. Needless to say the credit you have brought to yourself and this department." It's always nice when your hard work is finally recognized and any commendation is better than none. But, I have to admit Mike and I were both a little bit taken back by the apparent lack of effort Captain Braddock put into the commendation. Some supervisors were obviously better than others and he definitely was no Dan Vaniman or Joe Gerwens.

I don't know exactly when or even how it actually began, but sometime during this first thirteen months I almost became totally addicted to T.I.U. My work seemed to be the most important thing in my life now. I still loved my wife and daughters very much, but all my waking thoughts now revolved around T.I.U. and my work. My family, unfortunately, and through no conscious effort or desire on my part, took a backseat to my own selfish pleasures and gratification. Mike and I were both very good at what we did. We enjoyed our work immensely and we were having the time of our lives. Our normal work hours, 7:00 p.m. to 3:00 a.m., were really kind of shitty, but we could have cared less. We were doing the things most police officers only dream about and I admit I gave very little thought to what an adverse effect all this might have on my own family. Horrendous hours, all night stakeouts that seemed to occur more and more frequently, surveillances and lengthy investigations that sometimes lasted for days; all these things were now an important part of my life. What I obviously failed to realize though was that these things were now also a part of my family's life too. But, I was having a ball and that's all that seemed to really matter to me. My wife Pat hated these hours with a passion but she's an exceptional woman and never ever complained. My two daughters were still to young to fully realize what "daddy's job" really was. It wasn't until much, much later that I learned just how little they really did understand. Apparently, when I'd tell them I'd be going out on a "stakeout" they thought I meant I was gonna go and have a "steak out." They couldn't understand why I didn't take them along because they both liked to eat steak too.

As Mike and I continued to excel at work, and our efforts resulted in many more additional good arrests, I let several other important aspects of my law enforcement career lapse entirely. My overall priorities changed and things that had seemed important to me before were no longer important to me now. For example; I'd always wanted to be a sergeant someday, but now that I was in T.I.U. I had no real desire to be promoted at this stage of my career. I did go through the motions in February and took the sergeant's test but I didn't do that well. I didn't do bad on purpose though, because I would never do that. But, I know I didn't want to be a sergeant and maybe my subconscious feelings inadvertently influenced how I answered the questions. Whatever the reasons, I wasn't going to be a sergeant this time around! I was gonna stay right here in T.I.U!

My almost obsessive behavior involving T.I.U. eventually affected my own off-duty time as well. Because of the dangerous and unique nature of our work most of the members of T.I.U. felt a certain unmistakable kinship with each other. Like Marines, Green Berets and Navy Seals, we too were apparently some of the very best in OUR respective field of expertise. So, it wasn't a real surprise that we began to regularly bond together as a group, even when we weren't working. It began rather innocently at first; every now and then we would all meet after work for a few drinks, but then the occasional night out turned into once, twice, three times a week. Some weeks we might even make it every night! And, like most of the cops I've known we had our own favorite watering hole. Ours was called the "Plantation Inn" and it was located on State Road #7 in the City of Plantation, due west of Fort Lauderdale. For some reason, and I don't know why, it always seemed to me that most cops didn't like to do their drinking in their own city - and I guess us T.I.U. guys were no exception to this unwritten rule.

Once again, I was having such a good time "bonding" with my T.I.U. buddies I totally neglected to even consider what some of the more important negatives might be. I'd usually leave for work right around 6:30 p.m., so this meant I might, but I might not, have dinner at home with my family. Mike and I would work until 3:00 a.m., and then along with most of the rest of the guys, we'd probably head west to the "Plantation Inn" for some suds, fun and relaxation. It wasn't unusual for us to close the place and then we'd more than likely go out and have some breakfast. If I was lucky, I mean really lucky, I might even make it home before the sun came up. I didn't really believe it mattered what I did after work, or what time I staggered in. After all, if I went home right after work at 3:00 a.m., like I probably should have, my family would all be asleep anyway, so why not go out drinking with my brother officers instead? – that's what I kept telling myself! I admit, this stellar example of modern moral philosophy had me totally and thoroughly convinced! But, what I definitely failed to realize at the time, and I know I should have, was that my after hours off-duty activities with the guys couldn't help but have a negative impact on my family. I'd come staggering home, probably before anyone else was even awake, and then I'd plop myself down into our bed and stay there almost all day. Things that should have been done, like maybe yard work for example, never seemed to be that damn important to me. I also stopped going to college, because there was no way at all I could attend classes working this murderous 7:00 p.m. to 3:00 a.m. shift. Now I know I was really only fooling myself, though. The real reason I couldn't attend classes wasn't because of the shitty hours, it was because I was sleeping most of the day away, trying to recover from the night before, and then prepare for the night ahead.

One of the main things I really regret the most is the wasted time I could have spent with my wife and daughters, and didn't! Don't get me wrong, my family and I still did many things together, but we could have done much, much more! My nightly escapades at the "Plantation Inn" were very important to me at the time and I'll always fondly remember the closeness and comradeship these frequent outings helped foster. But, in the end, I think I paid a price for all the adventure, glory and good times I had during my time with T.I.U. - and unfortunately, my family paid a price too! An old French proverb wisely warns, "All the treasures of earth cannot bring back one lost moment."

13

SERGEANT DIERKZON

Sergeant Dan Vaniman left F.L.P.D. for bigger and better things with the U.S. Secret Service and his replacement in T.I.U. was a veteran officer named George Dierkzon. Like Sergeants Gerwens and Vaniman, and Lieutenant Bob Burns, I knew Sergeant Dierkzon quite well and had worked with him before. I hated to see Dan Vaniman leave but it wasn't because I dreaded who his replacement was going to be. I liked and respected Sergeant Vaniman and I knew supervisors like him didn't come along every day. I never will forget how he took my side against Sergeant Richardson, reference the "Lafayette Drugs" fiasco.

I'd known Sergeant Dierkzon since my first few days on the job, back in 1967. My experiences with the man had always been very positive. In fact, George Dierkzon probably taught me the most important and valuable lesson I would ever learn, and he never even said a word to ME in the process! I was a brand new rookie officer and I had absolutely no previous police experience, no formal training and not a clue about what makes a good officer. Then, without any warning at all, I was suddenly thrown smack dab in the middle of the annual Spring Break Invasion along Fort Lauderdale's famous beach. These were the years when hundreds of thousands of college students flocked to the city. Most kids just wanted to have fun but there were always others who couldn't stay out of trouble no matter what they did. The sheer numbers were overwhelming and eventually the situation turned into a complete rout.

At the corner of E.L.O. and A.I.A., right in front of the world famous "Elbow Room," the excited crowd stopped and looted a large bread truck. The police officers stationed there quickly lost control and now we had a major riot-like disturbance on our hands. It took us a number of hours to finally restore order. I'm glad most of the huge crowd wasn't hostile because if they had been I know I could have been hurt very badly. I did some extremely foolish things during this disturbance, things only a totally inexperienced rookie would ever do; like running after a fleeing suspect, then going into the massive crowd of humanity after him. Alone! If someone in the crowd had really wanted to they could have easily overpowered me. Then, they could have beat me to a bloody pulp and no one would have even known about it. I often think about these turbulent nights back in '67 and wonder how I ever managed to survive! Either God felt sorry for me and protected me, or I was just plain lucky! I suspect both were probably true!

After most of the crowd had finally dispersed, and had wisely decided to depart the beach area itself, our secondary role was to deal with the occasional stragglers who defiantly refused to leave. Everyone had been ordered away from the beach strip and this included most of the adjoining land area east of the beautiful Intracoastal Waterway. The I.C.W. separated the major sections of Fort Lauderdale from the beach areas and during this riotous disturbance it became its own Vietnam-styled D.M.Z. If an individual happened to be to the west of the I.C.W., then he was on relatively safe ground. But, anyone caught east of the waterway was still considered to be a threat and they were often dealt with rather harshly. Most of these remaining celebrants apparently realized this and there seemed to be a massed exodus of cars and even people on foot, westbound over the E.L.O. Boulevard Bridge.

During these later stages of this disturbance I was located on the east side of the I.C.W., right near the E.L.O.

Bridge itself. There were also at least another dozen F.L.P.D. officers all around me and George Dierkzon was one of these. A few people were still moving along the streets heading towards the bridge. I watched as one officer approached several subjects and told them to move a little faster. One of them responded with a rude and belligerent "Fuck You!" Under the circumstances that was definitely the wrong answer to give. The officer quickly gave the mouthy guy a very sharp whack across the seat of his pants with his nightstick. Both subjects moved forward now a little more diligently. A few more obnoxious individuals came along and when they began to verbally berate several officers for spoiling their evening out, they too felt the sting of the officers' nightsticks. I noticed that a few officers eventually began whacking some people even before they had an opportunity to mouth off. An officer would say something like, "Move faster," and then before the individual could resist, or even verbally respond, he'd feel the nightstick up against his butt. I'm not trying to defend these officers' actions but for the most part I don't really believe these were truly brutal officers. Oh, I'm sure there were some brutal cops out there that night, and they probably shouldn't even be police officers. But, on the whole, I think most of these men (in 1967 there were no female officers in patrol) were merely trying to do a very difficult job, the best way they knew how. Unfortunately though, they were also frustrated, angry and extremely tired. These factors, coupled with a definite lack of proper training in many cases, led them to react in a very unprofessional manner.

I've said it before but I think it is very important I say it once again - I am not a brutal person! In fact, I'm an easy-going kind of guy and it usually takes something major to really piss me off. You know, like maybe someone trying to shoot me, or run me over with a car! Those two things will definitely get my dander up! But, when I saw some of the other officers using their nightsticks on people who mouthed off, I just assumed that's what I was also expected to do. So,

I did! And, when a few unrepentant sinners gave me a dirty look, I also gave them a quick whack or two in return. My short time on the job, and my lack of training is obviously no excuse for my actions, but at the time I really believed I was doing the right thing. That's until Officer George Dierkzon let me know otherwise.

Dierkzon wasn't that far away from me so I had a good view of him and what he was doing. I saw him talking to many of the people who were walking by him. Most were on their way to the E.L.O. Bridge and although I couldn't hear what was being said it seemed he was merely telling them to move along more quickly. He wasn't having trouble with any of these people and I never ever saw him raise his nightstick to strike anyone. I know George saw the rest of us responding more aggressively than him but for the longest time he never said anything to any of us. An arrogant-looking biker cockily strutted past my position and I recognized him as a trouble maker I'd had some dealings with earlier in the evening. I didn't have anything to arrest him on then and unfortunately nothing had changed. Just being there on the east side of the I.C.W. wasn't a crime. I told him to move along faster and then, just as he curled up his lower lip to loudly protest his right to be here, I gave him a quick but admittedly undeserved whack right across his big fat butt. I know I didn't really hurt him though and I'm fairly certain this brute was in more pain each morning when he looked into his mirror to brush his rotten teeth.

"You guys shouldn't be doing that!" Dierkzon finally said. "It's not right!" He didn't say this loudly and he wasn't even talking to anyone in particular. He was expressing his own personal opinion about what he was seeing, reference what was happening there all around him. I was across the street from George and I could just barely hear him. But, when I looked over at him and saw the disapproval and disgust in his sad eyes, there was no mistaking what he really felt. I immediately knew exactly what George meant! He never directed any of his comments at me specifically but I still got his message just the same! It came through loud and clear! I may not have had any formal police training, but I definitely knew right from wrong. And, it WAS wrong to use unnecessary or excessive force, unless that force was required to effect an arrest. These people on their way to the E.L.O. Bridge weren't being arrested for anything so there was absolutely no justification at all for us to hit them with our nightsticks. I realized I was wrong, and I felt ashamed!

I never really forgot that fateful night at the E.L.O. Bridge. In fact, more than any other single event during my rookie years, and this included my eventual training at the Police Academy, my participation throughout "Spring Break 1967" left me with a new and better understanding of myself. Yes, I'd made some horrible mistakes - mistakes I wished that I could change. But I couldn't! This incident did change me, however. Before this night I'd always thought cops were perfect. Infallible. They knew everything and they had all the right answers. They never ever made mistakes. Now, thanks to George Dierkzon I suddenly realized how totally naive and foolish my previous thinking had been. Cops were human beings just like everyone else on this planet – and they weren't Gods. There were good cops, and unfortunately there were some bad cops. I still believed the overwhelming majority of men and women in law enforcement were good decent people and there were very few real bad apples out there. But, as much as it pained me to admit it, even good cops sometimes made mistakes! Big mistakes!

Even though I'd done wrong and I hit a few "innocent" people with my nightstick I still counted myself among the good guys category. I realized I could still salvage my own self-esteem if I learned from this experience and never made the same mistakes again. When I began to really critique the entire incident itself I found there was really only one major reason why I acted the way I had. The term "peer pressure" was not yet fashionable but that's exactly why I did what I did. I saw many of the other officers using their nightsticks and I didn't want to be different. So, I did things I knew in my heart were wrong. George Dierkzon, with his few well chosen words, intended for no one in particular, gave me a "wake-up call" I'd never forget! He showed me that being different wasn't always bad, and being wrong was even worse! That's the million dollar lesson George taught me and I'll be forever grateful to him because of this. Thanks to him, I think I became a much better police officer; and, even more important, a much better person!

After Dan Vaniman left T.I.U. and the department, and Sergeant George Dierkzon replaced him, most things still seemed to go along rather smoothly at first. This was a very pleasant surprise because I definitely had expected otherwise. Whenever a new sergeant took over a specialized unit, or maybe even just a regular squad, it always seemed as though they immediately had to show everyone that they were now in charge. There were many different ways of doing this but the usual way was to fix something that wasn't even broken. I was glad to see Sergeant Dierkzon was apparently immune to this often popular supervisory phenomenon. Instead, he seemed content, at least for the time being, to gently feel his way through a totally new assignment he knew nothing about. It was refreshing to see a supervisor who wasn't afraid or ashamed to admit he wasn't already an expert. So, in the very beginning Sergeant Dierkzon took on a more passive approach as he continued to quietly observe and learn. I'm sure Sergeant Joe Gerwens own powerful presence in T.I.U. also had something to do with the way George Dierkzon initially conducted himself. After all, from day one, Joe Gerwens had been the dominant supervisor in T.I.U., and now that Dan Vaniman was gone, and Dierkzon had taken his place, that still hadn't changed!

I can't say for sure when it actually started, and when the honeymoon ended, but Mike eventually began to get the distinct impression Sergeant Dierkzon didn't care for us. And, as far as Mike was concerned, I know this feeling was mutual. Mike didn't like our new sergeant all that much, but once again the specific reasons why weren't that clear. Even though Dierkzon carefully avoided any outward display of his true emotions there was still a certain amount of noticeable tension always in the air. At times, it almost seemed as if Mike and the sergeant merely tolerated each other. Initially, I didn't share Mike's opinion that Dierkzon didn't like us and I even felt he was being just a little bit unfair to our new boss. After all, there was no logical reason why the sergeant should dislike us so I really thought most of this negative karma was in Mike's head. I decided Mike was just imagining it.

When Sergeant Dierkzon suddenly exploded one night, and he showed exactly what his true inner feelings were, it didn't take me long to come around to Mike's way of thinking. Mike and I had worked a complex and involved investigation the night before. We made a few felony arrests, confiscated some property and a vehicle, and coordinated everything with several other local jurisdictions which were also involved. What complicated things even more was the fact Fort Lauderdale P.D. had just changed over to an entirely new report writing system. We had always typed our own police reports but now with the advent of this new system we would dictate our reports via phone, to special taped lines in the Records Bureau. These tapes were then transcribed by departmental stenographers and if everything went according to plan we would receive a finalized copy of our finished report a day or two later.

This new and modern reporting system was a giant step forward and once again F.L.P.D. seemed to be out in front and leading the way. As far as I knew no other police departments in Broward County had anything remotely like it. But, as modern as it was, our new reporting system didn't appeal to me that much. I, for one, didn't have any experience at all dictating reports, and I definitely liked to type my own. When I'd type a report I'd read and then reread the narrative as I worked and this almost always helped me to concentrate better. I didn't have any choice in the matter, however. The new system was here and I knew we had to use it! I know the powers to be realized it was going to take some of us a little longer than others to adjust to this new system. It was suggested that we initially write out our reports first in longhand and then read what we'd written. This way we could get use to the new system and eventually we would hopefully begin to feel more comfortable with it. So, when I needed to do the offense report reference the complicated arrests and property seizures Mike and I had made the night before, this is exactly what I did. It took me a little longer to do it this way but in the end we had a finished product I felt I could be proud of. I had survived my first real encounter with this new system.

The next night Mike and I walked into the T.I.U. office and reported in as usual. Sergeant George Dierkzon was seated behind one of the two desks and there were also maybe four or five other tac guys quietly standing around the small cramped office. After Sergeant Dierkzon finished putting out what information he wanted to disseminate he asked if any of us had anything else to discuss. If we didn't, then we could all "Hit the road." I handed the sergeant my overtime card from the night before. I needed him to sign it before I turned it in. He silently looked at it for a few brief seconds and then he suddenly threw it down onto the top of the desk. "This is fucking ridiculous!" he angrily ranted as the card skidded across the desk top like a rock skipping over a pond's still waters. The card eventually went over the edge of the desk and landed on the floor. "I'm not signing this fucking card!" he continued unabated.

I was shocked by Sergeant Dierkzon's outburst and I couldn't figure out what had pissed him off. It wasn't unusual for Mike and I to work past our normal quitting time as we had done the night before. In fact, there were some nights we'd do this even if we weren't involved in anything specific. Our normal time to 10-19 (return to the station) would arrive and Mike and I might decide to stay out just a little longer, if we both had a good feeling something "big" might happen. After these self-imposed extended shifts we never put in for overtime. Our working late wasn't about money. We stayed out because we liked our work, not to make a few extra bucks. This is why I was so puzzled by Sergeant Dierkzon's strange oddball behavior. Mike and I rarely put in for overtime, even when it was appropriate.

I could see the other tac guys getting very, very uneasy. Mike had been lucky though and he wasn't in the room when Dierkzon unexpectedly unloaded on me. He had gone up to teletype to get a criminal history so he missed the fireworks completely. But now, as Sergeant Dierkzon continued to vent his obvious anger, I began to block out most of what he was saying. He was still chewing me out for taking such a long time to finish the report and it seemed apparent that he felt Mike and I had "milked" our investigation for every minute we could. I don't know which emotion I felt more; embarrassment, hurt or anger. I was embarrassed because the sergeant had chosen to chastise me in front of my peers. Even I, who didn't do that well on the sergeant's test in February, knew this was a piss poor way for a supervisor to handle a subordinate! I was also deeply hurt, because other than a smelly goat on my grandfather's small farm in New York, when I was only thirteen, I'd never "milked" anything! Lastly, I was outraged that Dierkzon could be so unfair! Now, I was pretty pissed off myself!

When Sergeant Dierkzon finally stopped his tirade just long enough to catch his breath he looked at me with those hard and wicked-looking eyes and asked, "You got anything you want to say?" He seemed to be really pleased with himself and I even detected what looked like the initial beginnings of a smile. "This bastard enjoyed this!" I thought to myself, as I tried to decide what I should, or shouldn't do, next. My first gut reaction was to reach across the desk and punch his lights out but I quickly rejected this option as being totally out of the question. Even though I was sure I would enjoy it tremendously it would definitely create many more problems than it would solve. Besides, I'd already had my right hand broken twice before, and I didn't want to break it a third time, especially on Sergeant Dierkzon. He wasn't worth it. So, as I continued to think about how I should respond I bent down and picked up the overtime card. I folded it and put it into my shirt pocket.

I don't know why but I suddenly got the feeling I was being set up. Sergeant Dierkzon leaned all the way back in his swivel chair and waited and I realized he wanted me to tell him off. The other tac guys were all still there, even though a few of them were slowly but surely inching their way towards the safety of the hallway. If I told him what I really thought of him, in front of witnesses, I'd be falling right into his trap, and I knew he'd waste no time at all writing me up for insubordination. I realized this and quickly decided the best thing I could do was to keep my mouth shut. That wasn't always an easy thing to do, especially for a guy like me who usually liked to speak his mind! But, I remembered what the philosopher Cyrus Ching had once said, "Never wrestle with a pig. You get dirty, and besides, the pig likes it!" Well, I wasn't gonna be wrestling with no pigs today. And, I wasn't gonna wrestle with Dierkzon either!

"I've got nothing to say," I finally answered softly. I could see this wasn't the answer Dierkzon wanted, or expected. He seemed almost disappointed.
"Then get the hell out of here!" he shot back.

One by one all the tac guys left the room. I was the last one to leave. The minute I got out in the hallway though I knew I just couldn't let Sergeant Dierkzon get away with this kind of unjust and oppressive behavior. I had wisely held my tongue while the other guys were in the office but now that he was alone I knew I had to go back in there and tell him what I really thought. This wasn't any gut wrenching decision on my part, and I didn't spend a lot of time in the hallway building up my courage. Almost as soon as I had exited the T.I.U. office I made an about-face and went back in. That's how long it took me to think about what I had to do. Who knows, if I had taken the time to analyze all the possible ramifications I might not have gone back into the office to confront Sergeant Dierkzon. But I didn't - so I did!

Sergeant Dierkzon seemed to be surprised to see me again so soon. When I walked into the office he had been looking down at one of the reports on the desk so he didn't know it was me until he looked up and saw me standing there in front of him. As they say, the best defense is a good offense, so I really didn't give him a chance to start in on me again.

"You know sergeant," I began rather slowly. My overall tone may have been firm and steady but there was still nothing disrespectful about the way I spoke to him. "I have to tell you, I don't appreciate the way you talked to me in front of my peers." I could see he wanted to say something back but I never gave him the chance to respond. "You're my sergeant," I continued, "and you have the right, and the obligation, to point out any weaknesses I may have. That's your job, and I expect you to tell me when I'm doing something wrong. But, you don't have the right to purposely humiliate me in front of the men I work with. That was wrong! I came in here to tell you I'm writing a letter complaining about your actions tonight. I'm going to request an internal investigation! That's all I have to say."

I kind of expected another violent broadside from the sergeant but he seemed to take what I had just said rather docilely. I think he was stunned by my sudden outburst, even though it was nowhere near as explosive and degrading as his had been.

"Okay, fine," he eventually replied. This time however, in sharp contrast to his previous verbal exploits, I just barely heard him.

I turned and started to leave the office once again. I fully expected him to stop me. I didn't want him to, but I expected it. After all, most good supervisors will usually try to diffuse a problem with a subordinate before it gets totally out of control. Sergeant Dierkzon had the perfect opportunity to do just that but he failed to take advantage of it. I don't know if in his own arrogant way he still believed he was right and I was wrong, or maybe he did realize he had acted improperly, but his own stupid pride wouldn't let him admit his mistake. Whatever the reason, he let me walk out the door without another word being said.

After I finished telling Sergeant Dierkzon what I thought about his supervisory style I immediately felt 100% better. In fact, I felt so damn good I even decided against writing a letter of complaint as I'd originally told him I would. I believed I had made my point and hopefully given him something to think about. I was totally satisfied with this and I didn't think an official investigation was needed now. So, Mike and I went out on patrol and I tried to forget about this very unpleasant experience. What I didn't know however, was that Sergeant Dierkzon not only got my point, now he was worried silly about the letter he thought I intended to write. We never saw him on the road during the hours we were out there and we never even heard him on the radio either. It was as though he had disappeared. I learned later, from another tac guy who had gone by the T.I.U. office to pick up a piece of equipment for one of the VARDA Alarms, that Sergeant Dierkzon was busily working on his own letter, which was apparently intended to be a response to mine.

I know I probably should have cleared the air and informed Sergeant Dierkzon I no longer intended to submit a letter of complaint against him. That would have been the nice thing to do. But, I didn't feel nice! Telling him what I thought of him definitely made me feel better, but I was still just a little bit upset because of the humiliating way he had unjustly demeaned me in front of my brother officers. I suppose I enjoyed the thought of him worrying about my upcoming letter - the letter I now had no intention to write. This almost pathetic image of him struggling there at his typewriter, frantically pounding out the words that would hopefully justify his own actions, excited me in a strange perverted sort of way. According to my Mom, when I was growing up in California I sometimes exhibited a mischievous or even an almost sadistic behavior. She said I was an adventurous lad and when I got bored I'd often kill time by catching a fly or two. Then, very carefully, I'd remove the poor fly's wings and watch as it helplessly rolled around on the ground. A young boy's curiosity can sometimes be a very frightening thing! Now, Sergeant Dierkzon was my fly without any wings, and I admittedly enjoyed watching him suffer! Some boys never grow up entirely - and some things don't change all that much!

I should have known Sergeant Dierkzon wouldn't consciously allow me to have the last laugh. If he was going to spend the time and effort to put together a letter of his own I should have realized he'd turn that sucker in no matter what I did with my own letter. I hadn't heard anything for several days and the sergeant seemed to be cordial and polite. I really thought the entire incident had just gone away. But, when I found myself being called into the lieutenant's office, I knew it hadn't gone away at all. Dierkzon apparently wouldn't let it! I felt a bit uncomfortable as I entered the lieutenant's office. Bob Burns, T.I.U.'s first lieutenant, was no longer here, and he had been replaced by this new man. I felt uneasy for several different reasons. First of all, I believed Bob Burns had gotten a really raw deal when he was suddenly transferred out of T.I.U. As the unit's very first lieutenant he obviously had taken on an important assignment requiring a great deal of sweat, dedication and energy. Unfortunately however, Bob Burns didn't fit the stereotyped image some of the brass had of what the perfect tac lieutenant should look like. Bob was a large individual, so large in fact, he eventually earned the nickname "Massive Dude." One night several tac guys were interrogating a couple of subjects and up putt-putted Lieutenant Burns on one of the unit's very small Honda motorcycles. Bob's massive body totally obscured the cycle's metal frame and all you could see was Lieutenant Burns, two wheels, a white headlight and a red taillight. One of the two subjects quickly remarked, "Man, look at that 'Massive Dude' over there!" The catchy nickname stuck!

The only thing that really exceeded Lieutenant Burns' enormous size and weight was the tender heart inside the man itself. Like Sergeant Vaniman, Bob Burns was that rare supervisor; a man we respected and admired, and a man we would truly do anything for! No, I wouldn't have minded if Lieutenant Burns had been the one to hear Sergeant Dierkzon's complaint against me. I knew he would have been fair and objective. But, now that "Massive Dude" was gone my fate apparently rested with this new and totally untested police lieutenant. I worried that since he had been chosen to replace Bob Burns, for what I considered unwarranted and even stupid reasons, he might just be a "yes-man" and do the popular thing. The popular thing, of course, would be to back the sergeant, no matter what.

The lieutenant's office was small and cramped. Sergeant Dierkzon and I sat next to each other and we both faced the lieutenant who was seated behind the medium-sized metal desk. The sergeant said very little and initially the lieutenant did most of the talking. From his comments it immediately became clear he had either been thoroughly briefed by the sergeant, or at least he had read and digested the contents of Dierkzon's letter. I had not seen the letter myself so I had no idea at all what it said. I must say my initial misgivings were totally unnecessary because the lieutenant's overall manner was friendly and non-accusatory. Just from the way he spoke, and the way he carefully chose his words, I got the definite impression he really didn't want to be involved in such a trivial incident. After all, there were many other matters that were much more important, that deserved his attention. I'm sure he wondered why this incident had even been brought to him in the first place. Sergeant Dierkzon should have handled it himself!

When it was my turn to speak I tried to keep my explanation short and simple. I told the lieutenant about the complicated arrests Mike and I had made and then I went over each individual factor which contributed to the overtime we eventually accrued. Foremost among these, of course, was the simple fact F.L.P.D. had just switched to the phone dictation reporting system, and per the instructions we all received, I wrote my report out longhand before I actually called it in. This took an extra hour or so. I didn't go into a long boring monologue about how I felt Sergeant Dierkzon had wronged me. In fact, in my own clumsy way I even tried offering him an olive branch of sorts. Well, instead of a branch, it may have only been a twig!

"I'm sorry Sergeant Dierkzon believes our overtime request is unjustified," I began slowly, and deliberately. "It really bothers me that my sergeant would think I'd be 'milking' a call. That's not me, and it bothers me he would think I would do such a thing. This really isn't about money so if Sergeant Dierkzon doesn't feel I earned it, I don't want any overtime."

The lieutenant remained silent for several brief seconds and he seemed to be reading through a copy of the offense report I'd submitted reference these arrests. After he finished, he put the report down on the desk and began to speak. "Gary, the bottom line is you worked more than your regular hours, so you earned the overtime and you're entitled to it."

Out of the corner of my eye I could see Sergeant Dierkzon moving around in his seat. He appeared to be a little uneasy. I was sure he wasn't happy with what the lieutenant had just said.

"Sir, I appreciate that," I quickly answered back. Then added, "But, I really don't want it if my sergeant doesn't think I deserve it." I wasn't being openly rude or hostile, in fact my overall tone was soft and subdued. Sergeant Dierkzon never said a word!

"Well, I'm going to sign your card anyway," the lieutenant continued assertively. "You earned it. In the future though, I think you need to try and speed things up just a little. Okay?"

Dierkzon and I watched the lieutenant sign my overtime card. After he finished he reached across the desk and handed it to me. I appreciated the difficult and uncomfortable position the lieutenant had found himself in and I realized his last comment to me, about speeding things up just a little, was probably meant to be a bone thrown to Sergeant Dierkzon. "Yes sir, I'll do my best."

Okay Officer, It's Decision Time!

(Situation #15)

Sergeant Dierkzon's complaint against you, about your overtime card, has been resolved in your favor. The lieutenant signs the overtime card and gives it to you. What should you do next?

What is your answer? (put an "X" in the space in front of your answer)

❑ _____ You've won! Say "Thank you!" and then leave the lieutenant's office a.s.a.p. without any further comment. Consider yourself fortunate that the lieutenant is a fair and objective supervisor.

❑ _____ Because of the lieutenant's decision Sergeant Dierkzon has been humiliated and you'd like to appease him a little, if possible. You again advise the lieutenant you really don't want the overtime if your sergeant doesn't think you earned it. You eventually tear up the card to prove your point, but you make sure to do this in a very respectful way. The last thing you want to do is to alienate the lieutenant.

An analysis of this situation appears at the end of the book

(Do <u>not</u> go there until you have finished reading this chapter)

I probably should have just left the office and considered myself lucky. I mean, the lieutenant had been more than fair to me. And, contrary to my original fears he had reviewed this incident objectively and made his decision based solely on the facts and nothing else. This man was definitely no "yes-man," that was for sure! Even though I was enormously happy with the outcome; I hadn't been declared at fault, I wasn't going to be disciplined, and Sergeant Dierkzon had clearly been humiliated, I still felt the need to make one last final statement.

"You know lieutenant," I began confidently, "I've said this before, and I'll say it again, this really isn't about money! Mike and I like our work and we've worked overtime many other times and haven't even asked for compensation."

The lieutenant just looked at me without saying anything in return. I continued. "Again, if Sergeant Dierkzon doesn't feel we earned this overtime, I really don't want it!"

"Well Gary, I've signed your card so the overtime is yours."

"Sir, can I do anything I want with this card?"

I don't know if the lieutenant actually knew what was coming but he definitely had a "please-don't-do-anything-stupid" sort of look on his face. "Yes," he answered slowly.

"Good!" I responded, as I immediately took hold of the O.T. card with both of my hands and tore it in half. I then took these two pieces and tore them again. The card was now in four pieces. "I'm not going to turn this card in and I'd like to forget all about this incident completely. Is there anything else sir?"

"No, you can go."

"Thank you sir."

As I left the lieutenant's office Sergeant Dierkzon quietly remained seated. I knew damn well he and the lieutenant would discuss everything in much more detail after I'd gone. I never looked over at Dierkzon as I departed and I wasn't able to see his reaction when I tore the card up, so I really didn't know what he thought about what had happened. Had I been able to smooth things over a little? Or, by tearing up the card had I made things worse? I really didn't know. But, to tell you the truth, I also didn't care! I had done what I thought was right! No man ever needs to apologize or feel ashamed about his actions, not as long as he does what his heart and conscience tells him is the right thing to do!

This whole miserable affair died a quiet death, even though Sergeant Dierkzon vainly tried to keep it alive with his own unique brand of CPR. Later, "off the record," the lieutenant advised me Dierkzon had wanted me disciplined for tearing up my overtime card in front of them. The sergeant felt that it had been disrespectful and insubordinate for me to do this! The lieutenant obviously didn't want to openly criticize one of his own sergeants, especially to one of the man's subordinates, but in an apparent moment of weakness he did make the comment that Dierkzon was "a little bit weird." He also cautioned me that I should watch my butt because Dierkson seemed to definitely have it in for Mike and I. I appreciated the advice and filed it away in the back of my mind. I added Sergeant Dierkzon to that very short list of F.L.P.D. supervisors I knew I needed to be leery of when I was around them. Dierkzon's name now had the honor of being first, and K-9 Sergeant Richardson was bumped down to number two.

14

JIMMY HATCHER

With all its splendor and glory the summer of 1975 arrived in south Florida. And, on June 30, 1975, the motion picture "*Jaws*" made its nationwide debut. It was an instantaneous hit and an enormous success. Like millions of Americans all across this great country my wife and I braved the long lines to see this exaggerated tale about a large and totally neurotic killer fish. It seemed ironic this popular movie just happened to be playing at the same Lauderhill mall where T.I.U. had spent so much of its time following bad guys around. As Pat and I stood in line waiting for our turn to enter the packed theater I quietly looked south into the crowded parking lot where we had parked our vehicle. I thought of Wallace Tompkins and his dead buddy Carlton Johnson. Just prior to their ill-fated robbery attempt in November, at the drive-thru milk store across the street from the mall lot, they had also stopped their red Camaro in this same lot. In fact, I suddenly realized tonight I parked our car in almost the same exact spot they had. As I looked at the milk store across the street, I reminded myself how unpredictable life could sometimes be. I also began to think about the violent shooting itself but just then we reached the box office and I bought our tickets and we entered the theater.

Armed with a large buttered popcorn, a couple of Cokes, and a box of gooey but delicious Milk Duds, Pat and I located two of the last remaining vacant seats inside the theater. We made ourselves comfy just as the movie started. I enjoyed the movie's gruesome story line, even when the ocean turned red with the blood of the monster shark's many helpless victims. But, like many other cops my mind sometimes wandered and I'd find myself playing "what if" games at the most inopportune times. You know, "what if" games like: "what if" this restaurant I'm in gets held up while I'm eating here? "What if" someone tries to rob me while I'm out on the golf course? "What if" Jack the Ripper came to my house and tried to sell me some magazines? These mental exercises, though maybe a little absurd, helped keep me sharp and alert, and someday I knew they might even save my ass! They were also distracting though, especially when I was trying to watch a movie.

When the movie's Chief Brody tried to single-handedly kill *Jaws* by shooting the monster fish with his puny little .38 caliber Police Special, my mind began to wander. After all, I could relate to Chief Brody's total lack of success. I thought back to my 1968 car chase to Deerfield Beach when we shot one of the two car thieves in the head and our own .38 caliber round failed to penetrate the suspect's thick skull. I guess that's one unique thing some lucky bad guys and the Great White both have in common, their apparent ability to resist a would-be executioner's coup de grace.

Now, in addition to understanding how totally frustrated Chief Brody must be, I also suddenly received one of my "what if" kind of messages from my brain. "What if" someone was breaking into our car in the theater parking lot right now and I went outside and caught them in the act? - I found myself thinking. For a few intense moments my imagination ran completely wild with thoughts of foot chases, possible struggles, and yes, maybe even "Shots Fired!" I eventually tried to stop thinking about this "what if" scenario and concentrate on the movie instead. But, for some unknown reason this particular "what if" message almost seemed like a damn premonition and I really felt I should go outside and check our vehicle. Something deep inside me told me I should.

Pat and I were seated smack dab in the middle of the crowded theater and for me to get up and then out to the aisle meant moving right in front of many other people. I didn't want to do this. If I had been sitting in an aisle seat, where I usually liked to sit, I would have definitely left the theater to check on our car. I wasn't though, so I forced myself to ignore this enormously strong "gut feeling" and chalked this possible premonition up to my over active imagination. After a few more minutes I finally settled down and I was able to enjoy the rest of the show. I especially liked the ending when Chief Brody blew the shark up into a million pieces. That's one way to get rid of a shark, or maybe even a suspect.

I know it doesn't take an Einstein to figure out what Pat and I found when we eventually returned to our car after the movie was over. You guessed it; bigger than shark shit, our car had been broken into. When I saw that puddle-like mass of broken glass there on the pavement I immediately knew what had happened. I, who prided myself on being the protector of the weak and the abused, was now the victim! And, to make matters even worse I made it easy for the s.o.b., whoever the asshole had been. I don't know why I did it but I had left my briefcase on the back seat, right there in plain view for every Tom, Dick and Harry to see. Talk about being careless. If I could have done it, without turning myself into a human pretzel, I would have given myself a swift kick in the ass. I deserved it for being so incredibly stupid.

It's funny, but when the investigating officer routinely asked me if I'd seen anyone suspicious around our vehicle, or did I have any suspects in mind, I immediately thought of our dead guy Carlton Johnson! Maybe this was his way of getting even with us; we killed him, so he comes back and breaks into my car when I park it in his favorite spot at the Lauderhill Mall. Wow, talk about an over active imagination! I hadn't believed in ghosts, goblins or even monsters for a very long time; not since I was a wee lad growing up in Oakland. Now, I had to really laugh that I thought about the subject Johnson, even if only momentarily. I knew there was no way at all a supernatural spirit was responsible for the burglary of my vehicle. If any monster was involved I was sure it was the two-legged kind that breathed fresh air and walked upright. But, if Carlton Johnson had come back to haunt me, which I doubted, he'd done a really piss poor job of it. He was almost as bad a ghost as he was a robber. After all, he'd made a rather pathetic trade; he took my briefcase, yet we had taken his life. As the drive-thru milk store robbery had shown, Carlton never was much of a businessman.

So far, emotionally, the summer of 1975 had been a real roller coaster of a ride for me. It began on the extreme downside with the completion of the U.S. withdrawal from South Vietnam and the total collapse of the South Vietnamese government itself; but then things perked up just a little with the successful American effort to rescue the kidnapped crew of the *Mayaguez*. But, the burglary of my own vehicle at the Lauderhill Mall parking lot, while Pat and I watched "*Jaws*" and happily munched hot buttered popcorn, once again had a somewhat negative effect on my morale. Even so, I still tried to maintain an overall positive attitude because I realized for every up there was usually a down, and vice versa.

Mike and I continued to make our fair share of good quality felony arrests but that didn't mean we totally ignored the minor lawbreaker altogether. As long as we had a legitimate charge we would take anyone to jail for anything! Our overall philosophy was very simple; the more subjects Mike and I stopped and checked out, the more likelihood we'd find us a real live bad guy. Unfortunately though, if you ran enough clowns through teletype you'd eventually find some bozos who were wanted for some pretty strange things! Some of our not so memorable incarcerations included exciting offenses such as: Tampering with phone company equipment, Violation of the Financial

189

Responsibility Law, Urinating in the open and one of my own personal favorites, Failure to return a rental tool!

My arthritic-like right knee still bothered me some and I'm not exaggerating when I say I experienced a certain amount of pain each and every day. It was usually tolerable though and I still considered myself to be much luckier than most other people. Even so, maintaining a positive and optimistic outlook was sometimes just a little bit difficult. But, I'd decided long ago I would try and take one day at a time and not worry about what the future might bring. Even though I kept telling myself this was what I needed to do this was sometimes easier said than done. But now, several very important things suddenly happened, and each had a tremendous and immediate impact on me emotionally.

In late June Mike and I arrested a white male subject by the name of Jimmy Hatcher. Hatcher had walked into a small redneck type bar on Riverland Road (S.W. 27th Avenue), just a few blocks south of Broward Boulevard. He must have thought he was James Bond, or maybe even "Our Man Flint," because underneath his unobtrusive looking blue jean jacket was a rather large caliber revolver. I don't know if Hatcher was showing off and purposely let the barmaid see the butt of the handgun, or if she merely saw it by accident, but see it she did. She called the police without his knowledge and since we were only a few short blocks away we responded as a back-up to the marked unit that had been originally dispatched. We were out of uniform, so we entered the bar first. We quickly spotted our wanna-be secret agent sitting by himself at the bar. After we disarmed him without incident we carted him off to jail. In Florida, carrying a concealed firearm without a permit is a felony. End of story? Well, not quite.

Jimmy Hatcher pled guilty and he was quickly sentenced to a minimal security type facility. He was considered a low risk so part of his overall sentence included his doing road gang type work. This was hard back breaking work, especially during south Florida's long hot summer months. So, in mid-August, Hatcher, apparently not content to merely serve out the remainder of his sentence, suddenly walked away from the road gang and escaped. Mike and I immediately began looking for him and it didn't take us very long to locate him. In fact, Hatcher really made it easy for us. On the afternoon of August 16th, in broad daylight, another tac unit spotted Hatcher as he nonchalantly walked northbound along the west side of Riverland Road. He was only a few short blocks south of the bar where we had arrested him only six weeks earlier. Man, talk about a set of balls!

Neither Mike nor I, or any other tac guys for that matter, intended to take Jimmy Hatcher for granted. As we covertly moved into our positions to intercept him, we didn't need to remind ourselves that this particular fugitive had been armed the last time we encountered him. As far as we were all concerned, until we learned otherwise, Hatcher was a very real threat to each and every one of us, and we would treat him accordingly. As Al Smith and his partner slowly moved in from the south, and us from the north, I began to experience that same strange feeling of exhilaration I always seemed to get just before something big was about to happen.

When we finally pulled our unmarked vehicle up to the fugitive Hatcher he had just reached a side street that branched off Riverland Road and entered the residential area to the west. As Mike and I started to exit our car, a somewhat surprised Jimmy Hatcher looked straight ahead and directly at us. Then, he quickly took another uneasy look behind him and he saw Al Smith's vehicle coming at him very fast. I don't know if Hatcher recognized Mike and I from his previous arrest at the bar but I'm sure it didn't take him very long to realize just what was happening. He knew he couldn't go forward, he couldn't go backwards, and he also apparently didn't want to cross busy Riverland Road and go east, so his only logical choice was to run west into the residential area. He looked at us one more time and then took off like some world class sprinter bolting out of the starting blocks for the race of his life.

Hatcher ran west for one very short block, then immediately cut back southbound at the first cross street he came to. I don't know how I was able to do it but for that first short block I actually seemed to be keeping pace with the fast moving subject. He'd had a very good head start on us but the overall distance between him and I still didn't seem to be getting any bigger. However, it also wasn't getting any smaller. I'd estimate there were at least thirty to forty feet separating us as I turned the corner and now headed south like Hatcher had just done. I knew Mike was also chasing after him, and Mike admittedly was in much better physical condition than I was, and he didn't have a gimpy bum knee to slow his ass down, so I was a little bit surprised that I was still out in front. My temporary moment of glory was about to come to an abrupt end though.

I suddenly heard the unmistakable sounds of someone running off to my left, just behind me. I took my eyes away from Hatcher's backside for a split second and looked over my left shoulder. It was Mike!

"Go back and get the car!" he yelled, as he passed me like I was standing still.

I couldn't believe it! I had thought I was doing so good, keeping up with Hatcher and all, and being out in front, and now Mike had left me in the dust of southwest Lauderdale! It was a scene reminiscent of the famous story about the tortoise and the hare; Mike, of course, was the cocky and confident hare, and I was the hapless and slow-moving tortoise. I must admit, even with my bum knee and all, I'd never before thought of myself as an ugly green turtle.

I don't know if it was my own shattered ego, my foolish stubborn pride, or merely just a fierce determination somewhere deep inside me, but something definitely wouldn't allow me to stop my now faltering pursuit of the fleeing fugitive Jimmy Hatcher. When Mike yelled for me to go back and get our car, I never answered him. I couldn't. My right knee hurt me a little, but my lungs hurt a lot more, and they felt as if they were about to explode! There was no way I was gonna waste any precious energy trying to respond verbally to Mike's command. Even though I knew I wasn't going to catch up with the subject Hatcher, I also knew Mike was fast enough that he might just run him down and I definitely wanted to be there when Mike put the cuffs on him. This was immensely important to me and I needed to prove to myself, bad knee and all, that I could still cut it when I had to. Tactically, I suppose going back for the car might have been the wise thing to do, but it would have meant leaving Mike alone with Hatcher, without a back-up. So, I wasn't gonna stop! It was just as simple as that!

After Hatcher ran due south for one very short block he reached the next cross street which branched off to the west. He immediately changed his overall direction and headed westbound into this normally quiet and predominately middle-class neighborhood. Nice looking single-story homes lined both sides of the street. Now, as he ran westward, I lost sight of him completely. Seconds later, Mike turned this same corner and also disappeared from my view. I was still running as hard as I could, heading south towards the same corner where Hatcher and Mike had turned westbound. But between my bad knee and a definite lack of air for my oxygen starved lungs I was falling farther and farther behind.

Even though I no longer saw them, I believed Hatcher and Mike were still running on the paved roadway portion of the street. The house on the corner momentarily blocked my overall view of the suspect and Mike, but nothing else had happened that would make me think Hatcher had once again changed his direction. When I last saw him he had just started running westbound down the middle of the street and I believed he still was. I knew he wouldn't continue to do this indefinitely however, and sooner or later he'd turn to either the north or the south. If he continued running down the street itself I felt certain Mike would eventually overtake him and run his scrawny ass down. Therefore, instead of my staying on the street, like Hatcher and Mike, I decided I would parallel them by going through the backyards. That way, when Hatcher finally did turn north or south, I'd have a 50-50 chance of being right there to intercept him. Considering the circumstances, these weren't bad odds.

When I reached the corner house a second or two later I never even hesitated and I just aimed myself straight for the backyard and hoped my tired brain would be able to make the rest of my totally exhausted body cooperate. I was like a jet fighter in trouble; the auto pilot was on and working, but the engine had suffered a dangerous flameout long ago. As I entered the small backyard located just north of the corner residence I began to wonder if it was finally time for me to bail out. A waist high chain link fence separated the back yard I was in from the backyards to the north and it seemed to run westward for as far as I could see. But, there weren't any fences between the house I was behind, the one next door, or the one next door to that one. "Well," I thought to myself, as I continued to jog along slowly, "at least I won't have to climb any fences!"

I was still behind the corner house, smack dab in the middle of the backyard, making my way towards the backyard area of the house next door, when I first heard what sounded like someone huffing and puffing. My initial reaction was I was only hearing my own grunting and groaning. "God, I sound awful!" I thought. But, when the sounds grew increasingly louder, and closer, I realized they weren't coming from me. At this exact same moment I looked to my left between the two houses and observed the suspect Hatcher hauling ass for all he was worth. Just as I had anticipated he left the street and now he was frantically cutting back northbound between the two houses. He was trying everything he could to get Mike off his ass. It may have worked too, because Mike didn't seem to be anywhere around him.

Even though it was night, and the backyard was very dark, I'm sure Hatcher saw me at exactly the same time I first saw him. It was unavoidable and I'm sure he was probably shocked. I imagine he never expected to find someone there waiting for him in that backyard. When I observed him I immediately started to slow my forward progress down a bit, but this really wasn't that hard to do because by this time I wasn't moving that fast. Hatcher also tried to stop, but his herky-jerky actions were much more abrupt and sudden than mine. It's good we both tried to stop because if we hadn't, and if we both continued forward as before, we would have definitely collided with one another. I'm sure about that! I may not have been that proficient in high school geometry, in fact I even failed the course twice before I finally managed to get a passing grade, but I could still draw a straight line. Our two paths would have intersected and our bodies would have come together.

Having body-to-body physical contact with Hatcher was the last thing I wanted to do. There was no way in hell I wanted to get that close to him. After all, he was a fugitive and it was very obvious he didn't want to go back to jail. This meant he was desperate. And, to a cop, the word desperate was spelled only one way: D-A-N-G-E-R-O-U-S! In his bid to stay out of jail Hatcher could be capable of anything. I didn't intend to give him the opportunity to show me just how dangerous he might be. As we silently stood there looking intently at one another I suddenly realized I had my S&W 9mm Automatic in my right hand. I don't remember when I first pulled it out, and I'm not even sure if I had it in my hand all during the foot chase to the backyard, but somewhere along the line my instincts took over and the gun ended up in my hand. Now, I was ready for whatever Hatcher had in mind.

"Jimmy, give it up!" I ordered firmly. "You're under arrest!" I was almost totally out of breath but my words seemed to be clear and crisp and I was sure Hatcher understood their meaning. He just stood there frozen though, as if he were trying to decide what he should do next. There were less than ten feet separating the two of us and I still felt I was dangerously close to the suspect. It wouldn't take much for him to lunge at me and make a grab for the gun in my right hand. I found myself taking a few cautious steps backwards away from him. For the moment his hands seemed to be empty, but I still didn't know if he had a weapon or not. I reminded myself of one very important thing; last time we'd met, Hatcher carried a big, bad nasty revolver!

"Put your hands in the air!" I barked loudly. "Let me see your hands!"

Hatcher obviously was still undecided about what exactly he should do next. His favorite choices apparently did not include surrender, however. I watched him as he took a few steps back towards the south, in the same direction he had just come from. He suddenly stopped, turned back around towards me, and then began to move straight ahead, right at me. I yelled "Stop!" very loudly, and emphasized the foolhardiness of his actions by pointing the barrel of my automatic right at his head. If I had to shoot this stupid jerk the bullet would hit him right between the eyes! I didn't want to shoot him though, but I wasn't gonna back up any more either! And, I wasn't going to let him get close enough to hurt me! His choices now became fewer. If he made the right decision he would live; the wrong one, and he stood a good chance of dying.

Hatcher had stopped his erratic moving around and it seemed as if he'd finally made the decision to stand his ground. He wasn't running away, but he wasn't surrendering either. It looked as if he intended to go down fighting. I still had no desire to engage the s.o.b. in the gentlemanly art of fisticuffs or any other form of physical contact for that matter. That would put him way to close to my weapon and if he didn't have one of his own he might just be tempted to make a try for mine. No, I still intended to stay as far away from him as possible but take him into custody just the same. I knew this would be a neat trick if I could pull it off, because at this point in time Hatcher didn't seem to be that eager or willing to cooperate.

Now, he no longer faced me straight on and I didn't have a clear and unobstructed view of his right side. This concerned me! I also couldn't see his right arm and from his overall movements it looked as if Hatcher might be reaching for a weapon possibly hidden somewhere on his right side. Was I paranoid? You bet I was paranoid! The sheer exhaustion brought on by the long and stressful foot pursuit, the tension of a face-to-face confrontation with an unpredictable individual who refused to be arrested, the suspicious movements of an obviously desperate man, all these things definitely contributed to my paranoia!

I again found myself faced with the most momentous decision any cop will ever have to make; shoot, or don't shoot! Even though I hadn't seen a weapon, I still suspected Hatcher had one, and now it appeared he was reaching for it. Should I go ahead and shoot the bastard because I merely thought he might have a gun or should I wait a second or two more and make sure? I was torn between these two options. I knew that whenever you waited these few more precious moments, in addition to giving a suspect more time to surrender, you also might be giving him the advantage and the edge. If he chose to capitalize on your generosity, but not surrender, he might even be able to get off a first shot, if he's lucky!

Okay Officer, It's Decision Time!

(Situation #16)

The last time you arrested Jimmy Hatcher he was carrying a concealed firearm. You know he is an escapee and now he's resisted arrest by fleeing and you are in a face-to-face confrontation with him in the back yard of a residence. You have ordered him to surrender, but he hasn't. What should you do next?

What is your answer? (put an "X" in the space in front of your answer)

❑ _____ Because you can't see the subject's right side, and it appears he may be reaching for a weapon, you shoot the subject.

❑ _____ As much as you didn't want to come into physical contact with the subject, you rush and tackle him, and take him down to the ground.

❑ _____ You strike the subject in the head with your gun and this makes him fall to the ground.

❑ _____ You wait. You want to see what he does next. If he takes off running, then you'll have to chase him again.

Note: Even though you have been issued *Mace*, you don't have it with you tonight, so you can't use it to subdue the subject Hatcher.

An analysis of this situation appears at the end of the book

(Do not go there until you have finished reading this chapter)

Alright, it was decided; I didn't see a gun yet, so I wasn't going to shoot him! As a general rule, unless I actually saw a weapon in a suspect's hand I usually would hold my fire. But, I also wasn't going to let this bad guy get off the first shot either, not if I could help it. Once again my survival instincts took over. I quickly moved forward and when I was within arm's reach of the suspect I lashed out with my right arm and hand. The barrel of my 9mm impacted squarely against the left temple area of Hatcher's head. He was knocked off balance by the force of the blow and he immediately fell backwards and ended up on the ground.

"Let me see your hands!" I ordered again, as I now brought my weapon back up to the ready position. I also took several steps away from Hatcher, just in case he still might want to resist further. I hoped he wouldn't.

As I watched the suspect lay there on the ground in almost a half sitting position, for the very first time, out of the corner of my eye, I saw Mike approaching us from the south. He was running northward between the houses. Another split second and then Mike was there with Hatcher and I in the backyard. I knew he must have seen it when I popped Hatcher with the barrel of my gun and now I suddenly realized Hatcher must have seen Mike too. That's why he never ran back south towards the street even though he'd started that way just before I slammed him. I guess he knew he was finally cornered but I still couldn't figure out why he decided to fight us rather than surrender. Desperate men often do desperate things; and I'd learned long ago you can never really anticipate what a man like this will do. Next to women, small children and juries, desperate men were perhaps the most unpredictable and complicated creatures on this planet.

Hatcher didn't seem to have any real fight left in him now and I suspect he was just as tired and worn out from the foot pursuit as I was. Mike and I easily cuffed him and took him into physical custody without any further incident. After we put Hatcher into the back seat of a transport unit, Mike softly asked, "G.P.," - Mike liked to call me by my first two initials G.P., for Gary Phillip – "did you really have to hit him in the head?" I looked at him and smiled, because I knew he wasn't being judgmental or critical, he was just showing his frustration. "Now we'll have to take this s.o.b. to the hospital and baby sit him," Mike added, with a definite hint of disgust in his voice. I observed a small but steady trickle of blood seeping out of the left side of Hatcher's head and I knew Mike was right. The jail would never take him the way he was, so now we'd have to take him to the hospital instead. There, he'd be put on a waiting list, but the priority life threatening cases would, of course, be handled first. That meant we'd probably have to hang around the hospital for hours before they'd even begin to put the first stitch into Humpty Dumpty's broken head.

This was why Mike was upset and I knew Mike didn't mean anything personal by his comments. I had no qualms at all about my own actions. Some people might say hitting Hatcher in the head with the barrel of my gun was excessive force. I, of course, would strongly disagree! My choices involving the fugitive suspect had been very limited; I could have shot him, gotten into a wrestling match with him, let him run away again or did what I did. Shooting him, or wrestling with him, were out of the question! I didn't feel comfortable putting a bullet in him, and I didn't want to get so close to him he might be able to overpower me and take my gun, and then maybe put a bullet in me. Letting the punk run away was also unthinkable. What would happen if he took an innocent person hostage, or hurt someone else? No, Hatcher had to be taken into custody and we were empowered to use any reasonable force that might be necessary to complete the arrest. In my own mind, giving him a quick bop on the head was preferable to putting a 9mm slug into him. He might end up with a damn headache and lose some blood, but at least he'd still be alive.

After Hatcher's capture, I felt ecstatic! Immediately following my twin knee surgeries in 1971 my painful obsession with my arthritic right knee became sort of a living hell for me. I felt self-conscious and in the end became defensive and extremely secretive. I never complained about my knee or the pain I experienced almost daily. In fact, I'd do my best to avoid any discussion at all that had to do with my injured right knee. If someone happened to ask me how I was doing, I would quickly change the subject if I could. It wasn't that I was trying to be some super-macho type cop, oblivious to my own pain and suffering, because I wasn't! My right knee hurt - and I knew it! No, I was ashamed and scared; ashamed because I foolishly imagined my condition made me less than the man I had been before, and scared because I remembered all to well Doctor Pike's somber admonishment about my life as a cop being over. Now however, even our annoying but necessary detour to the hospital, so Hatcher's little boo-boo could be sewn up, couldn't rain on my parade. I caught the bastard and no one could take that away from me. I knew I didn't have the cheetah-like speed of a Mike, and I didn't actually run young Mr. Hatcher into the ground, but the tortoise had had his day anyway, and I crossed the finish line and secured the prize before the hare did! Oh, by the way, Hatcher did not have a weapon on him when we finally captured him this second time around!

The Hatcher arrest made me feel completely whole again, even if deep down I knew I wasn't. And, around this same time I also was approached by an influential detective sergeant I respected and admired a great deal. He said if I still wanted that coveted gold badge of a detective all I had to do was submit another short letter of request. This time, unlike the other two times when someone else had been selected instead of me, he guaranteed I would be the definite choice. I'd never known this man to promise anything he couldn't deliver and I was quite certain he probably knew what he was talking about. But, even though it was still my dream to be a hot-shot homicide detective someday, right now I was having way to much fun in T.I.U. After all, Mike and I were already doing a detective's work, without the added burden of a heavy case load and the pressure and stress that goes along with it. Right now, I had the best of both worlds, and I wasn't about to give it up so easily. I know my wife would have preferred me to work days, like most of the homicide dicks did, but I still made the selfish decision to stay right where I was for the time being. I knew there would be other openings and other opportunities in the future, but a dream assignment like I had now in T.I.U. only came along once in a lifetime. I planned to make the most of it while I still could. So, instead of a letter requesting assignment to the detective bureau, I wrote a brief letter asking that I no longer be considered at this time.

These two things; the successful apprehension of small-time punk Jimmy Hatcher, and the knowledge that now "they" wanted me to be a detective, both these things had an immediate and tremendous effect on my overall morale. I felt I had finally turned the corner and even though I still had to live with a very painful right knee, that never would be 100% normal again, I realized I no longer had to worry about proving my worth to anyone.

"Doctor Pike," I whispered to myself proudly, as I thought about his previous warning that my career in law enforcement was probably over. "I plan on being a Fort Lauderdale cop for a long, long time to come!"

15

OCTOBER 23, 1975

There really wasn't anything special that initially alerted Mike and I, just the fact these three guys seemed to be paying lots of attention to the late night store located on the corner at Davie Boulevard and S.W. 23rd Avenue. In fact, my first thought was that these three guys were more than likely just bums. I wasn't quite sure that they intended to rob the store but I did consider it a very real possibility they might attempt to shoplift some food, beer or wine. Once again, an arrest was still an arrest.

We had first seen them right around 10:40 p.m. as they walked through the residential area due south of the store. Mike and I lost sight of them for about five minutes but then observed them again as they walked back westbound towards the store. They crossed 23rd Avenue and headed north towards Davie and then they stopped in the small darkened parking area along the store's east side. They seemed to be hiding in the shadows right near some medium-sized bushes that separated the store property from the first house directly behind it. One customer's vehicle was still parked there at the east side of the building and it almost seemed as if the three subjects were waiting for this unsuspecting fellow to leave before they did anything further.

This last customer finally exited the store, got into his vehicle without incident, and then left the area. As the three subject's silently lurked there in the shadows along the darkened east side of the store, this lone male customer apparently never even knew they were there. It seemed these three guys weren't interested in robbing just any individual. If they had been, this had been the perfect opportunity. If they had been so inclined they could have easily jumped him and then quickly overpowered him. The all-important element of surprise had been on their side. As Mike and I continued to watch the suspicious trio I again thought to myself that these guys were more than likely just bums. But, they also appeared to be bums who were up to no good.

One of the three male subjects, apparently in his mid-20's and wearing a black and yellow baseball type cap, reached into his own pocket and handed one of the other guys something very small. I suspected it was only money and probably just coins at that. They talked among themselves for a few more seconds and then the fellow that had been given the money walked around to the front of the store and went inside. As he passed into the lighted area out in front of the store Mike and I finally got a better look at this guy. He was also in his early to mid-20's and he wore a light colored shirt and pants, and a blue denim flop brim hat. Although his clothes and his overall appearance appeared to be neat and clean to me he still looked like a damn bum!

While this first guy with the floppy blue brim innocently wandered around the store's interior for the next several minutes his two amigos outside remained hidden in the shadows. From our previous contacts at this particular store Mike and I knew there were only two female clerks inside; a 53-year old grandmother and her attractive 14-year old granddaughter. These were easy pickings for any would be robbers or thieves that might come along. The store's front faced Davie and we were located on the north side of that busy boulevard. We could see most of what occurred inside the main portion of the business, but not all. We couldn't see behind the counter where the cash register was situated and this was where the two clerks were usually located. We watched Mr. floppy brim approach the register, have some conversation with the clerks, and then apparently make a small purchase. Then he left the store and quickly rejoined his two compatriots along the east side of the business.

What we didn't know at the time, and what would have undoubtedly only bolstered my own "bum theory" even further, was that Mr. floppy brim had asked the grandma clerk how much one can of soda would cost him. She told him $.31 cents. He asked her if he could have it for $.30 cents because that was all he had. I don't know if she felt sorry for him, or what, but she told him okay. He happily left the store with his one "Coke" in hand. He quickly met up with his two friends and all three walked in an easterly direction away from the store. They remained on the south side of Davie, the same side of the street the store was on. After they had gone about a half of a block they all suddenly stopped. Mike and I couldn't tell if they were sharing sips from their one soda, but it appeared as if they were talking something over. After another minute passed all three began walking westbound again, back towards the store. They crossed 23rd Avenue and entered the store's front parking area. Except for the clerk's lone vehicle in front of the store there were no other cars in the lot. And, except for the two female clerks, the store was empty. Now, Mr. floppy brim, Mr. baseball cap, and the third banana entered the store. It was show time: time for these three bums to do whatever it was they were gonna do!

Mike and I had already requested assistance from any other tactical units in the area. Several other teams responded and these units were positioned both north and south of Davie Boulevard. Mike and I continued to maintain the "eye," however. After they entered the store, all three subjects walked to the back of the business where the coolers were located. They disappeared from our view for a few anxious moments and then they made their way back up to the front counter and entered a portion of the store which couldn't be easily seen from the outside. Eventually, they went back to the coolers again, and Mr. baseball cap opened up one of the large glass doors and removed a bottle of wine.

Mr. floppy brim walked back to the front of the store, opened the door and then took several steps outside. Once outside, he looked to the east, and then he looked to the west. I suddenly felt my heart begin to race excitedly as we advised the other tac units about what was happening. Things were beginning to look better and better, but I still wasn't totally convinced these three bozos really intended to rob the store. I thought they might just take the bottle of wine and then leave the store without paying for it. Even though I definitely preferred a real-life robbery arrest, instead of just a mere larceny, as long as we ended up making some sort of an apprehension I'd consider the surveillance to be at least a partial success.

When Mr. floppy brim finally went back into the store several seconds later he once again walked back to the rear area where the entrance to the counter was located. This was the area we couldn't see and Mr. floppy brim quickly disappeared. After a few more seconds the third suspect also disappeared from our view into the same general area where Mr. floppy brim had gone. Only Mr. baseball cap remained out where we could see him and it appeared he might be acting as a possible lookout. As he silently stood there just inside the store's front door, we watched him as he nervously looked up and down Davie. But, he never seemed to look straight ahead northward across the boulevard itself. If he had, he might have noticed Mike and I just sitting there in the darkened parking lot across the street, our headlights off, but our motor still running. Along with the other Yankee units in the area we patiently waited there like a couple of hungry vultures. We waited to swoop in on him and his two friends. If only they knew what lay in store for them!

With two of the three suspects now totally out of our sight and the female clerks also unseen and unaccounted for, we suspected something dastardly and illegal was definitely afoot. The lone bad guy standing watch there at the front door only reinforced this feeling that much more. If nothing changed drastically during the next few minutes, I knew we'd be faced with a very difficult decision to make; do we immediately move in and make sure the two female clerks were all right, or do we continue to do nothing and wait, and see what happens? It was a decision I hoped we wouldn't have to make. I didn't relish the thought of entering the store in search of three bad guys, especially when employees were still inside and might get caught in any possible cross-fire that might develop. No, I'd much rather let these three dimwits do their thing, then take them down after they exited the store. Inside the store they still had lots of cover to hide behind and if they were desperate enough they could even take the clerks hostage. But, once they were outside they'd be ours and they would be at our mercy. But, if things really turned to shit, and it seemed likely they were either abusing or hurting the two clerks in any way, then I knew we'd have to act immediately. We no longer would have the luxury of waiting.

Even though we obviously didn't know it at the time our suspicions about these three guys being involved in foul play inside the store were absolutely correct. Lacy Ann, the 14-year old granddaughter, later described in vivid detail the horrible ordeal she and her grandma had to endure. "The guy with the white pants on (Mr. floppy brim) came up behind the counter and grabbed me by the neck and shoved a gun into my face. I began gasping and he pushed me to the floor and told me to 'Shut up you fucking bitch!' And then, the other two guys came up onto the platform, the one with the gun, the same one that had grabbed me grabbed my grandmother and pinned her up against the cigarette rack by the neck and kept the gun pointed at her and then he told her, 'All right mother fucker, open up the cash register!' Then, I can't remember which one grabbed the money out of the drawer and one of them grabbed my purse and they began putting the money from the register into my purse." The young beauty went on to say, "They were all pretty mean the way they shoved us around and grabbed us, I feel they really meant business." When the detective taking her statement asked her if she was in fear of being harmed or killed she responded firmly, "Yes! I was definitely afraid of being killed if I would have screamed or not done as they had told me to do." When the detective later asked the grandmother this very same question, about was she in fear for her life, she replied succinctly, "Yes, I thought they were going to shoot us."

Our first actual confirmation that something wrong had just taken place inside the store occurred several moments later. Mike and I observed both female clerks walking in a very hurried manner towards the rear storage room located near the back of the store. The three suspects were walking behind them. When we looked at the females through our binoculars it appeared quite obvious that both were very frightened. We could easily see the fear and the stark terror in their faces. It seemed unlikely to me, and I'm sure Mike too, that both of the clerks would voluntarily leave the security of their counter area, unless they had been ordered to do so. And now, with all three suspects behind the two females, prodding them forward like experienced cowboys moving a herd of nervous cattle, I was sure in my own mind that a robbery had just taken place. I didn't see any weapons at this point, and maybe the three suspects weren't even armed - we really didn't know! But, because the suspects apparently were threatening the women with some sort of violence if they didn't obey their commands I knew we still had at least a Strongarm Robbery.

Okay Officer, It's Decision Time!

(Situation #17)

You are certain a robbery is in progress at the Davie Boulevard store and you observe both female clerks being taken to the back of the store. They look terrified! What should you do next?

What is your answer? (put an "X" in the space in front of your answer)

❑ _____ You still would like to avoid a hostage situation, if possible. Therefore, you decide to wait a few more moments to see what happens.

❑ _____ Fearing for the safety of the two female clerks you decide you must immediately take action and you give the order to "Move in!"

❑ _____ You're not sure what you should do, and because you don't want to be held responsible if anything goes wrong, you attempt to raise the sergeant on the radio to see what he wants you to do.

An analysis of this situation appears at the end of the book

(Do <u>not</u> go there until you have finished reading this chapter)

Once again we were faced with an awesome and possibly momentous decision to make; move in immediately, or continue to wait? I didn't like it at all that the three suspects were taking the two females to the back room. Were they going to shoot them there, rape them, or just abandon them? These troubled thoughts raced through my mind. Waiting was now clearly out of the question and even though we faced a possible hostage situation by moving in with the suspects still inside the store, it appeared we had no other alternatives. As I started to move our unmarked vehicle forward, in preparation for our dangerous dash across the width of Davie Boulevard, through the maze of traffic that always seemed to be there, we radioed the other tac units, "Move in! It's going down!"

I don't know how we managed to safely maneuver our way across Davie Boulevard without totally wiping ourselves out, or at the very least causing one or two multiple car fender benders. I mean, we were driving southbound through heavy traffic which was headed both east and west. Now I knew what it felt like to be a participant in a demolition derby! "This is crazy!" I thought to myself as we quickly avoided yet another unsuspecting motorist. His only crime had been his misfortune to have the right of way. I'm sure these other drivers thought we were insane and they probably decided all Fort Lauderdale was crazy when one or two more tac units quickly followed us southbound in our frantic flight across Davie. This amusement park-like ride lasted no more than ten or fifteen seconds and during these few precious moments we never ever took our eyes away from the front of the store. The other drivers and their vehicles became only secondary considerations.

It was midway during this hair raising ride across Davie Boulevard that we observed the three suspects now heading back towards the front of the store. Almost immediately after we gave the order to "Move in!" - and we ourselves started moving southbound, the bad guys left the two clerks completely alone and began making tracks for the store's front door. My worst fears, about the clerks being further victimized by this low-life scum, apparently were unwarranted, I'm happy to say. These three guys just wanted to get away and now the only thing standing in their way was us! But, this wasn't ABC's "Wide World of Sports" and before we'd let these guys experience the true ecstasy of victory, we definitely intended for them to learn about the real meaning of the term: "The Agony of Defeat!"

The first suspect to leave the store was Mr. floppy brim himself. We noticed he was holding a brown woman's purse in his hands out in front of him and the other two suspects were right behind him. One of them, the one wearing the black and yellow baseball cap, tightly held onto a bottle of wine. Mike and I rolled into the store's front parking area just as all three suspects came barreling out of the business. I know they saw us right away and I'm sure they quickly realized exactly who we were. We were the "P-O-L-I-C-E!" The clerk's vehicle was still the only car out in front of the store. Its front was all the way up against the sidewalk that separated the building from the parking lot itself. The vehicle's trunk area faced Davie. I pulled our unmarked vehicle into the lot and stopped. Our left front bumper almost touched the left rear fender of the clerk's vehicle. Our own car faced west and the two vehicles together looked a little like a large backwards letter "L".

If I'd had the time to think about it, and plan things out more thoroughly, I might have done a better job of positioning our unmarked vehicle after we entered the store's front lot. True, by pulling up to the left rear portion of the clerk's car I did cut off one possible avenue of escape. It now seemed unlikely they would attempt to run westward between our two vehicles. The spacing between the cars just wasn't there. They might try going west on the store's sidewalk, between the front of the clerk's vehicle and the building itself, but I doubted they'd get very far if they tried this. The building prevented them from immediately being able to change direction, and head back south into the residential area right behind the store. Also, I didn't think they'd want to turn north and try and cross Davie which was moderately congested. Not with Mike and I behind them and on their ass! No, I suspected once they saw the trap they were in they would turn to the east, back towards where they had originally come from. But, the thing that worried me the most, at least for the split second I had to think about it, was the vulnerable and completely exposed position I'd left myself in. When I exited our vehicle I suddenly found myself standing there with nothing at all between me and the three bad guys. There was no cover at all! Nada! Mike at least had our own car between him and the three robbers, but I was naked! If they had opened up on me, they probably would have gotten me.

Mr. floppy brim quickly dropped the brown leather purse onto the sidewalk next to a pay phone located there at the northeast corner of the building. I watched as he suddenly reached under his shirt with his left hand and pulled out what appeared to be a small caliber chrome revolver. But, he never raised the gun up and pointed it in my direction and before I could even react to this definite threat he changed his direction, like a determined fullback fighting off would be tacklers, and he headed away from me to the east. I, of course, already had my own weapon out and ready but before I could bring it to bear on the suspect he disappeared completely around the corner of the building.

My first immediate reaction was to go after this armed and dangerous individual. I was definitely lucky he hadn't taken a shot at me, and I knew it. At this close range, which was no more than 15-20 feet between us, he probably wouldn't have missed. Now, I wanted to go after him and make him pay for his crimes, one way or the other. But, there were several things that prevented me from doing this.

First of all, I knew T.I.U. Officers James Dawson and Walter Powell were located south of Davie and when we gave the word for everyone to "Move in!" I was almost certain they had strategically positioned themselves alongside the east side of the store. With any luck at all Mr. floppy brim would run right into their waiting arms. Yes, he was armed; but so were they, and they outnumbered his ass 2 to 1! Secondly, and just as important, was the fact we still had two more suspects here at the front of the store. If I ran off and left Mike he'd be all alone and then they'd outnumber him 2 to 1. Simple mathematics necessitated that I didn't chase after this first bad guy, no matter how much I might want to.

The other two suspects decided to run westward along the front on the convenience store. The youngest one led the way and the bad guy in the cruddy looking baseball cap followed along right behind him. When these two bozos were about twenty feet away from the store's entrance, and almost within arm's reach of the front of the clerk's vehicle, Mike and I heard a single shot suddenly ring out from the east side of the store. This was the same exact area where Mr. floppy brim had just disappeared. I recognized that this shot had definitely come from a small caliber weapon. My heart began to race even faster. I was sure this gutless punk had fired his gun, the gun I had seen him pull; and I knew all to well who his probable targets were, T.I.U. Officers Powell and Dawson!

A few seconds after we heard this single pistol shot we heard several more reports which were obviously very much louder. There was no doubt about it, these were shotgun blasts! Because I'd never seen Mr. floppy brim with a shotgun, and I didn't believe he had one secretly hidden underneath his shirt, I was reasonably sure these two blasts came from police shotguns. I strongly suspected Powell and Dawson were in the process of teaching this bad guy a very valuable lesson: You better not shoot at the P-O-L-I-C-E, not unless you don't mind getting your brim filled with little round holes made by OO buck!

The subject with the baseball cap was directly in front of the clerk's vehicle when he also heard the sounds of gunfire to the east. I don't know if he thought we were shooting at him, or if he just feared these distant shots being fired might be an ominous prelude to what was about to happen to him, but he suddenly stopped, bent down and attempted to seek refuge right there in front of the parked car. The other suspect, who was still a few yards ahead of Mr. baseball cap, continued fleeing west. I decided to concentrate all my attention on the one who had stopped. I knew Mike was somewhere off to the right of me and he could take care of the suspect who was still running westbound along the front of the store.

I aimed my 9mm automatic at the subject's head, which was still completely exposed, as he tried to hide the rest of his puny body behind the clerk's vehicle. I yelled for him to stand up and show me his hands, or I would open fire. I could see he was fumbling with whatever it was he had in his hands, and although I suspected it might just be a bottle of wine, I wasn't about to assume this automatically. Until I actually saw this item for myself, AND, it was no longer in his possession, I'd assume it was a threat to me and act accordingly. There wasn't time, of course, for me to verbally communicate all of this to the suspect. But, by my tone and the words I used, I was sure he understood what was going to happen if he didn't do as I told him. He was very close to getting his ticket punched - permanently!

Okay Officer, It's Decision Time!

(Situation #18)

You are certain a robbery has just occurred at this Davie Boulevard store and the first suspect to flee (Mr. floppy brim) WAS armed. This other subject now in front of you is trying to hide behind the front of the clerk's vehicle. You see that he has something in his hands and although you think it may just be a bottle of wine, you're really not sure. What should you do next?

What is your answer? (put an "X" in the space in front of your answer)

❑ _____ Because he hasn't given up, he continues to try and hide, and he definitely has something in his hands, which could be a weapon, you shoot the subject.

❑ _____ You fire a warning shot in an effort to show him that you mean business, and that he should definitely surrender.

❑ _____ You wait. You want to see what he does next.

An analysis of this situation appears at the end of the book

(Do not go there until you have finished reading this chapter)

I was almost ready to drop the hammer on this clown when he suddenly bolted upright into a standing position, as if his pants were on fire. The suspicious object he'd been holding moments before now crashed to the pavement and it sounded very much like a glass bottle breaking. But, before I began forward myself, I scanned his hands to make sure they were in fact empty. When I was confident he no longer had any apparent weapons easily within his reach I quickly moved forward and pushed him up against the front outside wall of the store. I didn't do this violently but I did use a certain amount of physical force just to let him know who was in charge. His black and yellow baseball cap came off his head and ended up on the ground very near the broken bottle of wine he had just dropped.

After I was reasonably sure I had my own suspect under control I looked to my right to check on Mike and his bad guy. His guy had continued to run along the store's front sidewalk. A small music store occupied the far west end of the same building the convenience store was located in. This portion of the building extended another ten to fifteen feet northward towards Davie Boulevard and this sidewalk the suspect was on only led to the music store's front entrance, nowhere else. When the suspect finally reached the end of this sidewalk he suddenly found himself completely trapped. He was in a corner; with the building on two sides of him, me behind him, and Mike there in front of him ordering him to surrender.

As I began to put the cuffs on the bad guy directly in front of me I noticed how he seemed to be more than eager to accommodate my every demand. This was almost comical because a few violent moments earlier he had been Mr. tough ass. Apparently he was a real pro when it came to pushing a few helpless females around but when he was faced with a true life-and-death challenge his backbone suddenly turned to mush. As I watched him tremble nervously I realized what a total chicken shit he really was. When I looked over to my right though, where Mike and his guy were located, it appeared his suspect was at least putting up some sort of resistance, even though it might be only minimal.

I suddenly sensed another individual right behind me. This unknown subject was running in my direction and I immediately became concerned. Had the first bad guy, Mr. floppy brim, who initially ran to the east, had he now changed direction and doubled-back towards me? To my delight, I quickly learned this new addition to our party was Officer Bill Stewart. Prior to the robbery he and his partner Ron Ray had positioned themselves north of Davie Boulevard. When the robbery finally did go down he exited their unmarked vehicle and proceeded to make his way across Davie on foot. I guess he felt this was much safer and definitely quicker than driving. He apparently didn't want to run the gauntlet like Mike and I had done. And, as Stewart played his own deadly version of tag with the confused and angry motorists clogging Davie Boulevard, Ron Ray haphazardly maneuvered their own vehicle southbound across the moderately congested thoroughfare.

"Help Mike with his guy!" I yelled to Stewart, as he began to assist me in my efforts to finish cuffing my suspect. Bill looked over to our right and observed Mike and his bad guy. They were at the far corner of the building, in the shadows where the sidewalk ended. Bill and I really couldn't tell for sure what was happening but it almost appeared as if Mike and the suspect were involved in a minor struggle. Without a word, Stewart left my side and ran the few short yards to where Mike and the third subject were located. This culprit was then subdued and taken into custody without any further trouble. While Mike and Stewart thoroughly searched their guy, cuffed him and advised him of his rights, I let my own gutless wonder know about the magical thing called Miranda.

Mike and I had been extremely lucky. We had been able to quickly apprehend the two suspects who fled westbound, but a totally different drama unfolded there along the darkened east side of the store. Just as I thought, when we gave the word to "Move in!", T.I.U. Officers Powell and Dawson immediately pulled their unmarked vehicle up to the east side of the store. But, by this time the three bad guys had already exited the business, and even before Powell and Dawson could get out of their car, Mr. floppy brim turned the corner of the building and they were suddenly eyeball to eyeball with each other. As the two tac officers tried their best to exit their vehicle as quickly as possible, Mr. floppy brim ran right by them. To say they were a little bit surprised would be an understatement!

Mr. floppy brim now headed in a southeasterly direction towards 23rd Avenue and the houses in the residential area right behind the store. Officers Powell and Dawson observed a chrome colored revolver in the suspect's left hand. He was still armed and potentially very dangerous! Both men began chasing after him, but when he reached the sidewalk just before getting to 23rd Avenue itself, and he started running south on it, he suddenly slipped in a small muddy area and fell down. "Police! Stop!" Officer Dawson ordered loudly. The suspect wasted no time at all and immediately began to get back up onto his feet. He wasn't ready to give up just yet!

Officer Dawson watched intently as the suspect turned and pointed the small revolver at him. As Jim raised his shotgun up to his shoulder the suspect fired off one quick shot at him. He missed! Officer Dawson later recalled, "The subject raised his left hand (and) pointed the revolver at me and fired one shot right at me. I observed the muzzle flash directly in front of me. I returned fire with the shotgun." By his own estimate, Dawson was approximately fifteen yards away from the fleeing suspect when he returned fire. It appears however, his first round of OO Buck unfortunately missed its mark, as the suspect continued to run due south along the narrow sidewalk. To his left was 23rd Avenue and to his right were the houses facing this usually quiet neighborhood street.

Mr. floppy brim had been almost directly in front of the first house south of the store when he suddenly fired his gun at Officer James Dawson. Officer Walter Powell had only been a few short feet to Jim's right when this had happened and he also saw the ominous looking muzzle flash of the suspect's weapon. He knew without any hesitation or doubt that the suspect had just tried to murder his partner. Like Officer Dawson, Powell also carried a shotgun. And, like Dawson, he too continued to actively pursue the armed suspect with reckless abandonment as well as with great vigor. Now, as the suspect passed by the second house south of the store, Officers Powell and Dawson prepared to unleash another deadly barrage. The distance between them and the bad guy was about twenty yards.

I'm not really sure who actually fired their shotgun first; whether it was Powell, or Dawson. They may have even fired their weapons simultaneously. I don't think they even know this themselves. No matter, Jim fired yet another round of OO Buck from his police shotgun, and so did Walt. The suspect, who continued to run southbound along the sidewalk, still had the gun in his hand! So, even though he was running away from these two officers he was still a very dangerous individual and a definite threat to any other officers or even civilians he encountered. Therefore, under the circumstances, these two additional shots by Powell and Dawson were indeed warranted and justified. Once again, it was totally unthinkable for us, as police officers, to let this scumbag escape. As long as he still had that gun in his hand, he had to be stopped!

Police buckshot from these two additional shotgun blasts successfully found its way to Mr. floppy brim's posterior. But, because Powell and Dawson both fired at the suspect at about the same exact moment, I don't believe we'll ever know for sure which one of the officers actually hit him. I know however, that Powell is certain it was him! In Walter's supplement report later he stated, "The undersigned took aim at the subject and fired. The subject

219

immediately jumped approximately 3 feet into the air and grabbed his buttox (buttock) and yelled." Even though the suspect appeared to be wounded he continued to flee from the two officers. He suddenly cut back to the right and headed off in a westerly direction between two houses. These were the third and fourth houses south of the store. Powell and Dawson lost sight of him. A perimeter was quickly established and K-9 was requested.

This last remaining culprit, who so far had successfully eluded all efforts to capture him, had been hit by buckshot and six of these deadly little round metal balls violently tore into his flesh. Two pellets hit him in the buttock, two more ended up in his groin, one hit the back of his right heel, and one did some damage to the underside of the middle finger of his right hand. But, even though he felt a painful bee-like sting when hit, he really didn't realize just how bad he'd been shot until a little bit later. While he was hiding in some bushes he felt his pants beginning to dampen, especially in the area of his groin. He knew he was bleeding and he was worried he might bleed to death. He began moving forward once again.

The "Tic-Toc Bar" was located only one short block to the west of the store which had been robbed. Like the store itself, the bar was also on the south side of Davie Boulevard, and on a corner. The bar, which catered almost exclusively to a redneck biker type clientele, was well within the police perimeter which had been established. An elderly female approached one of the uniformed officers guarding our two prisoners in front of the store and advised him that she had heard "something moving in the bushes on the east side of the tavern." Several officers, including our own boss, Sergeant Joe Gerwens, immediately responded to the area. They quickly observed the suspect "running in a northerly direction from the bushes, towards the street (Davie Blvd)." He "was shirtless and bleeding from the right hand and buttocks area," so there was little doubt this was our last remaining bad guy. Now, at gun point, they ordered the still fleeing subject to halt.

Sergeant Gerwens quickly took the now unarmed subject into custody, right there in front of the "Tic-Toc" and a small but vocal group of drunken rednecks who drifted out of the bar to watch what was happening. Joe advised this wounded bad guy of his Miranda rights and then the suspect was returned back to the front of the store where his two comrades awaited him. Even though we witnessed the robbery while it was in-progress the two female clerks were still asked to view and identify all three suspects. As silly as this might sound, this was departmental procedure, so we had to do it. The two women, who were both still a little bit rattled, positively identified all three men as the culprits in the robbery. I would have been shocked if they hadn't!

The wounded suspect voluntarily agreed to show us where he threw his gun down and the weapon, an old decrepit .32 caliber "Clerke" 5-shot revolver, was recovered near the southeast side of the store. It contained four live rounds in it, plus one empty casing located directly under the hammer. There was also residue very similar to burnt gunpowder clearly visible on the front edge of two of the projectile holes of the cylinder, as well as on the one spent cartridge itself. Yet, despite this evidence, and the accounts of Officers Powell and Dawson, Mr. floppy brim said he did not fire at the two officers. He did admit however, to having the gun in his possession during the robbery, as well as during his initial flight from the store. According to him, the gun accidentally went flying out of his hand when he slipped in the mud and fell down. I'm not quite sure if he was trying to say the gun went off by accident, or what, but it really didn't matter because I was sure the bastard was lying! He'd also said he decided to give up when he found out just how bad he was hit. I suspected this was just some more of his bullshit! In fact, I would have bet money he didn't decide to give up until he saw Sergeant Gerwens and our other guys closing in on him, and he was afraid if he didn't give up he might just get another load of police buckshot in his ass!

After his arrival at the scene our crime lab guy Ralph began taking photographs and collecting physical evidence. A tan colored leather purse, belonging to the youngest of the two clerks, was on the sidewalk at the extreme east corner of the business. This was where Mr. floppy brim dropped it. The now abandoned purse contained $76.90 in assorted bills and coins. Not bad for a night's work. After all, if these three bozos had been able to make good their escape, each would have netted a whopping $25.63, with a damn penny left for them to fight over. "Crime don't pay!" When I was growing up in California I remember my mom telling me this more than once. $25.63 each? Boy, was she right!

Ralph took the money from the purse so he could put it into evidence and then he returned the purse itself to the clerk. He also photographed the black and yellow baseball cap, and the now broken bottle of wine. Both lay very near the front of the clerk's vehicle which was only about thirty feet west of the store's front door. Ralph bent down and started picking up the individual pieces of the broken bottle. He looked up and saw me watching him and he must have read my mind.

"M.D. 20-20!" he remarked knowingly, then added flippantly, "A superb domestic wine with a brisk and lively bouquet."

"If you say so."

But, Ralph was on a roll, and he was not to be denied. "It's somewhat reminiscent of the more expensive French imports and it's ideal with either fish or fowl," he concluded, as he took a final whiff from the last piece of broken glass he'd just picked up.

"Foul is right!" I shot back sarcastically.

Things around us started returning to normal and I began a silent critique of my own performance; before, during and even after the robbery. Overall, I was pleased. Once again, instead of being dispatched, or advised of the suspicious suspects by some third-party reportee, Mike and I had taken the initiative. We had spotted the three bad guys on our own without having to be told about them. Again, I felt this alone was a major accomplishment. But, the one thing that did bother me just a little was my incorrect assumption about the suspect's apparent vagrant-type lifestyle; these guys might have looked it, but they weren't bums. Admittedly, the one clue I'd misinterpreted was the fact these clowns were on foot and not in a vehicle. Almost all our previous bad guys had used a car, but apparently not these three. This could mean they lived somewhere nearby. It's not really smart to shit where you eat, I thought to myself, but whoever said robbers were smart.

This mini-mystery of the missing car took on a different twist when we suddenly found keys to a 1973 Chevrolet in the pocket of one of the three suspects. The Chevy, which was white and had a blue vinyl top, was eventually located almost two full blocks east of the store. It was parked there in the shadows, to the rear of a closed business, which was located on the north side of Davie Boulevard. When other tac officers searched the car prior to having it towed they found a book of American Express Travelers Checks and a Social Security Card in the vehicle's glove compartment. None of these items belonged to any of our three suspects so they were confiscated and placed into evidence, to be released to the rightful owner only upon valid proof of ownership.

Later, detectives learned Mr. floppy brim snatched another woman's purse shortly before the ill-fated Davie Boulevard robbery. The identification and travelers checks in the Chevy's glove compartment belonged to the victim of this other Strongarm Robbery. But, for whatever reason, this other victim did not wish to prosecute. So, in exchange for his just admitting to this other robbery, and another purse snatch as well, Mr. floppy brim was not actually charged with any other additional crimes. This might seem like he got a big break he really didn't deserve, and maybe that analysis would be accurate, but the fact is he already had much more trouble than he could handle. Reference our own little robbery, which would have netted him a kingly sum of $25.63, if they'd been able to get away with it, now instead he would be charged with Armed Robbery and Attempted Murder of a Police Officer. Neither charge was anything to sneeze at and he was facing some very heavy time if convicted. And, in addition to all this, we also received an early Christmas present as well; Mr. floppy brim was on probation reference a previous burglary. The real laugher was that this stupid jerk's probation was scheduled to end in just a little over one week, on November 1st. If he could have kept his nose clean for just a few more days his probation would have been over and done with. But now, in all likelihood he would probably be violated, and have to face these additional sanctions as well. The inner workings of the criminal mind never ceased to amaze me.

Tac officers at the hospital with Mr. floppy brim eventually reported his wounds were much more serious than originally thought and he was going to be admitted. His wounds required surgery so he wouldn't be going to our jail anytime soon. He was stripped of all his bloody clothing so it could be placed into evidence and arrangements were made for a 24-hour guard to be placed on him until his release. We didn't want him getting restless in the middle of the night and taking a midnight stroll.

===

The shooter, Mr. floppy brim, pled guilty and received fifteen (15) years on each count. He was adjudicated guilty and the sentences were to run concurrently. The other two culprits also received prison sentences.

*   *   *   *   *

Mike and I received a much appreciated Departmental Commendation from Chief of Police Leo Callahan. We were also named Police Officers of the Month for December, 1975.

16

THE LAGO MAR HOTEL

A few of the tactical guys, myself included, kept track of T.I.U.'s overall statistics on a semi-regular basis. You might say we were the self-appointed, yet unofficial, historians of our small but potent little unit. We were all extremely proud of T.I.U.'s outstanding record and I'm sure this was partly why we eagerly spent this extra time calculating and analyzing T.I.U.'s impressive totals. We finished our latest analysis midway through November of 1975. T.I.U. had been in existence now for almost two full years (21½ months) and during this short period of time our tac guys arrested 870 people. Most of us still tried to concentrate on quality rather than quantity and as a result almost 45% (388) of T.I.U.'s total arrests were for felony type crimes. Again, not bad for six two-man teams.

Mike and I still continued to have better than average luck when it came to finding real nasty bad guys and we continued to perform at right around the 28% to 29% marks. We accounted for about 28% of T.I.U.'s total arrests (246 of 870), and for about 29% of the unit's felony arrests (114 of 388). If nothing else, Mike and I were at least consistent. Robbery was still our number one priority, just as it was with the rest of the guys in T.I.U., and during this 21½ months Mike and I accounted for 31 robbery arrests. We were also responsible for 25 burglary arrests; 10 residential, and 15 business. There were 26 felony narcotics arrests, 28 misdemeanor narcotics arrests and then finally rounding out our stats, another 34 arrests for various other felony charges.

It wasn't any big secret that Mike and I preferred working robberies rather than burglaries. I'm sure most of the other tac guys felt this way too. Robberies, of course, more than likely involved armed and dangerous individuals and the potential for a deadly shoot out was always there. I'm sure the extra danger, stress and uncertainty that almost always went along with an in-progress robbery apprehension made it that much more attractive than just a mere burglary arrest. The adrenaline rush I'd experience when I'd have an armed robber squarely in my sights was a unique and awesome feeling I really couldn't explain. True, we'd almost always take burglars down at gunpoint too, because you never really knew if one of them might be packing, but the "rush" you felt just wasn't the same.

Maybe this is why Mike and I initially weren't that enthusiastic about our new assignment. The fact Sergeant Dierkzon specifically picked Mike and I for this "important mission" also made us feel just a little bit suspicious too. We still felt that Dierkzon didn't care for us and it was only a matter of time before he made another move against us. I know this sounds paranoid, and we were! But, he had already tried once to get me, reference the infamous over time card incident, and he had failed miserably. I strongly suspected he wasn't about to give up that easily. So, when he advised Mike and I that we would be working days, trying to catch a burglar who apparently specialized in hitting one particular high-class beach front resort, the Lago Mar Hotel, I was sure in my own mind he wasn't trying to do us any favors. I'm sure most normal guys would probably have wanted to kiss their sergeant, not question his motives like Mike and I did. After all, what could be so bad about working straight days for a week or two and hanging around the beach getting a nice tan? This was the kind of cream puff assignment most guys fantasized about. Mike and I weren't like most guys though and we felt if Dierkzon wanted us to work the hotel stakeout then there must be something wrong with it and it had to be a shit detail! I guess to be a good cop, I mean a really, really GOOD cop, it helps if you're a little bit neurotic too.

I know Sergeant Dierkzon thought Mike and I were a couple of annoying prima donnas, but we really weren't. We were just two guys trying to do a difficult job the best way we could. Sure, we liked our work, and it showed. Damn right it showed! I'm sure that's why we were almost always there among our unit's top producers, because we liked what we did. At times though, it seemed as if our over abundance of enthusiasm and energy actually bothered the sergeant. Now, it finally hit me why the sergeant probably picked Mike and I for this daylight burglary detail at the Lago Mar Hotel and it had nothing at all to do with us being the best men available for the job. I believed this was Dierkzon's way of getting rid of us, even if it was only for one or two weeks.

The beautiful Lago Mar Hotel was only a short mile or two south of Fort Lauderdale's famous "strip" on a very large and expensive piece of beachfront property. To get to this exclusive hotel, which was located north of the busy Port Everglades Inlet, you had to drive east from A1A into the quiet residential neighborhood that surrounded the hotel on three sides, the fourth side being the ocean. This affluent section of the city provided the hotel with a sort of free buffer and effectively separated it from most of the outside world; specifically the hustle, bustle and congestion of the South Beach area itself. There weren't any Holiday Inns here, no Ramadas, Best Westerns or Hiltons, just towering condominiums, luxurious apartments and townhouses, and the Lago Mar which catered mostly to the very well-to-do. The Lago Mar's primary source of competition, at least close by, probably came from the world famous "Pier 66 Hotel" located about one mile to the west on A1A, right at the bridge where the highway crossed over the Intracoastal Waterway. Pier 66 had a unique and totally awesome revolving restaurant and lounge at its top, but the Lago Mar still had that magnificent stretch of beach and the peace, quiet, and solitude that went along with it. If I had my choice; I'd dine at the Pier, maybe even have a few drinks there, but I'd stay at the beautiful Lago Mar. As far as I was concerned she was definitely the crown jewel of hotels in the entire Fort Lauderdale area.

There had been five hotel room burglaries at the Lago Mar during the past two months and all these B&E's had a few specific things in common. For example: none of the rooms showed any obvious signs of forced entry so they were either key jobs or the victims left their respective rooms unlocked while they were away from them. I doubted the latter possibility, especially since the reported losses in each of these offenses were large amounts of jewelry. Even though the first offense took place late last year, on December 23rd, a Tuesday, and the victims did not return back to their two rooms until well after dark, the rest of the Lago Mar burglaries definitely occurred during the day. The last three B&E's occurred somewhere between 10:30 a.m. to 2:30 p.m. Mike and I had been briefed on all of this but our biggest surprise came when we read each of these B&E reports ourselves. The most significant piece of information, which hadn't been passed along to us verbally, concerned the dates and the day of each of these last three B&E's; December 24th, January 7th and January 21st. All three of these dates were a Wednesday. I might not be Sherlock Holmes, and Mike definitely wasn't Doctor Watson, but we both recognized the importance of this information. The last three burglaries at the Lago Mar, where jewelry in excess of $36,000 was reportedly stolen, all took place on Wednesdays. And, these Wednesdays were always two weeks apart. That sure sounded like a damn pattern to me!

Even though there wasn't any description of the Lago Mar burglar we still weren't completely blind and we did have one possible lead. Back on Friday, December 19th, which was during this same period of time when the Lago

Mar was being routinely targeted, there was a hotel room B&E at another nearby South Beach hotel. This other hotel was about a mile or so away from the Lago Mar, heading back north towards the beach "strip," just off A1A itself. This burglary had occurred sometime between 9:30 a.m. and noon and it appeared to be a possible key job. The loss was reportedly $4,000.00 in expensive jewelry. The overall similarities to the crimes at the Lago Mar were indeed striking. We were in luck too, because this time someone had been able to get a good description of a possible culprit. He was described as:

White Male, 35-40 years old, 6'1", 195-205 lbs.
Brown eyes/Dark black curly hair/Mustache
Dark complexion/Good build/Scar on right cheek

January 27th (Tuesday)

This was the first day Mike and I worked the Lago Mar surveillance. I'd been at the hotel a few times before but only as a rookie patrol officer to handle reports. Mike and I turned onto South Ocean Lane and we headed northbound down the long dead end street towards the hotel itself. The Lago Mar was on the right, midway down the street. On the left was a large and beautiful lake and across this lake was the quiet residential area we had just driven through after we'd left A1A. If you wanted to get to the Lago Mar it was almost essential that you knew your way around the south beach area. Most visitors to Fort Lauderdale didn't and you could always count on a large percentage of these out-of-towners getting lost. I wondered about our burglar. How had he managed to stumble upon the Lago Mar? "I bet he's a local," I silently thought to myself.

Even though there was a large parking lot located just north of the Lago Mar complex, adjacent to the hotel's tennis courts which separated the parking area from the beach itself, Mike and I pulled our unmarked vehicle into a vacant spot right in front of the hotel's main entrance. The front of the hotel was deceiving and it lacked much of the modern elegance of Pier 66 and gave no hint at all to what lay beyond. Mike and I quickly made contact with the hotel manager and advised him we would be hanging around the hotel for the next week or so. He, of course, already knew about the string of burglaries at his hotel and he seemed to be very happy to have us there. He gave us a key to one of their vacant rooms and told us we could use it until they needed it back for a paying guest. The hotel wasn't sold out yet but January was always prime time in south Florida and we knew it wouldn't be long before they would be.

Mike and I spent most of our first day at the Lago Mar getting acquainted with the hotel itself and the unique little niceties that went along with it. I admit, the thought of us laying by the pool all day suddenly seemed to appeal to me a little bit more than it had before. Or, maybe we'd just sit there at the pool side patio bar, watching all the lovely ladies, and sipping delicious Margaritas, one after another. These enjoyable thoughts, as tempting as they were, never really materialized though. I know it's going to sound square but Mike and I knew we were there at the Lago Mar for a reason and we both took this assignment seriously. So, we spent this first day checking out each of the rooms that had been previously hit by our elusive burglar and we tried to see if there was any sort of apparent pattern to his, or maybe even her, modus operandi. But, other than the burglar's definite preference for Wednesdays, we really couldn't find any other common denominators.

Mike and I did come to two very important conclusions. Number one, if our crafty burglar continued to follow his, or her pattern, we predicted there would be another hotel room B&E at the Lago Mar on Wednesday, February 4th. Number two, we needed more tac guys to adequately cover the huge hotel and all of its spacious grounds. The hotel itself wasn't a towering skyscraper-like structure but its three stories were spread out over an area of several city blocks. There were gift shops, tennis courts, the pool areas, the beach, and all these areas needed to be watched if we were going to find our bad guy. Just two men, Mike and I, couldn't possibly do it alone. Mike and I figured up a plan of action and we decided we would be able to do a fairly adequate job with just two more men.

Our simple plan called for one of us to always be positioned somewhere out in front near the main entrance to the hotel. From this location this tac officer would be able to easily monitor all the hotel's parking areas and observe almost everybody as they came and went. Hopefully, and with a little luck, this plainclothes officer would be able to spot our bad guy when he arrived at the hotel. This portion of our plan, of course, made two major assumptions; first, that our tac guy would always be alert and paying attention, and second that our would-be burglar would arrive at the hotel by car. If either one of these two things didn't happen then we stood a very good chance of missing our bad guy entirely. And, if he covertly came ashore from the ocean side, a la the James Bond style of unique and surprising entrances, we had another problem.

A second tac officer would walk around the hotel building itself. It would be his job to roam all three floors of the hotel's main building, as well as the smaller annex to the north. If the man out front spotted a possible suspect this second tac officer would try to keep the potential bad guy under surveillance. The third tac guy had perhaps the toughest duty of all; staying there by the always busy pool side patio bar. From this ideal location, which seemed totally awash in a sea of colorful bikinis, magnificent cleavage and slippery sun tan oil, our third man could easily watch most of the hotel's rooms that faced east towards the beach. He could also watch the south side of the annex and the rooms facing the pool. North of the annex, out of sight of our man at the pool, were the tennis courts and parking lot. The second guy who would be roaming would have to check on these north side rooms, when possible.

The last of our four tac guys would also roam around the hotel grounds whenever possible but we would mainly use him for relief. The tac guy at the patio bar probably wouldn't mind staying put there all day, but the man out by the street, who'd be in the open sun watching the hotel's proverbial front door, would definitely need to be relieved sooner or later. That's why Mike and I put this fourth man in the equation, just to take care of this eventual requirement. We both knew our overall plan wasn't perfect and it obviously left a great many things to pure chance, fate, luck, or anything else you might want to call it. But, given the huge area we had to cover, our almost total lack of knowledge about the perpetrator we were after, and the nature of the crime we were trying to prevent, we believed our plan was at least workable.

Our first full day at the Lago Mar had been a long one; 9:00 a.m. to 4:00 p.m. We returned to the station and eventually initiated a Police Information report. The first four pages of this report covered everything we had learned and done so far. We detailed the dates, days and times of all the previous burglaries, the losses involved in each, and our own personal theory that another burglary would occur on Wednesday, February 4th, if our bad guy continued to stick to his pattern as we hoped he would. I also made sure our report was stamped "CONFIDENTIAL" so it wouldn't become public record without our approval. Mike and I made contact with Sergeant Dierkzon and we tried to explain our analysis to him. We told him about the pattern we had discovered, although in my own mind I couldn't figure out why he hadn't noticed it himself. I assumed he'd read all the burglary reports before he assigned Mike and I to the Lago Mar surveillance and the information about the dates and times was right there in front of him, in black and white. As far as I was concerned Dierkzon's apparent failure to recognize the importance of this information, and his subsequent failure to pass this information along to us if he did notice it, either one of these failures was just another black mark against him!

After we finished describing the burglar's apparent pattern to Sergeant Dierkzon, Mike and I waited for the sergeant's response. But, neither Mike nor I were really fully prepared for what happened next. The sergeant's overall reaction was less than enthusiastic. In fact, it almost seemed as if he could care less. I wondered if he was so incompetent he couldn't recognize a good piece of information, even when it was explained to him. Mike and I were both very disappointed because we had expected much more. We persisted however, and we went ahead and explained our plan to the sergeant anyway. We described how four men, not just the two of us now assigned, could provide adequate coverage at the hotel if they were strategically positioned. After all, the idea was for us to catch the bad guy responsible, wasn't it? Four tac guys, positioned the way we wanted them to be, would give us at least a fighting chance. Sergeant Dierkzon politely listened to our sales pitch and never said a word and I really began to wonder if any of what we were saying was sinking in. I soon found out.

"You guys are just tokens," Dierkzon stated matter-of-factly. "We really don't expect you to catch anyone. You're just there so we can say we tried to do something about it."

I didn't know about Mike, but I was in shock! Even though things were going along extremely well for Mike and I, and we were at a high point in our law enforcement careers, these demeaning comments by Dierkzon were undoubtedly some of the bitterest I had ever had to endure. T-O-K-E-N-S! Was this what our sergeant really thought of us? Mike and I were two of our unit's top producers, yet the best use the sergeant could make of us was to assign us to the

Lago Mar as a couple of damn tokens! In addition to being in shock, I was also livid. How could he be so thoughtless? Didn't he care about our feelings? Couldn't this man, who was a supervisor, and who was supposed to know how to motivate and inspire the people under him, couldn't he see that Mike and I took great pride in our work and our accomplishments, and we'd never be satisfied doing meaningless or unnecessary work? Did Dierkzon really think we'd walk away all happy now that he told us we were only tokens? Not hardly! Then it suddenly hit me, Dierkzon didn't have a clue he had just insulted us. I could tell by his own demeanor that he had no idea at all. This leader of men, who once wanted to be a preacher, but became a cop instead, didn't even know how negatively his remarks had effected us. I almost felt sorry for him. Mike and I didn't argue our point because we knew that would accomplish nothing. Dierkzon's position was very clear and we knew he wouldn't change it just for us, so Mike and I would have to approach this matter from a different angle.

January 28th (Wednesday)

Mike and I were back at the Lago Mar for a second day of poking around and we began our day's work at 9:00 a.m. But, thanks to Sergeant Dierkzon's obvious lack of vision there were still only the two of us, and not the four we had requested. It really didn't matter though because if our bad guy held true to form this Wednesday would be a day off for him. Mike and I still believed in our analysis of the data from the previous burglary reports and we weren't about to let the matter die just because our pigheaded sergeant couldn't recognize a good lead even after it was shown to him. I've never liked back dooring a supervisor and I usually would not do it, no matter what the circumstances. But, in some extreme cases you sometimes had no other alternative. As far as Mike and I were concerned this was one of those times. So, we approached Sergeant Joe

Gerwens with our analysis, plan and recommendations. He seemed interested and although we were putting Joe in an awkward position we knew he would do the right thing.

Even though the Lago Mar was crowded, this second day was rather uneventful. We did follow a few individuals around the grounds, both guests and some visitors too, but nothing came of these efforts and we secured for the day at 3:00 p.m.

January 29th (Thursday)

When 9:00 a.m. rolled around this bright and sunny morning Mike and I were no longer alone. Sergeant Gerwens hadn't let us down and Tactical Officers Bill Stewart and Ron Ray were now assigned to work the Lago Mar surveillance with us. We never did hear any of the specifics about what actually transpired between Sergeants Gerwens and Dierkzon that suddenly caused them to adopt our plan. I suspected Joe Gerwens used some of his charisma to convince Dierkzon that our plan seemed plausible, but I also knew that Joe was the senior sergeant and if he had to he would make Dierkzon accept it, whether he liked it, or not! No matter what had happened though, whether Dierkzon voluntarily changed his mind, or even if he grudgingly went along with it and only gave tacit approval to our plan, Mike and I both knew we had not made a friend by doing what we had done.

We explained our overall plan to Officers Stewart and Ray and then we all got down to business. I ended up doing much of the duty out near the front entrance of the hotel. Don't get me wrong though, this was just fine with me and I volunteered for this important position when we were trying to decide who would do what assignment. I knew the tac man out front of the hotel would be in a very good position to see the bad guy first and I wanted that tac man to be me!

True, no one really knew what the bad guy looked like because the Lago Mar culprit, or culprits, had never been seen. What a challenge! It was me against a totally unknown adversary; an enemy that might be a man, a woman, a man and women working together; who knows, the possibilities were endless. This was the perfect opportunity for me to test my powers of observation, to apply all I had learned and experienced since I became an officer just a few short years ago, and now I would be competing against a professional criminal; someone skilled in the ways of avoiding detection, someone clever enough to never even leave behind a damn clue. Yes, I wanted to be the first one to spot this bad guy!

As I sat there alone in my unmarked vehicle I tried to watch as much of South Ocean Lane as I could. Anyone driving up to the Lago Mar would have to use this dead end street and from my present position I would be able to see them long before they pulled up to the hotel itself. I also had a very good view of all the parking areas out in front of the hotel, as well as most of the parking lots located to the north of the Lago Mar complex. Anyone wanting to park their vehicle in any of these lots would have to drive by me first. One added bonus we hadn't even thought about involved the large lake across South Ocean Lane from the hotel. A series of canals connected the Intracoastal Waterway and this lake, so it was also possible to reach the front of the hotel by small boat. But, because low bridges crossed over most of these narrow canals larger yachts couldn't make this short journey, but smaller speed boat type craft could. From my excellent vantage point near the hotel's front entrance I was now also able to spot any individuals who might arrive by boat.

Today was more active than our other previous days at the Lago Mar. Things started out on a very positive note and I really thought we had something. Right around 10:20 a.m. a white male subject was observed as he hurriedly left the third floor of the hotel. This was the open side of the hotel that faced the beach and he left the same general area where several of the previous burglaries had taken place. He was approximately 38 years old, 6'2", 210 pounds, and he had dark hair and a mustache. He fit the description of the possible suspect from the other hotel B&E back on December 19th. He got into an orange Chevrolet Monte Carlo, which had a Broward County rental tag on it. I don't know how it happened, but he left the area so damn fast we weren't able to follow him. But, about fifteen minutes later this same guy suddenly returned. After he parked, we followed him back up to room #333 which he promptly entered with a key. The hotel manager confirmed this man was registered in that room. I sure am glad, because the four of us would have looked pretty damn foolish if this guy had been our burglar.

Once the four of us actually got our act together and began working as a team we did a little better. The fact there were now four of us working the hotel stakeout allowed us a little extra freedom and we conducted several short vehicle surveillances that Mike and I probably would not have been able to do if there had been just the two of us, like before. Although we remained busy most of the day, watching and following several different individuals around, nothing positive developed and we once again terminated the hotel surveillance at 3:00 p.m.

February 3rd (Tuesday)

Our supervisors now decided we would go for broke and we would put all our eggs in just one basket. So, on January 30th (Friday), and then February 2nd (Monday), none of us worked the Lago Mar Hotel surveillance. It had already been decided, back before we even started the surveillance, that we wouldn't work weekends because none of the previous burglaries occurred on either a Saturday or Sunday. Missing the weekends didn't bother me and I knew it made good sense not to work them. But, I would be lying if I said I wasn't just a little bit uneasy when we also skipped that Friday and Monday too. Sure, Mike and I were still fully committed to our plan and we were both convinced our bad guy, whoever he was, would still appear at the Lago Mar on Wednesday, February 4th; but, what if he didn't! What if, for whatever unknown reasons, he changed his M.O. entirely and decided to hit the hotel a day or two early. This possibility bothered me all weekend long, but when there weren't any reports of any new burglaries on Friday, I breathed a little easier. And today, before I did anything else, I checked to see if there were any new reports from yesterday. There weren't. Apparently our bad guy hadn't changed his style after all and now I knew he'd definitely be back here at the Lago Mar tomorrow; Wednesday, the 4th.

Don't get me wrong, even though we were convinced tomorrow would be our lucky day, we still didn't let our guard down. We followed the usual subjects around; guys who looked a little out of place, vehicles that came and then went suspiciously, and when time and circumstances permitted, we even did some follow-up investigation on the few promising leads we had developed during our previous surveillances. We kept busy, but in the back of my mind I still couldn't wait for today to end. I wanted to get at tomorrow in the worst way. I was sure tomorrow would be the day. It seemed to take forever for 3:00 p.m. to finally arrive.

February 4th (Wednesday)

We began at our usual time, right around 9:00 a.m. And, once again four of us worked the Lago Mar surveillance: Bill Stewart, Ron Ray, Mike and I. I was excited about the upcoming day, and I think Mike was too. We realized today could be a very important day for us, and for T.I.U. too. But, I really couldn't tell if Stewart and Ray felt the same way. They were both good men and Mike and I enjoyed working with each of them. Maybe it was just my imagination but they didn't seem to be as enthusiastic about our plan as Mike and I were. Maybe they didn't believe any professional burglar could be so stupid to hit the same hotel every other Wednesday, four times in a row! They did have a point.

As I settled down in my favorite spot out near the front entrance Mike began roaming the hotel's grounds. Stewart and Ray would take turns watching the pool side patio bar area and providing relief. At approximately 10:00 a.m. Mike thought he had a possible suspect when he observed a white male subject quickly exit room #338. This guy, who was 45-50 years old, sported a two day old growth of beard, and he was holding a flight bag under one of his arms. When Mike tried to follow him, he disappeared. Mike and the other two tac guys spent some time looking for this elusive fellow, but eventually gave up. But, as so often happened, all of a sudden this subject reappeared, almost as if by magic. He was followed as he went back to room #338. He seemed to be staying there in that room and we quickly eliminated him as a probable suspect.

Throughout the remainder of the day we continued to watch and follow a number of other individuals, all of whom looked even more suspicious than the one we'd just followed before. Unfortunately though, none of these new subjects appeared to be our bad guy either, and as the day wore on I began getting more anxious and impatient with each passing minute. "Damn, maybe today isn't going to be day!" I thought to myself. I started getting a little depressed and disgusted, especially when I thought about Sergeant Dierkzon. I knew he'd probably be very happy and even gloat when he found out Mike and I had been wrong about our prediction. I could just visualize him standing there all cocky and smug. And, I was sure I even knew what he would say - "I told you guys so! I told you, you're only tokens." I got pissed and immediately tried to think about something else. It didn't work!

Then, right about 2:20 p.m. I observed a 1970 Ford Mustang, convertible, white top over a brown bottom, slowly heading northbound on South Ocean Lane. The Mustang was operated by a white male and it appeared he was alone. The vehicle and subject passed by the front of the hotel itself and although there were several vacant parking spaces out front the Mustang did not stop. Instead, the white male subject drove into the Lago Mar's northernmost parking lot and then he drove around the lot until he found a space that suited him just right. The narrative of my police report, which I completed later, told the rest of the story - "....he was very careful to back his vehicle into a parking space so that the tag was more difficult to see. The W/M then exited the vehicle and he walked towards a hallway that exited onto the pool area. He was observed to just stand at the hallway, looking all around, and he appeared to be watching several couples that were playing tennis. He then walked to the stairs and went to the 2nd floor, again looking all around as he did. There was a maid on the 2nd floor and he almost immediately returned back to the ground floor and he then went through the hallway to the pool area. He continued to look all around as if he might be looking for someone. He walked through the grounds of the hotel to the 2nd pool that is located nearest the restaurant of the hotel. After staying there for several minutes, he again walked back to his vehicle. He got into the car and then drove off."

The thing that amazed me the most, about how we first spotted this W/M subject, was the way Mike and I both picked up on him almost simultaneously. I saw him first, of course, when I saw him back his car into a parking space so the rear was up against some bushes and the tag couldn't be seen. Then, when he left his vehicle and walked onto the hotel grounds, I followed. I wanted to find Mike, or one of the other tac guys, so they could help me watch this guy. To my surprise and delight it didn't take me very long to locate my partner Mike. In fact, he found me! He had seen the W/M entering the hotel grounds and immediately sensed there was something about this guy that warranted further observation. Once again, both our radars functioned perfectly!

When this W/M left the Lago Mar area, I followed him. I was able to stay with him and his vehicle as he headed northbound on A1A for a number of miles, but eventually lost him as he headed back westbound over the East Sunrise Boulevard Bridge, that crosses the Intracoastal Waterway. This didn't really matter though because I had already gotten the tag number from the rear of his Mustang, and the vehicle's registration told us a whole lot more about this suspicious individual. William "Bill" Mason was 35, 6'1", 195 lbs., and he did fit the description of the suspect that had been seen at the other hotel burglary back on December 19th. Mason lived in a very nice house in one of the better sections of northeast Fort Lauderdale, less than a mile from the beach itself. "Not your typical burglar's abode!" I thought to myself. But, when we ran the subject through our teletype, to see what our good friends at N.C.I.C. might tell us, we hit the jackpot! This guy might live in a nice respectable neighborhood, but he wasn't a saint. Bill Mason's most recent arrest was in May of last year, in Fort Lauderdale, for Indecent Exposure and C.C.W. He also had an arrest in Cleveland for Assault and Battery of a Law Enforcement Officer, and one in Florida's City of Hollywood for Careless Driving and Fleeing a Police Officer. The bonus? He had a past burglary arrest in the State of Ohio!

Mike and I both felt there was a strong possibility Bill Mason could be the culprit responsible for all the previous B&E's at the Lago Mar Hotel. His overall actions had been very suspicious and we definitely felt he was looking the hotel grounds over. If Mason had been looking for someone in particular it seems he would have done much more walking around than he did, or he would have made contact with the hotel front desk, or other hotel personnel. Instead, we watched him as he purposely avoided making contact with a maid. No, this guy was up to no good! The question was, what should we do about it? The decision was finally made that we'd all work the Lago Mar surveillance at least one more day, to see if Mason might return, or who knows, maybe he wasn't our bad guy after all, and maybe the real burglar would show up. No matter what happened, working the hotel surveillance one more day seemed to be the logical thing to do. I know I was all for it, and I'm sure Mike was too. And, after the appearance and actions of Mason today, even Stewart and Ray seemed to be much more excited and eager.

February 5th (Thursday)

Today's activity started off just a little bit different than normal. At approximately 9:15 a.m. Patrolman Howard Smith, who was the zone unit assigned to the South Beach area, advised us of a white male subject who was a known burglar and who was in the area of Pier 66 in a 1962 Red Rambler. After Officer Smith F.I.'d the subject we began a brief surveillance of him and his vehicle. We followed him until we were certain he had left the beach area for good and then he was dropped and we returned back to the Lago Mar Hotel. We didn't believe this W/M subject was the one responsible for the string of burglaries at the Lago Mar and Mike and I were still putting our money on the subject Bill Mason from yesterday. We spent the rest of the day wondering if he would return.

When 2:00 p.m. finally arrived, so did the subject Mason! Once again, he was driving his white/brown Ford Mustang, and he was alone. Just like he did yesterday, he parked his vehicle in an out of the way spot in the northernmost parking lot of the Lago Mar complex, and after he left his car we watched him as he again wandered around the hotel grounds. He finally ended up at the pool area nearest the hotel's restaurant. Again, he did not make contact with anyone at all, but he continually looked around as if he were looking for someone. Mason did sit down on a lawn chair near the pool and he just sat there for about 45 minutes watching all the happenings going on around him. Then, at approximately 3:10 p.m., he got up from the lawn chair and started walking around the hotel again. Several times he started to go up the stairs to another floor, but each time he unexpectedly encountered a maid or someone else and he'd come back down to ground level. He eventually ended up back at his original position in the lawn chair by the pool. Stewart, Ray, Mike and I had Mason pretty well covered and we could see most of his actions. I felt confident that if he were indeed our guy, and if he tried to pull anything he shouldn't, between the four of us we'd see it go down. But, I guess things just didn't click for Mason because at approximately 3:30 he left the pool area and returned to his vehicle, and then drove off out of the area. He was, of course, followed. With the invaluable aid of "Aerial 1," our department's single engine Cessna, we tailed Mason as he drove directly back to his residence in the northeast section of the city.

17

HAIL TO THE CHIEF!

We all felt Bill Mason was more than likely the culprit responsible for the recent rash of burglaries at the Lago Mar Hotel. There didn't seem to be a good reason why Mason had come to the Lago Mar these past two days; he never made contact with anyone, and his overall actions were definitely suspicious. For these reasons, the decision was made that T.I.U. would now initiate a surveillance of the subject Mason himself.

February 6th (Friday)

This was T.I.U.'s first full day watching Bill Mason and two things were different; the surveillance itself started earlier than usual, and Mike and I weren't there. Just in case Mason was an early riser, and he might be on the prowl early, by 8:15 a.m. Bill Stewart had a good "eyeball" on the subject's residence. Other tac guys would join him, but not Mike and I. As much as we would have liked to work each and every day, this just wasn't possible. We all thought, and this included our sergeants, that this surveillance wouldn't take very long and we'd probably catch the subject in a B&E in a day or two. But, just in case, our supervisors still had to plan for the long haul and that meant we needed to take a day off whether we wanted it or not. Tired cops make mistakes and one mistake could easily blow the entire surveillance.

Right around 9:50 a.m. a white female left the residence in a brown Ford Country Squire station wagon. She had some children with her and Officer Stewart rightly assumed this was the suspect's wife and kids. There wasn't any sign of the suspect however, and Bill didn't see Mason himself until approximately 10:45 when he too left the residence. The suspect was operating his now familiar looking white/brown Ford Mustang convertible. He slowly drove eastbound over the Oakland Park Boulevard Bridge which spanned the Intracoastal Waterway. This bridge quickly brought him to Fort Lauderdale's busy but beautiful North Beach area. This always crowded section of the city was a complicated mixture of businesses, hotels, condominiums and residences. A1A ran northward through the entire length of this area, from down south in the city where it began, until it entered Fort Lauderdale's smaller neighbor to the north, Lauderdale-by-the-Sea.

Jutting off A1A itself, just north of Oakland Park, and then running parallel along the main road, was Fort Lauderdale's well known gem, the Galt Ocean Mile. The first several buildings along the magnificent Galt Mile were elegant and very expensive hotels. These hotels sat there on the beach itself, with many of their fine rooms overlooking the beautiful Atlantic Ocean. They were truly omnipotent and supreme! Well-to-do tourists, many who came here from far off and exotic places, were more than willing to pay almost any price to stay at one of these luxurious American retreats. After these first few hotels there was an imposing array of large almost skyscraper-like condominiums which extended northward along the entire length of the Galt Mile, almost all the way up to nearby Lauderdale-by-the-Sea. These mammoth structures, standing there tall, stately and erect, like a modern day Stonehenge, seemed to have some mystical power all their own. Every now and then though, another hotel would be hidden there among these towering giants. But, when all was said and done, and even as impressive as the Galt Mile truly was, if I had my choice where I'd like to stay, I'd still pick the lovely Lago Mar. It had one thing these beauties here on the Galt Mile didn't have. It was isolated and away from the maddening crowds that routinely flocked to the North Beach area every tourist season.

The Beach Club was the first hotel on the Galt Mile and it was located there at the major intersection of North Ocean Boulevard and East Oakland Park. This often hectic intersection, where these two congested roadways came together, was the busiest road junction in the entire North Beach area. And, this was where the subject Mason finally ended up. After he drove back and forth along the south side of the hotel several times, he parked his vehicle in the lot and entered the huge building by way of a side door. Once again, his actions appeared to be a little suspicious. After all, why hadn't he just entered through the front entrance and gone into the hotel's main lobby area? Could it be he didn't want anyone to see him? Bill Stewart and Al Smith quickly exited their own unmarked vehicles and started to follow Mason around on foot. He only stayed inside the hotel for approximately 4-5 minutes though and when he got back to his Mustang he got in and then he drove off northbound on the Galt Ocean Mile.

Mason drove past all the other hotels and condos along the Galt Mile, and even though each one seemed to be an inviting and tempting target, it was apparent he had some other unknown destination in mind. At Fort Lauderdale's northernmost city limits, east of the Intracoastal, where the Galt Mile ends and you're once again on A1A, you suddenly enter neighboring Lauderdale-by-the-Sea. This is what Mason did. Just north of the city limits was a modern new Holiday Inn Hotel. The suspect parked his vehicle there, got out on foot, and began walking around the outside of the hotel. He seemed to be looking over the various rooms. He never entered the Holiday Inn itself and he just looked all around the area. He eventually walked eastbound away from the hotel towards the north/south boulevard located between A1A and the beach. This quiet area sported dozens of other smaller motels and now Mason seemed to be looking these over too. However, nothing apparently looked good to him, because at approximately 11:30 a.m. he returned to his Mustang at the Holiday Inn and he drove off southbound on A1A. He drove directly back to his residence which was several miles south, and arrived there right around 11:45 a.m.

At approximately 12:50 p.m. Mason again left his residence. Even professional hotel burglars have to eat and I suppose he probably went home to have some lunch. Anyway, now he was back out and about, and once again our tac guys eagerly followed along behind him to see where he would lead them. It didn't take them very long to find out. He drove directly back to the North Beach area and the Beach Club Hotel. Mason stopped his Mustang right near the side entrance he had used before, but this time he even backed it into a carefully selected spot so no one would be able to see his vehicle's tag. He exited his car and entered the hotel. Our police plane "Aerial One" was overhead and assisting in the surveillance and they observed Mason as he wandered around an outside courtyard area near the hotel's pool. Stewart and Smith again attempted to follow Mason on foot but they weren't able to locate him inside the huge hotel. After he walked around the hotel property for about ten minutes, the suspect Mason went back to his vehicle and left. It was now 1:05 p.m.

As Mason drove southbound on A1A our tac units, along with "Aerial One" obediently followed along behind him. There was no doubt about it, this guy was good! He was also apparently very cautious. But, we knew he still didn't have a clue he was being followed by some of Fort Lauderdale's best. Mason drove up and down a number of side streets in the area between Sunrise Boulevard to the north, and East Las Olas Boulevard to the south. This specific area east of the Intracoastal Waterway was heavily saturated with hotels and motels of all shapes and sizes. He never did see anything that apparently tickled his fancy and he slowly continued heading south towards the Lago Mar Hotel. He arrived there at approximately 1:20 p.m.

As he had done on his previous visits, Mason parked his car in an out of the way spot in the northernmost lot. He walked to the pool and he again looked all around. He seemed to be watching the rooms, but after only twenty minutes he left the Lago Mar and drove to another large hotel complex located across the street from Pier 66. This hotel also didn't seem to turn Mason on and after only about five minutes walking around the pool area there, and looking over the individual rooms, he left this hotel too. This was Mason's routine for most of the remainder of the surveillance. He did the same thing at several more large hotels before apparently deciding to call it quits for the day. At about 2:30 he stopped at a small shopping center near the Gateway Interchange, made a purchase of some groceries, and then he went home. He arrived there at approximately 2:50 p.m.

Mason seemed to be up to no good, that was obvious! The tactical guys working the surveillance met with Sergeant Gerwens and advised him about the specifics of Mason's movements and actions. Joe decided the surveillance should continue until dark, just in case Mason had second thoughts and tried again. The tac guys continued to watch his residence until approximately 7:00 p.m., but when there was no further movement they secured. Joe decided we would continue the surveillance the next day, which was a Saturday.

The Next Six Days

Bill Mason's actions this next week pretty much mirrored his suspicious activities on Friday. Except for Saturday (February 7th), when he stayed home and played the role of devoted husband and father, and then Sunday

(February 8th), when we didn't even bother to watch him, during the rest of the week he almost ran us ragged as we followed him to dozens of different locations he seemed to be casing. Most of these locations were in the North Beach area of Fort Lauderdale but we also followed him back to Lauderdale-by-the-Sea, to the north of our own city. He seemed to be a real creature of habit and he apparently had a few favorite areas where he liked to roam.

Mason's overall actions this week did nothing to alleviate our concerns that he was indeed a professional burglar. Almost everything he did, every move he made, only seemed to reinforce this opinion. On Tuesday (February 10th), Mason parked his Mustang to the rear of a hospital located on A1A, just south of Oakland Park Boulevard. He slowly walked through the parking lot until he reached the hospital's north ramp. This elevated ramp provided direct access to the hospital's emergency room which was located at the northern end of the huge building. The rear parking lot was at ground level, but the entrance to the E.R. was one story higher. Mason began walking up this north ramp to the E.R. but he quickly did an about-face when he suddenly saw a marked police unit parked there right at the E.R. entrance. The officer was more than likely inside the E.R. taking a break, or maybe even handling one of the many reports that originated at the hospital. No matter what the officer's reason for being there it was very obvious Mason did not want to accidentally run into him. He walked back down the north ramp, then southbound through the parking lot until he reached the hospital's south ramp. He used this south ramp to get to the A1A side of the hospital. Once he reached the sidewalk, then he walked back northbound along the front of this very large and impressive structure. It was amazing; from just the mere sight of an EMPTY police car, Mason had taken the long way around the hospital, to reach A1A and the sidewalk out in front of it.

In addition to all the casing he did of motels, hotels and condominiums, Mason also managed to find the time to take care of some of his personal business too. One day he stopped at the public library on East Sunrise Boulevard, on another day he did some shopping at a local bookstore, and then a nearby drugstore, located just northwest of the Oakland Park Bridge. One day he even found the time to take in an early afternoon movie. As far as we could see, Mason had no visible means of support, and he certainly lived in a nice house, in a very nice neighborhood. Mason had previously listed his occupation, on an old arrest card, as "Self-employed/Real Estate." Yeah, right! During one of our many surveillances, when Mason had been away from his vehicle, I walked by it and I observed a real estate sales contract laying in plain view on the right front passenger's seat. There was a name of a local real estate firm at the top of this form and we eventually got an address for this company from the ever-handy Yellow Pages. We didn't really need to let our fingers do the walking though because we already knew that Mason hadn't been anywhere near this business, at least not while we'd been tailing him. In fact, we never had seen him near any real estate offices at all. No, we suspected this supposed occupation as a real estate broker or salesman was just a cover. And, the more I thought about it, the more I realized what a damn good cover it really was. It gave Mason the perfect excuse to walk around many of the expensive pieces of property he liked to frequent, and if he were stopped he could just say he was thinking of buying the place - or, "I've got a buyer who's interested."

"Aerial One" did an outstanding job of following the subject Mason when he was on the move in his vehicle and without their help we wouldn't have been able to keep him under such close surveillance as we did. But, whenever he got out on foot, especially when he wanted to walk around a hotel, at least one of the tac guys usually became his shadow. We always tried to maintain a very loose tail, but sometimes this was easier said than done. On Wednesday (February

11th) I learned firsthand how true this was. Mason was out on foot walking around a few of the hotels and condos along the Galt Mile and I was one of the tac officers trying to keep tabs on him. After walking between two of these structures he turned a corner and disappeared onto the beach. I quickly walked to that same corner so I could see where he went. Just as I reached the end of the building though, there was Mason coming back around the corner and walking straight towards me. He had reversed his direction and I was caught cold turkey dead! He never said a word as he passed me by, but he sure did look me up and down. I stopped at the corner and began taking pictures of the beach with the 35mm Canon I was carrying. Maybe he'd think I was just another dorky-looking snowbird in awe of the sun, the beach and the waves. I never looked behind me to see if he was looking at me, but I could almost feel his eyes burning a hole into the back of my neck.

Also on Wednesday (February 11th), Mason added a new wrinkle to an already complicated puzzle. Officer Ron Ray, Mike and I, had watched Mason all day long. Even after I had had my brief face-to-face encounter with him he seemed undeterred and he continued to roam the hotels and condos along the Galt Mile, and then north into Lauderdale-by-the-Sea, and then even further north to Pompano Beach. He returned back to his residence right around 3:15 p.m. and we were relieved by T.I.U. Officers Al Smith and Guy Freeman at approximately 7:00 p.m. We were headed back to the station when Freeman suddenly advised over the radio that Mason was once again on the prowl, but this time he was riding a 10-speed bike. This was definitely a new twist!

Mason was lost for a short period of time but then Freeman spotted him again about 10-15 minutes later. He was standing at a telephone booth at the southeast corner of his favorite intersection, A1A and East Oakland Park Boulevard. We couldn't tell if he was actually talking with anyone but there was no mistaking the fact he was looking all around. Was he looking for a tail? When Mason finally left the phone booth he rode northbound to two of his favorite hotels at the south end of the Galt Ocean Mile. He slowly cruised around each hotel's parking lot and then he stopped and hid his bicycle in a row of bushes separating the two huge pieces of property. Mike observed him placing something into the rear waistband of his trousers and this unknown object was totally concealed underneath the white nylon jacket he was wearing. He entered the southernmost hotel by way of the side entrance at the north end of the building, and disappeared. By this time, a number of other tac officers had also responded to the area to assist with the surveillance. This included our lieutenant, "Yankee-1", and our two sergeants; Gerwens and Dierkzon.

Two minutes after Mason entered the hotel, five of our T.I.U. guys also went in, via the same side door. A systematic search of each floor was conducted by these officers, however Mason could not be located. A search was also made of the pool and patio area, the lobby and yes, even the restrooms. The subject, although we knew he was still somewhere inside, could not be found. While the five tac guys searched the interior of the hotel the rest of us maintained a watch on the various exits, as well as the subject's hidden getaway bike. Approximately fifteen minutes after Mason had entered the hotel one of our tac guys observed him coming down a stairwell at the north end of the building. He had apparently been up on one of the upper floors. We knew these upper floors had all been checked by our guys inside and none of them had seen Mason in any of the hallways or stairwells, so it seemed a pretty good bet he might have been inside a room doing his thing. Again, we didn't see him do it, so we could only speculate. That wasn't good enough!

When Mason got back to his bicycle he opened a small pouch located at the rear of the bike's seat. Pouches like this usually contained small tools which could be used to make emergency bicycle repairs, if needed. We watched as Mason now put some unknown object, or objects, into this pouch. We had no idea at all what it was. It could have been the "fruits of the crime" from a burglary he may have just committed, or maybe even burglar tools he may have used. Or, it could have been just a box of damn cough drops! We didn't know! After he snapped the pouch shut, he looked all around the parking lot for a few seconds, and then he took off riding his bike southbound on A1A.

For the next hour or so the subject Mason rode up and down a number of streets, doubling back at times, and often just riding around in circles, almost as if he might be looking for someone following him. We didn't think any of us had been spotted though because for the most part our ground units maintained a very loose tail and most of the actual surveillance itself was carried out by "Aerial 1", which remained overhead throughout. I believe Mason was just being extremely cautious. But, in addition to being careful, he was also quite good and we knew it wasn't going to be easy catching him in the act. Tonight, the subject Mason was giving us a refresher course titled: Burglar 101.

Mason continued his roaming and prowling and for the first time I admittedly was getting a little frustrated. T.I.U. had spent hundreds of hours trying to catch this guy doing his thing and we still didn't have anything concrete to show for our efforts. Now, a new and totally different factor complicated the picture even more. In a few short days President Gerald Ford would visit Fort Lauderdale and T.I.U. had been chosen to provide additional dignitary protection. This meant us pulling off the Mason Surveillance completely.

February 13th (Friday)

T.I.U. watched Mason one more day on the 12th, but nothing more happened. I guess I should really say nothing "new" happened! There was just more of the same old stuff; his endless fascination with the exclusive hotels and high rise condos that saturated Fort Lauderdale's entire North Beach area, plus his occasional side interest in the inviting targets located to the north, in our neighboring jurisdictions that also had beach front property. But, all that was behind us now. Tonight, we would instead concentrate on just one important thing; protecting the most powerful man on the face of the earth, the President of the United States!

As I arrived at the hotel for the presidential reception President Gerald Ford was to attend I wondered how we would look to the President, the U.S. Secret Service and yes, even the general public too. I mean, some of us looked pretty damn scruffy and this ritzy presidential reception was being held at the Bahia Mar Hotel and Yatch Club, one of Fort Lauderdale's finest beach side hotels. Most of us, myself included, needed at least a good haircut and a few of the guys hadn't even picked up a razor in many weeks. Beards were a definite no-no for all uniform personnel and I could just envision some sharp eyed newspaper photographer snapping a quick picture of President Ford and one of our unshaven or bearded tac guys in uniform. If that happened, I knew the Chief would go berserk! But, I hoped the Chief, or anyone else who might question our overall appearance, would take the time to remember what our normal everyday assignment was; we worked almost exclusively in plainclothes, in a semi-undercover capacity, and the more unpoliceman-like you looked, the better. Tonight we were guarding the President of the United States, but in a day or two we would be back following the subject Mason again, and prowling around the often danger filled streets of Fort Lauderdale. Most of our tac guys took this challenge very seriously and unless you knew who they were beforehand, you'd probably have a tough time picking any of them out of a crowd and identifying them as being cops. Now, the F.L.P.D. brass was gonna clean all of us up, they hoped, put us back in our nice clean fresh uniforms, and then put us out smack dab in the middle of the public guarding the most visible person in America. Sounded like a good plan to me! There was just one more minor problem; entry to this reception at the Bahia Mar was by "White House Invitation Only", and I really wondered if after they saw us, if we would be able to get in ourselves!

The next thought I had was just an extension of my original concern about how we all looked. I knew some of us might not be that damn pretty, you know all spit and polish like the motormen always were, with their fancy black boots and shiny white helmets, but we still could boast we were the best of the best. That alone made me proud! But, sometimes being the best just wasn't enough. The Bahia Mar Hotel complex was an immense multi-building structure and I knew there were dozens of important access points that needed to be covered during the upcoming reception. I began to wonder if the brass might not decide to stick us unsightly tac guys at some of these less visible and out of the way locations that needed covering. This way they wouldn't have to worry about how we looked and we could still get the job done. This, of course, was all well and good, and I would obviously do anything they told me to do. But, if I had to pull off the Mason surveillance for this presidential detail, then I didn't want to be hidden away in some dusty out of the way cubbyhole somewhere. I really didn't want to be on some lonely rooftop looking for possible snipers, or at some forgotten loading dock checking out deliveries and watching for the uninvited. I wanted to be near where the main event was taking place and if I was lucky I might even catch a glimpse of President Ford himself. That's what I really hoped for.

I should have given our brass much more credit though, because as it turned out none of us were hidden away anywhere. When the Secret Service Advance Team of agents came to town several days before the affair itself, our supervisors went over every inch of the hotel with them. All the important locations were identified and our T.I.U. guys were assigned to many, if not most, of these key positions. The perfect example, which showed just how visible some of us were, was the fact my partner Mike was stationed right at the front main entrance of the ballroom where the reception was being held. He was to standby there and assist the Secret Service personnel who were screening the guests as they entered the ballroom. This included looking through all the women's purses. I'm sure the U.S. Secret Service was still just a little gun shy because of the two recent and, thank God, failed assassination attempts on President Gerald Ford. Both these attempts occurred in California. On September 5th, 1975, in Sacramento, Lynette Fromme was arrested after she pointed a loaded handgun at the President. Then, two weeks later, in San Francisco, Sara Jane Moore missed when she actually fired a single shot at the President. Both these would-be assassins were woman and each had used a handgun. So, it didn't surprise me at all that my partner Mike would be at the main entrance checking women's purses for weapons. It seemed the prudent thing to do!

I found myself situated outside the large ballroom, right by the main rear entrance. With my back up against the outside wall of the hallway I was in, I could easily look into the ballroom itself, because the rear door was initially left open. Hotel service personnel catering the reception used this rear entrance, and the hallway where I was located, to come and go from the ballroom at will. This way they avoided the guests arriving at the main entrance at the front where Mike was located. I was extremely happy with my assigned position there outside the ballroom's rear door because I knew I'd get a very good look at the

President. He was scheduled to come down the hallway towards my location and then enter the ballroom through the rear door I was guarding. I couldn't have asked for a better position.

I really liked President Ford! Never mind he was the so-called "accidental" President, or that he pardoned Richard Nixon, AND the Vietnam draft dodgers to boot! Thanks to his handling of the Mayaguez affair I still gave him very high marks. Sixty-two years young when he entered the White House, President Ford was an easygoing and unpretentious individual. I once read he was in very good physical shape and he was supposedly the most athletic president since Theodore Roosevelt. Like all presidents though, Gerald Ford had his detractors. Lyndon Baines Johnson, our nation's 36th President, once reportedly said that Ford "is so dumb he can't walk and fart at the same time." That didn't matter to me though, cause I still liked Gerald Ford anyway!

I had no trouble at all spotting the President and his impressive looking entourage. They came down the hallway heading towards my position at what seemed to be a very brisk pace and I immediately noted President Ford was several steps out in front of the rest of the group. There was one man following along right behind the President, almost on his heels. If the President stopped suddenly, I'm not sure this other man would have been able to avoid bumping into Gerald Ford's rear. That's how close he was to him. I was pretty sure this guy was a Secret Service man. There were also two other men trying to keep up with the President; one was off to his right, and the other was to his left, but both men were a step or two in back of him. I had seen these guys before and knew for certain they were with the Secret Service. The rest of the group, maybe another four or five individuals, who all seemed to be dressed alike, followed along silently behind the President and his Secret Service protective umbrella.

Before the President's arrival I had been standing in a relaxed parade rest type of posture. I wasn't at full attention but I also didn't look sloppy or uninterested either. However, when President Ford suddenly came down the hallway towards my location I automatically snapped to a higher level of awareness. I don't believe I did this consciously, it just seemed to happen. After all, this was our nation's Chief Executive, the Commander-in-Chief of our armed forces, and I wanted to show him the respect he deserved. Strict military dogma, I suppose, dictated that I should have been looking straight ahead, not to my left at the approaching President. But, to be quite honest, this was a very thrilling moment for me. Being this close to the President of the United States was not something that happened to me every day of the week and I found it hard to take my eyes off the man.

As President Ford got even closer to my location I continued to study the man intently. He looked supremely confident and there was no doubt at all about who was leading the group headed towards the ballroom. I suddenly realized several things, however. First of all, it hit me just how vulnerable the President actually was. Here he was, only a few precious feet away from me, and if I'd been some crazy or whacked-out cop hoping to make a name for myself, there was nothing to really stop me. I could have easily shot the President, if that had been my intention. Luckily, I liked the man, and I wasn't crazy! I also noticed though, that the Secret Service agents with President Ford seemed to be eyeballing me, just as much as I was eyeballing him. It occurred to me they couldn't take anything or anyone for granted and I realized they were sizing me up to see if I posed any kind of a threat to the President. Was I a real cop, or some nut impersonating a police officer? I'm sure the Secret Service also warned their agents they might some day encounter a rogue cop, and by the way these men watched me, I knew they didn't automatically discount this possibility as a potential threat. It was definitely a somber thought, that I, the protector of the President, was now being looked at as a possible threat to the President.

"Good evening Mr. President!" I said proudly, as I simultaneously snapped off a very smart salute with my right hand. I wasn't really sure if saluting was the correct thing to do but it seemed right at the time. I sometimes worked an off-duty detail at a local stadium where high school football games were played. I worked these events in uniform and I always saluted the American Flag when they played The Star Spangled Banner, so why not the President of the United States? President Ford was almost abreast of me now and he suddenly veered to the right and he came straight at me. The Secret Service men, and the rest of the people with him, also altered their course accordingly. It seemed as if they hadn't anticipated this move by the President and it took each of them a split second to react. It also took me just a moment or two before I fully realized what was happening too. President Ford, on his way to mingle with the affluent and other influential members of the Republican Party faithful, was apparently making a slight detour to shake my hand! My God, what an honor!

President Ford extended his strong right hand out in my direction and then, without even breaking stride, we shook hands, he said "Hello!", I nodded and smiled, and then he was suddenly gone! I watched as he and his entire ensemble quietly moved away from me. They continued to move as one, like a well tuned machine. As President Ford finally disappeared into the large ballroom opposite where I was standing I began to return to my previous relaxed but attentive state. I've always been a very patriotic individual and getting to shake the President's hand definitely meant a lot to me. It was truly the experience of a lifetime. But, what made the occasion even more memorable was the fact it had been totally unexpected. I had always hoped to see the President, but never thought I would really get close enough to him to shake his hand. After all, not many of our tac guys did. Also, the President had gone out of his way to do this simple thing and this made the moment even more important to me. President Ford might shake several hundred hands tonight at the reception, yet I ventured to say he probably wouldn't even remember most of these people by nights end. I, on the other hand, would shake only one hand tonight, but it would be an experience I would never forget!

Hotel personnel working the Presidential reception continued to come and go through the rear entrance I was guarding and I had a pretty good view of the crowd gathered there inside the huge ballroom. But, my main responsibilities were still the hallway and the rear entrance, not what was happening inside the ballroom itself. So, as I watched the guests jostle, cavort and mingle with one another, I tried to keep my mind on MY number one priority. I wasn't going to let any unauthorized individuals get by me and into the Presidential reception where they didn't belong, not if I could help it. I still had my own natural curiosity to contend with however, and from time to time I found myself a little distracted and not totally concentrating on my own duties as I should have been. Every so often I would find myself staring blankly at one or two of the guests. These were nameless faces that meant absolutely nothing at all to me, but a few times I did manage to make some eye contact with a few of these people. This wouldn't last for that long, of course, and before you could even say Lee Harvey Oswald, the person I might be watching would suddenly disappear. I'm sure they'd go off looking for President Ford, where ever he might be. I don't know if any of these people ever found him, but I know I never saw President Ford again, and I was looking for him too!

By now most of the people who were coming to the reception were already there inside the ballroom. I couldn't see the main front entrance where Mike was stationed but I guessed he was still there and probably dealing with any late comers who might be arriving. I suddenly experienced a very strange sensation and it's really kind of difficult for me to accurately describe what this specific feeling felt like. One moment I was standing there; calm, cool and relaxed, enjoying myself as I watched the reception's guests who were mingling near the door I was guarding. Then, the next second I felt a definite chill run up and down my spine, and I realized something was dreadfully wrong! At first I didn't know exactly what was wrong, but then after a few more precious seconds I finally began to understand just what had happened to make me feel this way.

As I quietly stood there at my post, staring intently into the stranger's eyes, it suddenly hit me. This man was no stranger at all and I had seen him before. Many times! Now, he was looking through the open door, right at me. I thought this a little odd at first because most of the people inside the ballroom were so preoccupied with their own presidential pursuits they had no time for anything else. But, not this man. He seemed to be more interested in me than he was in finding and meeting President Ford. Maybe it was the uniform I was wearing, I thought to myself. Whatever it was, it only took me a few precious seconds to realize just who this individual was. "Jesus, it's Bill Mason!" I muttered excitedly. It was a purely spontaneous utterance and I really hadn't planned it. In fact, immediately after I said it, I regretted that I did. True, even if someone had been standing there beside me, I doubt they would have been able to make out exactly what I'd said. But now, I had to hope and pray that Mason, among all his many other talents, couldn't read lips too! "What the hell is he doing here?" I silently asked myself, as I quickly turned away from him so he wouldn't be able to look at my face any longer.

I moved several steps to my left and pretended I was looking at something down the long hallway. After about fifteen seconds or so I turned back around towards the ballroom and carefully scanned the crowd just inside the doorway. Mason was no longer there. He was gone from my view entirely, but I knew he was still there somewhere inside the ballroom itself. I got on the radio and tried to alert the other tac guys inside the ballroom, as well as Mike at the main entrance, about Mason's unexpected presence at the reception. I guess I should have realized they already were well aware of this fact! Mason and his wife had entered the reception by way of the main front entrance and Mike had spotted them as they patiently waited in line. He had even been the one to check Mrs. Mason's purse, just to make sure it did not contain any weapons. Even though we still thought he was a professional hotel room burglar and jewel thief, he and his wife had a valid White House Invitation, so they were allowed to enter the ballroom unmolested.

Mason, of course, wasn't alerted to the fact his presence at the reception caused additional concern and consternation among the security detail guarding President Ford. Mike hadn't shown any outward signs he had recognized him and as far as Mason could tell everything seemed to be completely normal. But, everything wasn't normal! We quickly advised the Secret Service of Mason's unexpected presence and of our suspicions he was a professional crook. The Secret Service, obviously much more interested in would-be assassins, rather than mere burglars or jewel thieves, decided not to take any chances. So, for the rest of the evening, wherever Mason and his wife went in the crowded ballroom, at least two Secret Service agents went with them. They didn't know this, of course, but these two agents were there just the same. I guess you could say it was like suddenly having an extra shadow, and not even knowing it!

The reception lasted a few more hours and then it ended like it began, quietly and without the hint of any trouble. I don't think the Masons had a very good time though and I was later told they even left the reception just a little bit early. I think the large crowd may have had something to do with this, because between the guests and then their Secret Service bloodhounds, Mason and his wife must have felt like a couple of damn sardines in a can! I can't say this made me feel bad!

February 16th (Monday)

Seeing the subject Mason at the reception for President Gerald Ford had been a real shocker. But now, after this initial shock had finally worn off, T.I.U. went back to work and immediately began watching the suspect Mason once again. Some changes had to be made, of course. For one thing, of all the tac guys Mason may have seen, he got the best look at Mike and me. After all, he and I had walked right by each other that day at the beach, when he suddenly reversed his direction and I had almost walked right into him. Now, here at the President's reception, he had seen me again. And, this time I had been in full police uniform. To make matters even worse though, I also thought I saw the slight glimmer of recognition in Mason's eyes when he and I exchanged glances at the Bahia Mar. No, something definitely had to be done to make sure I didn't run into him again, and even more importantly still, to make sure he didn't get another good look at me. For this reason, Sergeant Gerwens told me to take this Monday off. Obviously, if I stayed at home there should be no way in hell Mason would be able to see me again. That is, of course, not unless Mason decided to come to MY neighborhood and break into MY house. I knew I could never be so lucky!

Mason had also seen Mike up close at the reception. Mike had been stationed at the main entrance and Mason had been near enough to my partner to smell what brand after shave lotion he was wearing. So, it was also very important that Mike be kept away from Mason too. For this reason, Sergeant Gerwens assigned Mike to the Aviation Unit for the day. Veteran F.L.P.D. Officer Ken Peterson would be the plane's pilot and Mike would be his observer. From this somewhat precarious perch 500 feet above the surveillance it seemed a safe bet that Mason wouldn't be getting a good look at Mike again. I have to admit, if I had had a choice between sitting at home all alone, which also meant missing out on all the action, or being up in the police airplane with Ken Peterson, I definitely would have taken the assignment up in the air, in a heartbeat! I wasn't given a choice however, and I wasn't asked for my opinion or preference either. So, stay at home I would! For me, I knew today would be a very long day.

Monday's surveillance of Mason's residence started right around 9:30 a.m. and about forty-five minutes later T.I.U. ground units reported the suspect leaving. Mason was wearing long brown pants, a burgundy striped shirt, and he was driving his 1970 white/brown Ford Mustang convertible. He drove north to Pompano Beach and prowled around the beach area there for about thirty minutes, before he drove back home. He arrived there right around 11:25 a.m. Mason left his residence a second time, at approximately 12:18 p.m. This time it appeared he had changed at least part of his wardrobe. He still wore the same burgundy striped shirt he had had on before, but now instead of the long brown pants, he was wearing a more casual pair of brown khaki shorts. Was there a reason for this change? I suspected Mason wanted to look more like a tourist and he realized khaki shorts were less conspicuous looking and would help him fit in better. Whatever the reason, it seemed today was going to be another long fun-filled day full of activity. As I continued to monitor the surveillance from my home, by way of my hand held police radio, I began to envy Mike even more. He might be 500 feet above the action, but at least HE could see what was happening!

Mason parked his vehicle within sight of the Oakland Park Boulevard Bridge. He spent the next thirty minutes out on foot prowling around one of his favorite hunting grounds; the popular Oakland Park and A1A area. At 12:40 p.m. Mason returned to his vehicle, started it up and drove off. The ground units reported Mason continued to act suspiciously and everything still seemed to indicate he was indeed a burglar in search of an easy mark. The police plane, with Mike overhead as the observer, continued to follow him as he headed north to the Galt Ocean Mile. At 12:45 p.m. Mason stopped his vehicle in the parking lot of the Ramada Inn Hotel, located in the 4200 block of the Galt Ocean Drive. During our previous surveillance last week, Mason had also visited here too.

For approximately the next 2½ hours Mason roamed all around the Ramada Inn almost at will. Mike, in the police plane overhead, maintained a watchful eye on Mason's parked vehicle. Numerous T.I.U. officers on foot and inside the hotel tried their best to keep Mason under surveillance. Our probable bad guy resumed his old tricks and he walked all around the hotel and its grounds, watching the rooms, guests and the hotel employees who crossed his path. He definitely appeared to be up to no good! It soon became apparent that Mason seemed to be paying a great deal of attention to the hotel's first floor area. He was observed there in that same first floor hallway a number of times. Anticipating Mason's strong interest in this one specific area Sergeant Gerwens made contact with the hotel management and they gave him a key to a vacant room. This was Room #121, and it was now 2:30 p.m.

At approximately 3:20 p.m. Sergeant Gerwens and his partner exited room #121 where they had been waiting. Mason had just passed by #121 again and both of these officers now walked east and then around the interior corridor. This eventually put them right in front of room #127. They noticed the door to #127 was partially open and they now observed the subject Mason standing there just inside the door. To their amazed delight they also saw him wiping the metal door knob with a white colored handkerchief. Mason looked up and saw the two plainclothes officers and although he obviously did not know they were the police he immediately shut the door anyway. Joe Gerwens and his partner proceeded past the room and positioned themselves directly west of the door itself and they waited. They didn't have to wait very long though. After about ten brief seconds the door to #127 once again opened and out walked our now verified bad guy Bill Mason. Sgt. Gerwens immediately identified himself as a police officer and ordered Mason to "Halt!" because he was under arrest! At gun point Mason was placed up against the corridor's wall. Moments later Mason was placed prone onto the floor and then searched. This is when Sergeant Gerwens first learned even professional jewel thieves sometimes have trouble controlling themselves in very stressful situations. The subject Mason, who had literally rubbed elbows with President Gerald Ford, as well as many of south Florida's Republican elite, had pissed his pants!

Mason was advised of his rights at 3:35 p.m. The actual search of the subject Mason turned up an unexpected smorgasbord of new evidence. This helped to seal Mason's fate even more. By far the most damning item they found was a Ramada Inn Hotel pass key Mason had in his possession. This particular key fit the lock on the door for room #127, which he had entered illegally, and it also fit several other rooms in this same general area. But, in addition to this pass key he also had a metal key ring with a maroon colored tag on it from this same Ramada Inn. There were nine keys on this ring and a few of these were even numbered (#230, #113, #330). These numbers seemed to be scratched in, almost as if by hand. Mason also had a pair of golf gloves with him, a homemade key-type pick, a pocket knife, a screwdriver and the white handkerchief he had used to wipe his prints off of #127's door knob. Today, for all the good it did him, he could have left the damn handkerchief home! He had been caught in the act and we really didn't need any prints to convict him. He was going to be charged with Burglary and Possession of Burglary tools, both felonies, and there was nothing at all he could do about it! He was bought and paid for!

Efforts were now made to locate the person who was registered in room #127. This turned out to be a 46-year old white female from Manchester, Connecticut. She arrived back at her room approximately twenty minutes after Mason had been taken into custody. The situation was explained to her and she advised she had not given anyone permission to enter her room in her absence. After she checked her room she stated that although a suitcase in the closet had been ransacked, which was also visibly apparent to the tac officers at the scene, nothing appeared to be missing. How ironic! After the Lago Mar stakeout, and then many days of following the subject Mason around, during which he cased literally hundreds of hotel rooms, Mason had been caught in the act and he hadn't even gotten anything for his trouble - other than a wet pair of under shorts! Man, life is sometimes just full of unusual and unexpected surprises!

Mason's 1970 Ford Mustang convertible was towed from the Ramada Inn parking lot and instead of going straight to the wrecker compound which was normal s.o.p., the vehicle was brought to the rear of the police station. The subject Mason was also transported to the P.D. and at approximately 4:15 p.m. he was brought to the second floor detective bureau and turned over to several burglary detectives there. They had eagerly been awaiting his arrival. Mason had already been advised of his rights when he was arrested back at the hotel so he wasn't immediately advised again at the detective bureau. When Det. Ed King asked Mason if he would sign a search waiver form, so our officers and King could search his home and his vehicle, I think to everyone's surprise, Mason agreed. We probably could have searched his vehicle anyway, as part of the towing procedure, but a search waiver was definitely the better way to go.

Detective King asked Mason how much stolen property was at his residence and Mason admitted there was some there, but there really wasn't that much. At approximately 4:45 p.m. Detective King attempted to obtain a sworn statement from the subject Mason and he advised him of his rights again. Mason stated he would not make any further statements about his arrest at the Ramada Inn until he conferred with his attorney. At this time the interrogation was concluded. At 5:25 p.m. Mason's Mustang was searched by Detective King. This was at the rear of the P.D. and it netted us a little more evidence which could be considered burglar paraphernalia.

After Mason completed the routine booking process at Fort Lauderdale P.D.'s Jail Ron Ray and Det. King transported him to his home in the northeast section of the city. They arrived there right around 6:15 p.m. Sergeant Joe Gerwens, Mike, and several other officers were already there waiting for them. Also waiting was Mason's wife and an attorney who was one of Mason's close friends. This attorney indicated he himself wasn't there to represent Mason, but Mason's attorney of record, a well known and popular local attorney named Howard Zeidwig, was enroute to the Mason home and he requested we delay the actual search of Mason's residence until Mr. Zeidwig could arrive. Zeidwig arrived shortly thereafter, at approximately 6:50 p.m. And now, for the next half hour or so, Zeidwig conferred in private with his client.

Even though none of the Fort Lauderdale police officers present were privy to their conversation it really wasn't that hard to guess what the two men were talking about. The main topic of conversation more than likely centered around

Mason's previous decision to allow us to search his home without a warrant. Mason probably had second thoughts now, and I'm sure his attorney Mr. Zeidwig also regretted his client's hasty decision too. Yes, Mason could now change his mind if he wanted to, and refuse us entry into his home, but Mr. Zeidwig also probably advised him we had more than enough Probable Cause to secure a search warrant, if we had to. After all, in addition to being caught in the act, and also having burglar tools in his possession, Mason verbally admitted to Det. King that there was more stolen property at his residence. These circumstances alone would have been more than enough to convince most Broward County judges that a search warrant was indeed appropriate.

At approximately 7:30 p.m. attorney Zeidwig and Mason advised that Mason would still waive his right to a search warrant and he would voluntarily allow our officers to search the interior of his residence. It was quite apparent Mason, or at least his attorney, realized the difficult spot he was in. And, a little cooperation now might just help him out in the long run. If they agreed to cooperate, instead of playing hard ball, they might just be able to make a deal. Zeidwig was good, and he knew his stuff!

Due to Mason's continued cooperation, it was agreed that any stolen property recovered from his residence, which had been taken in previous burglaries he had committed, would not be used against him for prosecution purposes. Mason also agreed to assist Detective King in his efforts to locate the rightful owners of this recovered property, and this meant eventually driving around with King and pointing out all the past burglaries he had been responsible for. But, Mason and his attorney were also warned that if he failed to advise us of certain B&E's he was involved in, and it was later learned he was involved in these other offenses, he could and probably would be charged with these additional crimes. Both men stated they understood this. Once again however, Mason's attorney advised him not to make any statements reference the burglary at the Ramada Inn, where he was caught, or about the burglary tools he had had in his possession.

The actual search of Mason's home took almost two full hours to complete and it ultimately resulted in the recovery of large quantities of stolen property. We eventually located guns, cameras, credit cards, an oil painting in a gold frame, a calculator, and even a Florida license plate belonging to a subject who lived in nearby Pompano Beach. There were also large amounts of United States coins of various denominations. Most of these coins were wrapped, but a few weren't. The total value of these coins was almost $1,000. This amount included the few foreign coins we also located. But, the real prize of the search was the tremendous amount of ladies' jewelry we located and recovered. And, much of this jewelry appeared to be valuable and quite expensive.

When we eventually did our police report the recovered jewelry found inside Mason's home filled seven full supplement pages, and part of an eighth one too. There were eighty-six (86) different pieces of jewelry and other assorted items described in these supplement pages. This included dozens of rings, broaches, necklaces, bracelets, and earrings. Most of this gold and silver jewelry sported expensive looking stones; and there was no shortage of diamonds, emeralds, rubies, opals, jade and even ivory and black onyx. There were also a couple of rings that had so-called mood stones in them and I had no idea at all what kind of stones these really were. They certainly were pretty though. Some of the more notable miscellaneous pieces included; a solid sterling silver ingot, stamped "The Franklin Mint," and guaranteed to be at least 1000 grains; a brown jeweler's type felt bag, which contained numerous assorted stones, many of which were apparently diamonds; and a ten dollar gold piece dated 1894, which was made to hang from a necklace. The catch from inside Mason's home was definitely a jeweler's delight and it seemed as if our bad guy had fibbed to Detective King when he said there really wasn't that much stolen property there inside his residence. I don't know why that should have surprised us.

Finally, the search of Mason's home turned up even more burglar tools and paraphernalia. Again, we found numerous keys to various Fort Lauderdale hotels and motels and most of these were beach front locations. Ironically, one key we found at his home belonged to room #125 at the Ramada Inn on the beach. This room was just down the hall from where he had been arrested earlier today. Perhaps most interesting though was the black camera carrying case we found. It didn't contain a camera, but what we did find inside was very enlightening just the same. There were three different sets of gloves, one for each occasion I suppose, and a blue with red trim pullover ski mask. And, there was an approximately 18-foot long length of white rope, knotted, with a homemade three-pronged grappling hook attached at the end. The last item in the case was a pair of channel lock pliers. It seemed we may have really underestimated our subject Mason. A ski mask? A James Bond-style grappling hook? Shit! This guy was definitely more than just your average burglar and these were apparently some of the tools of his trade!

The search of Mason's residence was concluded at approximately 9:00 p.m. Before everyone left though, Mason and his attorney Howard Zeidwig agreed to meet with Det. Ed King the next morning at 10:00 a.m. at Fort Lauderdale P.D.'s 2nd floor detective bureau. With Mason's continued assistance detectives would begin the attempt to locate as many previous burglary victims as possible and then return their stolen property to them. Considering the massive amounts of property recovered from Mason's residence, it seemed to be an almost impossible task!

The surveillance of Bill Mason, and then his arrest, was a huge feather in the T.I.U. cap! Not bad for an assignment Sergeant Dierkzon originally felt only merited a couple of "TOKENS." Now, as we all continued to bask in the glory of Mason's arrest, which was probably one of the best damn pieces of teamwork F.L.P.D. had ever seen, we tried to return to our normal routine and responsibilities. It wasn't going to be that easy though, in fact, it wasn't going to happen. Even though the Mason surveillance and arrest had been one of T.I.U.'s ultimate achievements to date; T.I.U.'s biggest challenge, its boldest adventure and eventually its greatest glory, still lay ahead of us!

===

Bill Mason admitted to our detectives that he was responsible for forty-five (45) different burglaries. This included both hotel rooms and some houses too. The stolen property recovered from Mason's home after his arrest was estimated to be valued in excess of $40,000, which was considered to be a rather large amount back in 1976. In today's dollars this loot would be valued well in excess of $130,000.

*   *   *   *   *

Bill Mason admitted to being an active burglar for only a couple of years, but the burglary detectives working the case felt that he had been active for as many as four or five years. Mason admitted to forty-five burglaries, but the detectives suspected this was just the tip of the iceberg and the true number would never be known, and probably numbered in the many hundreds.

*   *   *   *   *

Bill Mason later co-authored a book about his extensive life of crime, which he admitted had spanned three decades. This non-fiction book ("Confessions of a Master Jewel Thief") was released in 2004 and it will probably eventually be made into a movie. In his book Mason never did admit to the total number of burglaries he committed during his criminal career, but he did admit that the loot from all of these offenses numbered into the many millions of dollars (a few people have even suggested that Mason stole in excess of $35 million dollars in jewels during his criminal career).

18

HOME INVASION

Jack and Nicole Collingwood lived in a modest residence in southeast Fort Lauderdale. Many houses in this older section of the city had been remodeled and upgraded but for the most part it was still just a typical middle-class neighborhood. It seemed hardly a likely target for greedy thieves in search of gold, jewels, and other valuable treasures. But, back on the evening of February 11th, while T.I.U. was still following Bill Mason around, the Collingwoods, along with their friend Richard Cone, learned firsthand just how fragile and insecure their friendly little neighborhood really was.

On that date the Collingwoods and Cone were seated in the family room having a friendly conversation. When you entered the house the family room was located just to the left of the front door. Cone suddenly heard movement near the door and he looked up to see three masked individuals standing there in the doorway. All were wearing ski-type masks, black ski jackets, dark colored trousers and gloves. At least two were armed with handguns. Jack Collingwood and Cone were forced to lie face down on the floor. Then, while Mr. Collingwood was handcuffed behind his back with a pair of cheap Japanese handcuffs, Cone was tied with a drapery cord cut from the drapes in the family room. Nicole Collingwood, who was laid face down on the sofa, was securely tied with a piece of telephone wire cut from one of the phones in the residence. As two of the intruders quickly went about their deadly serious business of ransacking the entire Collingwood home, the third kept watch over the three helpless and terrified victims.

One of the first items seized during the rape of the Collingwood's home was a large solitaire diamond ring from the hand of Nicole Collingwood. The ring contained a baguette on each side and was almost five carats. There was also a matching wedding band containing numerous diamonds in it and both rings were valued in excess of $10,000. The three robbers made a few threats, warning the victims not to do anything foolish, or to hold anything back, but overall they remained very calm throughout the entire ordeal. One of the three even demanded, "Where's the good stuff?" Mrs. Collingwood eagerly told him and the thug told her if she continued to cooperate they wouldn't be harmed.

The three armed intruders remained in the Collingwood home for about fifteen minutes. When they were finally satisfied they had gotten every valuable piece of Nicole Collingwood's jewelry they gagged the three victims and then quietly left. The Collingwoods and Cone waited just long enough to make sure the three had left for good and then they freed themselves and called the police. When the first Fort Lauderdale patrol units arrived in the area the three culprits were nowhere to be found. They had vanished. But, even though they were gone, Jack Collingwood was still handcuffed behind his back and he would continue to be a victim long after the three armed men had left his home.

The first break in the case occurred the very next day when one of our detectives received an unexpected phone call from a female probation officer. This probation officer had a confidential informant who was feeding her some very valuable information. The C.I. informed her that one of the three culprits of the Collingwood robbery was a 43-year old parolee named Henry C. Parker, who had been arrested in the past for B&E of a Dwelling. He had also served time at Florida's State Prison before being released early in March of '72. According to the probation officer's C.I. Parker had gone out on the night of the Collingwood robbery and he had been with two other white male subjects. When Parker had left his residence in nearby Davie he had been packing a handgun and he also had a ski mask with him. This mask had supposedly been made for him by his loving wife. They had used a pair of lady's stretch ski pants, putting two holes in them for the eyes, and then sewing them up at the top.

Henry C. Parker was known to be an active dinnertime burglar. Veteran detectives familiar with his M.O. advised he was always armed, almost always carried a ski mask with him, and he was constantly checking his vehicles for electronic surveillance devices. These modern devices had been used successfully on him in the past. Parker would usually work with one or two other individuals. They would meet at a local restaurant, drive to the target area, and then make several passes by the residence they intended to burglarize. He would never park his vehicle anywhere near his intended target. Instead, he would usually park a block or two away and then walk in. Parker had a huge set of balls! If he were suddenly surprised by the occupants while inside a residence he wouldn't flee and he would just go ahead and rob them. He was a dangerous individual and he once told a girlfriend he knew he would eventually end up killing someone during one of his jobs.

During the next several days, while T.I.U. finished up our surveillance of the subject Bill Mason, our Fort Lauderdale robbery detectives gathered as much additional intelligence about Henry Parker as possible. The probation officer learned from her C.I. that Parker was armed with a silver colored snub-nose revolver, which had white pearl handles. Parker had also moved out of his residence in nearby Davie and now he resided farther south in a portion of Miami. The probation officer also provided current information about one of Parker's main associates. It seemed he liked to work with another ex-con by the name of Ricky Cannonier. Parker was indeed a bad guy, there was no doubt about that, but Ricky Cannonier was even meaner and nastier. Cannonier's F.B.I. Rap Sheet listed arrests dating back as far as 1959. This imported piece of white trash was originally from England but he had apparently spent all his adult and criminal life right here in the good old United States – the land of milk and honey, and opportunity for crumbs like Parker and Cannonier.

Like Henry Parker, Ricky Cannonier was your typical career criminal and he had been in and out of jail almost all his adult life. He was also currently on parole reference several burglaries, robberies and rapes he had committed in Miami in 1966. He was convicted, sentenced to twenty years and then eventually incarcerated at the Florida State Prison at Raiford. But, thanks to Florida's overcrowded prison system, in 1971 Cannonier was released early. Since his release he had again been arrested by another south Florida police agency for a new charge of B&E. He was out on bond awaiting trial when the Collingwood home invasion occurred.

* The Surveillance (Week One) *

Ricky Cannonier lived in Sunrise, Florida, which was located about thirty minutes west of downtown Fort Lauderdale. Because Parker now lived in Dade County, in Miami, it made much more sense for us to watch the suspect Cannonier who was local. T.I.U. began our surveillance at Cannonier's residence on the afternoon of February 19th (Thursday), one week after the Collingwood home invasion robbery, and just three short days after our arrest of professional burglar Bill Mason on the 16th. Right around 6:30 p.m. Cannonier left his single story apartment riding a 1972 red Honda motorcycle. We followed Cannonier to *Lester's Diner*, a popular 24-hour restaurant on busy State Road #84. He cruised around the parking lot looking for someone or something in particular and then he parked his motor and entered the diner and met with another white male subject.

None of us had ever seen the subject Parker so we had no way of knowing if this individual inside *Lester's* was him or just an innocent person not involved. Jim Kriner, one of the newer members of T.I.U., had seen a poor quality photograph of Parker and he was of the opinion this was not the subject Henry Parker. The unidentified subject was basically the same age and height as Parker, and even his hair was similar, but his weight was considerably different. This excited us because we knew we might now be looking at the third culprit involved in the Collingwood robbery.

After Cannonier and this unknown subject conversed for about fifteen to twenty minutes, both men left the restaurant. Cannonier departed on his red motorcycle and the other white male left in his vehicle, a 1975-76 Olds Cutlass Supreme, with a white landau roof over a white bottom. Both subjects proceeded eastbound to the nearby Harbor Beach area, an affluent residential neighborhood right near Pier 66 and the Intracoastal Waterway. They stopped near a deserted public boat dock and then both men walked to the westernmost end of the parking lot. As they conversed with one another it also appeared as if they may have been looking over the expensive houses located across the narrow canal there in front of them. They remained in the Harbor Beach area for another twenty minutes.

This time, when they drove off, they did something that was definitely different and very suspicious. Each man drove off in a totally different direction; Cannonier going westbound, and the other white male subject heading eastbound. T.I.U., with the added help of our police airplane overhead, followed along behind both of them. To our surprise and delight both subjects ended up in a Publix parking lot located one mile west of the I.C.W. This was definitely a planned meeting and not just a chance encounter. Cannonier got into the other subject's vehicle and they remained there in the parking lot, inside the Olds Cutlass talking, for approximately twenty minutes.

When each man drove away from the supermarket parking lot he was, of course, followed. The unidentified subject who had met Cannonier drove southbound into Dade County and he was eventually followed to a residence located in Opa Locka. The tag on his Cutlass was registered to this address, but to a 1964 Dodge, and not to the Olds he was driving. It was also registered to a female with the last name of Perkins and we suspected this was probably the suspect's wife. Cannonier, on the other hand, rode his motorcycle home to his residence in Sunrise. Once there, he covered it with a canvas and then he even chained it to a pole, apparently so no would-be thieves would be able to steal it. Both subjects appeared to be in for the night so at approximately 10:00 p.m. the surveillance on both was terminated and we called it a night.

The next day, February 20th (Friday), at about 5:00 p.m., T.I.U. again set up on Cannonier's residence in Sunrise. At approximately 6:10 p.m. the subject left his apartment. He was alone. He climbed onto his red Honda motorcycle but this time, instead of heading southeast towards nearby Fort Lauderdale, he headed due south to Dade County. With the assistance of "Aerial 1" we followed Cannonier to the same residence in Opa Locka where the still unidentified second subject from the night before had ended up. A cross reference of this address, run through Dade/Metro P.D., revealed that this house was listed to a subject by the name of Robert Perkins. When we ran that name through Dade/Metro Records, using an approximate age of 35, we hit pay dirt! 36-year old Robert Perkins had made a criminal registration with Dade County as required by law and he did have a past history of burglary. When we checked further with our own F.L.P.D. Records we learned that he had had at least eight arrests in Florida, which included two previous convictions for B&E. Everything seemed to point to the fact that Robert Perkins was one of the three participants in the home invasion at the Collingwood residence. But, only time, and our surveillance, would determine whether or not we'd ever be able to prove this.

When Cannonier arrived at Perkins' Opa Locka residence, right around 7:00 p.m., we observed there were several other vehicles already there. One was Perkins' Olds Cutlass but the other was a 1974 Ford Gran Torino with a tan vinyl top and a dark brown body. This vehicle belonged to the subject Henry C. Parker! As Cannonier got off his motorcycle and entered the residence we all tried to control our obvious excitement. Parker, Cannonier and Perkins were all career criminals and each man seemed capable of doing the worst deeds possible. Now, having all three of these rotten apples in the same Opa Locka barrel just seemed to confirm what we already suspected. These were the three bad guys responsible for the Collingwood robbery.

The three suspects remained inside Perkins' residence for almost two full hours. At about 9:00 p.m. a white male subject exited the residence and got into Parker's Gran Torino. We couldn't be sure, of course, but he did fit the description of Henry C. Parker. This vehicle and subject were followed out of the area and when it appeared as if the driver was indeed headed towards Parker's last known Miami address, the surveillance on the Gran Torino was terminated. Meanwhile, the subject Cannonier was also followed when he left Perkins' residence and the Opa Locka area. The surveillance involving Cannonier wasn't as short and as sweet as it had been with Henry C. Parker and on his way back home to Sunrise he made a few brief stops along the way. He cruised through a medium-size trailer park and he apparently wanted to meet with someone that he knew. He didn't stay put long enough for us to actually determine which specific trailer he had visited. I guessed that he probably had a girlfriend stashed away in one of these trailers; a girlfriend I was sure his wife knew nothing about.

It was also during this end-of-the-night surveillance of Cannonier, as he slowly but surely made his way back home, that we first learned several more important things about this wicked man and his sometimes almost compulsive behavior. For one thing, Cannonier had a penchant for donuts. Tonight, when he first stopped at a donut shop on his way home, we really didn't think that much about it. But, over the next several weeks, during countless hours of almost endless surveillance, we learned much more about his strong and seemingly irresistible craving for donuts. Whenever he passed by a *Dunkin' Donuts*, or any other donut shop for that matter, he just had to stop. Because of this funny little habit, which really wasn't that healthy and which I'm sure contributed to Cannonier's overweight condition, we eventually nicknamed him "D-O-N-U-T." It would be a name that would stay with Cannonier until the day that he died!

Throughout Cannonier's northbound trek from Dade County, back to Broward County, he drove like a man possessed with paranoid thoughts of being followed. Without warning, and for no apparent reason at all, he would suddenly slow down so other traffic would have to pass him. He would also occasionally pull his motorcycle over to the side of the roadway and then just sit there for a minute or two. These maneuvers clearly enabled him to get a good look at all of the vehicles right behind him. There was no other logical explanation. We were still almost certain that Cannonier had not seen any of us because "Aerial 1" had really done most of the surveillance. They would usually take over when Cannonier was moving and when he would stop one of the ground units would move closer to get an "eyeball" and see what he might be up to. So, if he hadn't really seen us, then why was he being so cautious? I suppose the simple truth was that he was a bad guy and a crook, and HE knew it! He was apparently worried that the police knew it too. Eventually, when he finally arrived home, we put

Cannonier to bed for the night and then we secured ourselves.

February 21ˢᵗ and 22ⁿᵈ (Saturday and Sunday) were the third and fourth days of our surveillance and there really wasn't that much noteworthy activity to report. We still set up on Cannonier's residence but there was absolutely no in-person contact between any of our main players; Cannonier, Parker and Perkins. As promising as the first two night had been, these two days were just downright depressing, and they brought this abbreviated first week to a very anti-climatic end.

* The Surveillance (Week Two) *

This week began like the first week ended and on February 23ʳᵈ (Monday) there was a definite lack of noteworthy activity to report. Things picked up a little on February 24ᵗʰ (Tuesday), but as far as we could tell Cannonier still did not make any in-person contact with either Parker or Perkins. He left his residence at 8:45 p.m. but this time he was driving his vehicle, a 1974 Chevrolet Monte Carlo, and not his red motorcycle. He drove to the Riverland Road area in southwest Fort Lauderdale, cruised suspiciously up and down several streets there, made a phone call to an unknown individual, then visited an apartment in a small duplex-like building. He left the duplex after only half an hour and then drove to another nearby apartment complex which consisted of two separate buildings. After exiting his car he walked back and forth by these two buildings. I quickly reminded myself Cannonier had been arrested twice before for rape and he was currently on parole from Raiford after being convicted of rape! Now, who knows what perverted thoughts flowed through this creep's polluted mind as he continued to watch the two buildings there in front of him.

Cannonier's next move was a little more predictable. He got back into his car and then he drove to the *Mr. Donut* located at Andrews Avenue and Oakland Park Boulevard, in the City of Wilton Manors. After getting his fill of donuts he drove to another nearby apartment complex, visited someone there for approximately thirty minutes and then picked up his wife at *Dania Jai alai* where she worked. When they stopped at a restaurant to eat we terminated our surveillance for the evening.

On February 25th (Wednesday), Cannonier and his wife left their apartment at approximately 6:15 p.m. He again drove to *Dania Jai alai* and dropped his wife off at work and then he proceeded to a *Mr. Donut* located on State Road #7. This particular donut shop was located quite a distance away from Dania and there were several others he could have gone to which were much closer. When he finally arrived at the State Road #7 location we found out why he had made this long drive. Robert Perkins, the subject from Opa Locka, was there at the *Mr. Donut* waiting for him.

Both men remained in the donut shop for about twenty minutes. They were doing lots of talking and we could even see them drawing and writing things down on several napkins. A treasure map? Probably! But, I wondered just whose treasure these two bums were after this time. "Donut" and Perkins eventually left the donut shop and each man drove off northbound on State Road #7. They then met up again just a few moments later at a nearby shopping center parking lot. They talked to each other for about ten more minutes, outside their vehicles, and then they drove off together in Perkins' Olds Cutlass.

The two subjects drove around to several different locations and even made a phone call from a 7-11. Eventually, they returned to where they had left Cannonier's vehicle and then they talked there for another twenty-five minutes. Perkins also removed two small bags from the trunk of his vehicle and handed them to Cannonier. None of our ground units were close enough to see exactly what these two items were and it was also impossible for the observer in the plane to see this too. They looked like small camera bags, or something like that, but we really couldn't be sure. "Donut" took these two objects and placed them in the trunk of his own vehicle. With both trunks now closed, "Donut" and Perkins got into their respective vehicles, and then each left the area. Perkins drove home, but "Donut" went to Fort Lauderdale's South Federal Highway area where he suspiciously prowled around for another seventy-five minutes.

"Donut" eventually drove back south into nearby Dania and he picked his wife up from her work. They arrived at their Sunrise apartment right around 1:00 a.m. Normally, the surveillance would have been terminated but because of his persistent prowling earlier it was decided we would maintain the watch on his apartment a little longer, just in case he got the urge to wander again after his wife was safely asleep. Two of our tac guys maintained this lonely vigil until approximately 3:00 a.m.

19

CORAL GABLES CAPER

February 26th and 27th (Thursday and Friday) were both a total bust and there wasn't any noteworthy activity to report. "Donut" did not have any in-person contact with either Parker or Perkins. But, February 28th (Saturday), all that would change dramatically. "Donut" and his wife left their residence at 6:15 p.m., and they headed south. None of us were surprised when he dropped his wife off at her place of employment at *Dania Jai alai*. Then, when he was all by himself again he headed southbound and we all knew we were headed back to Opa Locka and a rendezvous with Perkins, and maybe even Parker too.

Just like we thought he would "Donut" drove straight to Perkins' residence. They didn't stay there very long though and right around 7:15 p.m. both men left. They were in Cannonier's Monte Carlo and now they headed westbound on the 826 Expressway, which eventually curls into a mammoth ninety degree left turn to become the famed Palmetto. This is when our lives suddenly became very complex and things began to turn to shit real fast! My favorite President, Gerald Ford, was back in south Florida to complicate our lives once again! This time however, President Ford was not actually stopping in our city, so T.I.U. wasn't needed for dignitary protection duties as we had been during the Bill Mason surveillance. I wasn't even sure exactly what President Ford's specific itinerary was, but I was certain it did not concern us this time around and that was good enough for me. I knew he would be landing at one of the major airports in the area and then motorcade to another destination in a nearby jurisdiction, where he would then give a speech. The March primary wasn't that far away and President Ford was trying to woo every Florida voter he could. It wasn't any secret that his strategists viewed Florida as a critical state in the upcoming election.

Even though T.I.U. wasn't needed this time around, our department's motorcycle unit was. The President's motorcade would be passing through portions of our city so our motors would be needed to assist with traffic control and escort duties. This is where things suddenly got very complicated. Large-scale operations and other special events, such as President Ford's motorcade, were almost always handled on the tactical radio channel, not on the regular dispatch channels where the normal day-to-day business was conducted. That way these important operations could be carried out more efficiently and without any unnecessary interference. But, T.I.U. also needed to conduct its surveillances on the tactical channel, away from the near chaos that sometimes seemed to be so prevalent on the regular dispatch channels. Most of our surveillances were at night during time periods when activity was usually at its peak throughout the city and that's why we needed to be on our own radio channel. Normally, there wouldn't have been a problem. Tonight however, would be a different story.

"Donut" and Perkins continued to stay on the 826 and after they completed the entire westbound leg of the expressway they headed south on the Palmetto. Traffic was extremely heavy and it was your typical south Florida Saturday night. We didn't know where they were going, or why, but this one particular trip seemed to be something significant and maybe even special. As we silently followed along behind the suspect's vehicle at a discreet distance, we intently listened to "Aerial 1" as the observer routinely called out the vehicle's location every mile or so. Everything was running smoothly and as long as our guys in the plane overhead maintained the "eye" we could just tag along completely out of sight. But, when we suddenly heard the unmistakable voice of Captain Warren Braddock come across the tactical channel, we had our very first clue we were in for some deep, deep shit tonight! His message was simple and short, "All units stay off this channel until further advised!"

I didn't know what to make of the captain's message. The brass were well aware of our surveillance involving Parker, "Donut" and Perkins. They knew these three guys were all mean and nasty and that our surveillance could turn deadly at any given moment. Therefore, it was vital that we maintained radio communications with each other, and with "Aerial 1" overhead. Our very lives depended on this! Now, Captain Braddock was advising us to remain off the channel. "It must be a mistake," I mumbled to myself. I was not alone in my confusion and disbelief, so none of us really stopped what we were doing. For the next several minutes the observer in the plane continued to report on the subject's southbound progress, while Mike, George Long and I acknowledged each of these transmissions. It was just the three of us on the ground tonight, so we were in three separate solo cars. After all, it was Saturday night and we hadn't expected much activity, so our sergeants assigned only the three of us to watch Cannonier. Now, we continued heading south on the Palmetto, deeper and deeper into Dade County.

When I heard Captain Braddock's stern sounding voice again I immediately realized his initial transmission was no mistake. He meant business! "All Yankee units (T.I.U.), refrain from using the tactical channel until further advised! This will be a working channel! Stay off it! We need to keep it clear for the motorcade escort!"

Captain Braddock definitely sounded a little irritated and maybe even angry too. I didn't know what the hell he was angry about though, because we were the ones being castrated, not him! By taking the tactical channel away from us the captain had totally deprived us of our ability to communicate with each other, and the police plane overhead.

Our modern communications system was extremely state-of-the-art and high-tech. Each Fort Lauderdale police officer was equipped with their own personal two-way radio. Gone were the almost ancient days when officers had to stay in their individual squad cars to communicate with the station, or with their fellow officers. Now, an officer could be alone in a backyard, an alley or on a rooftop, and still call for "Help!" if he needed to. But, no matter how sophisticated our radio system might be, there still weren't any written guarantees that everything would always turn out right. I still remembered Walter Ilyankoff's desperate plea for assistance back on that painful day in July of 1974. His radio, which was part of this fantastic system, worked exactly as it should have, but unfortunately for Walter, it still couldn't save his life!

Fort Lauderdale's radio system was unique in several different ways. When an officer transmitted the signal did not go directly from the officer's radio to police headquarters. Instead, the signal from an officer's radio was captured by the nearest repeater. There were a number of these repeaters strategically positioned around the city and most were located on very high buildings for better reception. These repeaters would then instantaneously relay these radio signals to the Communications Center at police headquarters. This was done via regular telephone lines and not through the airways. I'll admit, I'm definitely not an expert on our radio system. I know it usually worked and it was much better than our old system which required the radios to be permanently mounted in our patrol cars. But, there were still some major drawbacks. For one thing, the farther away you got from the repeaters, the worse the reception. Throughout most of Broward County the system functioned okay and you could even go into south Palm Beach County, or north Dade County, and the system would usually still let you communicate with the P.D. most of the time. But, if you went to far north into Palm Beach, or to far south into Dade, as we were doing now, you might be able to hear the station, but the station more than likely wouldn't be able to hear you. That was our main problem tonight! We were definitely getting out of repeater range!

Normally though, even if we were out of repeater range this would not have caused us any great concern, not as long as we had "Aerial 1" overhead. These guys were our Ace in the hole! Thanks to one of the very dedicated pilots assigned to the Aviation Unit, who also happened to be an amazing wizard when it came to electronics, "Aerial 1" had its own mini-repeater in the plane. The pilot, with some extra special help from a buddy who worked at Motorola in Plantation, built the repeater himself. It worked perfectly! Now, we could go almost anywhere in south Florida we wanted and as long as the plane was up and overhead, we had radio communications. The only negative thing about the plane's mini-repeater was it only worked on our department's tactical channel. This was the main channel we did all our surveillance work on, so this was the channel the pilot built the repeater for. So tonight, when Captain Braddock rudely ordered us to stay off of the tactical channel, we couldn't just switch to another radio channel and continue to conduct our important business as usual.

Most hand held walkie-talkies have a minimum range of at least a few miles, so it would seem we still should have been able to communicate with each other, as long as we remained in close proximity to one another. But, this wasn't the case with our hand held radios. Without the all-important repeaters to intercept our transmissions our radios became just so much useless junk for us to carry around. Mike and I could have been standing side-by-side, but without the repeaters to make our radios work, we wouldn't be able to even talk to each other. This was extremely frustrating! Here we had all this sophisticated and expensive equipment, yet we couldn't make it work no matter what we did. None of us were quitters however, and we quickly decided we would just have to adapt and do the best that we could. After all, it wouldn't help for us to complain because without our radios no one would be able to even hear us.

It was remarkable the way this metamorphosis suddenly occurred. One minute Mike, George Long and I were tagging along behind the surveillance at a discreet distance, totally content to let the pilot and his observer in "Aerial 1" maintain the "eye" on our two southbound bad guys, and then, after Captain Braddock's surprise order for us to stay off of the tac channel, all three of us quickly moved up closer to the suspect's vehicle. Now, all three of us were right there on their ass! There were no further radio transmissions by any of us and I guess all three of us feared the captain's possible wrath if we disobeyed him. I, for one, didn't believe it would do any good at all to plead our case to him right then and there over the radio. I'm sure it would have only pissed him off more and I felt he would write us up if we tried to transmit again. I'd already had two previous supervisors, Sergeants Richardson and Dierkzon, try to bring me up on charges of insubordination, and I'd been very fortunate to come out of both of those incidents with my skin still intact. So, I definitely didn't want to tempt fate again and take Captain Braddock on. I felt this was just another good example of piss poor planning and preparation by the brass, and as usual the lowly grunts in the trenches were the ones who ultimately had to suffer for this occasional incompetence.

Cannonier's Monte Carlo continued south on the Palmetto past all the exits for the City of Hialeah. Mike, George and I remained right behind them and when I say we were on their ass, that's exactly what I mean! If "Donut" had slowed down for any reason at all; one, two, or maybe even all three of us would have probably ended up inside his damn trunk. I've never seen the Palmetto when it wasn't heavily congested and luckily for us, tonight was no exception. I knew this would help us and tonight this usual negative would hopefully work in our favor. With all these other vehicles around us I hoped our two bad guys wouldn't notice Mike, George and I. For the time being though, things seemed to be going okay. And, even though the three of us were busily buzzing around them like honey bees guarding the hive, "Donut" and Perkins seemed totally oblivious to our presence.

Without radio communications we obviously didn't have a way to coordinate our activities and the three of us just had to wing it the best way we could. We'd take turns getting into the spot directly behind their vehicle, but this wasn't always that easy to do. If George was the one right behind them he would stay there until he felt he'd been there long enough, then he would pull off and Mike, or I, would immediately take his place. We repeated this dangerous routine over and over again and each of us had our turn in the barrel right behind Cannonier's Monte Carlo. Quite a few times! It was a little unnerving having to do some of the hairy things we were doing and not being able to talk to one another beforehand. We almost had to read each other's minds and sometimes we seemed to be reading from totally different pages. Once, when Mike felt he'd been in Cannonier's rear view mirror longer that he should be, he changed lanes and pulled away so George or I could take over. George and I both tried to slide into the now vacant space right behind our bad guy's chariot and we almost had a real meeting of the minds. And bodies too! Our two cars came very close to one another and only our quick reactions saved us from having one very nasty wreck. But, this wasn't our only close call. We also had to be especially weary of the other motorists too. When you drove the Palmetto you literally ran the gauntlet and there didn't seem to be such a thing as courtesy.

We still headed southbound, going deeper into Dade County than we'd ever gone before. As we approached the western edge of the Miami International Airport I suddenly thought about "Aerial 1" and I wondered what had happened to them. After Captain Braddock advised us to stay off the tac channel, the second time, we hadn't heard anything further from them. I suspected they may have tagged along with us and if they had I was sure they were totally frustrated just like we were. Now however, as we headed southbound by the huge airport, and a large four-engine commercial jet passed directly over us as it made its final approach, I was almost certain they weren't overhead now. I knew they couldn't be. There was no way in hell they could continue to circle us without flying directly into the path of these planes which were landing. I knew the air traffic controllers at the airport would never allow this. Unless it was an extreme emergency, and our surveillance wasn't, "Aerial 1" would have been told to avoid the airspace immediately around the airport. So, I reasoned they may have stayed with us for a little bit, but I was almost certain they weren't with us now.

The three of us continued playing our grown-up's version of the kid's game of leapfrog. We weren't leaping over other kids though; the large over-sized frogs we were trying to get around were made of metal and steel, and usually weighed a couple of tons. Now we passed over the Tamiami Trail. If you went westbound on the Tamiami it would take you into the once forbidden land of the mighty Miccosukee – the Everglades! But, the Tamiami Trail was now also State Highway #41 and it went all the way across the width of Florida and ended up at the west coast City of Naples. I was relieved when we passed the Tamiami Trail exit because I really didn't want to end up on the west coast of Florida if I could help it.

I knew this southbound trek wouldn't last forever though, and sooner or later we would have to exit the Palmetto. Unless these two guys were going to take us all the way south to Key West, eventually we would have to exit. This was inevitable and I began to dread the thought of us having to do this. Even if we did go all the way to Key West the Palmetto still came to an abrupt end down in the Kendall area due south of Miami itself. This is where it suddenly merged into busy U.S. Highway #1 which did go all the way south to Key West. Again, I had no desire to make such a lengthy trip and I hoped these two guys were getting close to where they wanted to go. All of a sudden they seemed to be driving much slower and I suspected they were looking for the exit they wanted to take. When they finally came to the exit for Bird Road, which was also S.W. 40th Street, I knew I had been right. The subject's right turn blinker told me so.

The Monte Carlo now headed eastbound on Bird Road, towards Coral Gables. This busy street was your typical south Florida boulevard. It was several lanes wide in each direction, with almost bumper to bumper traffic moving slowly along for as far as the eye could see. Because of this heavy Saturday night congestion, which was normal, the three of us were forced to stay much closer than we wanted to the subject's vehicle. And, we couldn't change our positions frequently like we had been able to do on the Palmetto. Unfortunately, this increased the possible chance our two bad guys might spot us, but this was still a chance we would have to take. The two subjects continued driving east for a few more miles and they soon arrived at the lovely little City of Coral Gables.

The subject's vehicle eventually pulled into a small shopping center located right there on Bird Road, around 67th Avenue. Before they went and did this though, they took us on a very brief tour of a nearby residential area. I didn't immediately recognize the true significance of this short trip around the block, but the homes in this area looked moderately expensive and I suddenly realized this was probably the kind of neighborhood that would appeal to our two thugs in the Monte Carlo. But, before I could get to excited about this, they finished their drive around the block and then they pulled into the shopping center parking lot and parked, not to far from a Winn Dixie supermarket. They exited the vehicle and walked to a nearby pay phone. This is when things began to get interesting again.

"Donut" and Perkins were met there at the pay phone by two other white male subjects. One was definitely our original bad guy Henry C. Parker, but the other one was a brand new face we had never seen before. The four subjects stayed there together and talked for about five minutes. "Donut" also went to the nearby pay phone and appeared to be making a call. We really couldn't tell for sure but it didn't look as if he actually spoke with anyone. He may have been pretending to make a call, just for appearance sake, or maybe no one was home at the place he called. Whatever the reason, he didn't stay at the phone for very long.

Once again, Mike, George and I were having an extremely difficult time just keeping the "eye" on our four bad guys. Without radios we couldn't tell each other what was happening, or what each of us was doing. Each of us was on his own. We were able to see the vehicle Parker and the other unidentified subject were driving, which was a 1976 yellow Pontiac Ventura, with a Dade County tag on it. The vehicle's registration showed it belonged to a female who lived in Hallandale, but we didn't get this information until much later. The four subjects got into their respective vehicles and the two cars then pulled out of the shopping center parking lot and back onto Bird Road. They apparently had places to go and people to see. Again, we were right behind them. They only drove a couple of blocks and then they pulled into the rear parking lot of a Lums restaurant.

Things began to happen very fast now but because of the obstacles we had to contend with there was also a great deal of confusion and uncertainty too. "Donut" and Perkins left the rear of the Lums in the Monte Carlo and it initially seemed Parker and the 4th guy stayed behind at the restaurant to wait for their return. In reality though, Parker was probably with "Donut" and Perkins in the Monte Carlo, and we just didn't see him in the vehicle. Only the 4th bad guy apparently remained at the rear of the busy restaurant. The Monte Carlo drove straight to the same residential area we had briefly toured before and it seemed that our bad guys had a specific target picked out. The short phone call from Cannonier, just a few minutes earlier, was probably to see if anyone was at home. If they weren't home then this might simply be a burglary, or it might not go down at all. But, if someone was home, then a home invasion, like the Collingwood robbery, was probably about to occur!

Grandy Boulevard seemed to be the street they were most interested in. Mike and George managed to covertly position themselves in a driveway located on the west side of the street and they watched as the Monte Carlo circled the block at least twice. Both times they observed that "Donut" was driving, with Perkins being the passenger. Again, Parker was probably also in the vehicle, but he just wasn't seen. The third time the Monte Carlo came by their Grandy Boulevard location Mike and George observed only "Donut" still in the vehicle. Perkins, and probably Parker too, had been let out of the vehicle somewhere nearby and they were now out on foot. Mike went to a nearby residence and asked to use their phone. He called the Coral Gables Police Department and related the details of what was now occurring. Coral Gables immediately sent one of their plainclothes detectives to meet with Mike, and as an interesting footnote, this detective said he was very familiar with the subject Henry C. Parker.

Fifteen agonizing minutes went by before the Monte Carlo suddenly reappeared again. It didn't take that long to drive around the damn block, so it seemed a good bet

"Donut" had probably pulled over and stopped somewhere. More than likely this was all part of their grand plan; "Donut" would wait close by in their getaway vehicle while Perkins and Parker were out on foot doing their thing. Problem was, we had no way of knowing exactly where they intended to do "their thing" at. They obviously seemed to like Grandy Boulevard but we still didn't know which specific residence they had targeted. The Monte Carlo now pulled onto Grandy from the side street and when "Donut" came to the next cross street in front of him, he stopped there at the stop sign. Then, the Monte Carlo began to back up!

Mike and George were almost on top of the target residence and didn't even know it. But, when the Monte Carlo suddenly began backing up they immediately realized just how close they really were. One subject, and maybe even two, quickly scurried from the adjacent back yard, but all Mike and George could see were a person's legs through a thick hedge. That person, who had to be either Perkins or Parker, quickly got into the waiting Monte Carlo, which then headed off back towards Bird Road. We now observed that there were three subjects in the vehicle. The vehicle again pulled in behind the Lums and George observed all four subjects standing there outside the Monte Carlo, which was parked right next to the yellow Ventura.

Even though it was possible they may have done "their thing" while they were out on foot, because they definitely had the time to do a burglary or even a home invasion robbery, it seemed unlikely that they had. The mere fact the four of them now stood there calmly at the rear of the Lums, which was almost within sight of Grandy Boulevard itself, seemed to be a strong indication that nothing had gone down. They had either been scared off by something or someone, or they might have been out on foot just casing the target residence up close.

After about ten minutes of talking "Donut" and Perkins got into the Monte Carlo and left the area going eastbound on Bird Road, headed towards U.S. Highway #1. Parker and the 4th subject got into the Ventura and they headed westbound on Bird Road, in the opposite direction. Without the plane or our radios it was totally impossible to follow both suspect vehicles at the same time so we concentrated on Cannonier's Monte Carlo. "Donut" dropped off Perkins at his residence and then, like he had done so many other nights before, he began to cruise and prowl once again.

Before leaving the City of Coral Gables Mike went back to the Grandy Boulevard residence to check it out. He had the Coral Gables plainclothes detective still with him. No one was home at the residence and the homeowner's absence probably saved them from becoming victims and another south Florida crime statistic. Mike found some fresh footprints in the rear yard and it appeared our bad guys may have been looking over the home's modern alarm system. They didn't do it tonight, but that didn't mean they wouldn't be back!

20

BRACKMAN'S

This was a leap year and <u>February 29th (Sunday)</u> was an uneventful day with nothing noteworthy to report.

* The Surveillance (Week Three) *

<u>March 1st (Monday)</u> started off just like almost every other day of our surveillance with us patiently sitting on Cannonier's west Broward County residence in Sunrise and waiting for him to make a move. We began at about 4:30 p.m. and then at approximately 5:50 things started looking better for us. He exited his apartment and walked directly to his 1974 Monte Carlo which was parked out in front of his building. What got our adrenaline really pumping was the fact he was carrying some extra clothes and a pair of boots. When he got to his car he carefully placed these items into the vehicle, right behind the driver's seat. It almost looked as if he were trying to hide them. He also put some other unknown item in the trunk of his vehicle and we could only speculate wildly about what that was. I quickly remembered what happened just two short days ago, on Saturday (February 28th). That was the night we followed "Donut" down to Opa Locka where he picked up his sleazy buddy Perkins and then they both drove all the way down to Coral Gables where they eventually met up with their mentor Parker. That night "Donut" also took some extra things with him when he left his apartment. And, from the prowling around they did in Coral Gables it looked like they either cased a residence in that city, or intended to do a home invasion robbery but backed out at the last minute. Yeah, today was looking real good and I even wondered if this

would finally be our D-Day, and maybe Cannonier's Waterloo too!

Twenty minutes later, at approximately 6:10 p.m., "Donut" again left his apartment and headed for his vehicle. This time however, he had his wife with him. I think we all knew what was going to happen next; he drove her down to her place of employment at *Dania Jai alai* and dropped her off. Then he headed southbound. This was another one of those sure things I might have bet on. "Donut" was headed south and we all knew he was going to Perkins' Opa Locka residence! As our ground units played tag and then hide-and-seek with our bad guy's taillights, "Aerial 1" overhead maintained a firm "eyeball" on his maroon over white Monte Carlo. Tonight, we were not going to have any unexpected catastrophes because of President Gerald Ford! "Aerial 1" was with us and we knew they would be all the way. And, the tactical channel was ours too. It belonged to us completely, 100%. It had been cleared for our surveillance and other than "Aerial 1" and our tac units on the ground, there wasn't another sole using it. No, tonight there wouldn't be any important motorcades that would be given priority over what we were doing, like what happened to us two days ago Saturday night.

During the drive down to Opa Locka "Donut" did make one brief stop. You guessed it - a damn *Mr. Donut*! When he pulled into this *Mr. Donut* on U.S. Highway #1 and went inside I began to wonder if this fat guy we were following around might not have some stock in the company. He didn't stay very long though, just about ten minutes, and then he was off again on his way to Perkins' house. I wondered if he was bringing Perkins any donuts. I didn't think so. It really didn't take him that much longer to get to the Opa Locka address and when he got there it immediately became apparent Perkins had been expecting him. As "Aerial 1" climbed to a higher altitude, so Perkins and "Donut" wouldn't hear the sounds of their engine, our tac guys quickly established the "eye" on the ground. They saw the subject Perkins walk out of his residence carrying a briefcase in one hand, AND, an extra set of clothes in the other!

Perkins and "Donut" got into Cannonier's Monte Carlo and they headed west on the 826 Expressway, and then south on the Palmetto. I don't believe any of our tac guys had extrasensory perception and I know I didn't have ESP, but I think we all knew we were again going to the City of Coral Gables! The two bad guys continued south on the Palmetto until they came to the Bird Road exit. Now they exited the north/south expressway and headed eastbound on Bird Road, which would eventually bring them to Coral Gables. They came to the same Lums they had been at Saturday night and they pulled into the rear of the restaurant and parked. Almost immediately two white male subjects approached "Donut" and Perkins. It was quite obvious these two men had been waiting there at the rear of the Lums for Perkins and "Donut" to arrive.

We immediately recognized both these men. One, of course, was our original bad guy Henry C. Parker. We didn't really know the name of the other suspect, but we had seen him two days ago at this very same Lums. He was the 4th subject involved with our other three bad guys that night, so we were pretty damn certain he was dirty too! Saturday night he had been driving a yellow colored Pontiac Ventura, but tonight he was in a different Pontiac, which was blue. We ran the tags on these two vehicles and found out they both belonged to the same address in nearby Hallandale. We suspected this 4th guy was probably named Charlie Middleworth, because that's what the tag information advised us. This also seemed to confirm some more of the original intelligence we received reference Parker and his possible associates. We had been told Parker may have been working with a subject named Charlie, who lived in Hallandale. Now, we strongly suspected that this guy Middleworth was that Charlie!

"Donut" and Perkins stayed in their vehicle, while Parker and the 4th subject leaned in the windows talking with them. It appeared they were having some sort of disagreement and it also looked as if the 4th guy, thought to be "Charlie," was upset over something. After approximately 10-15 minutes of conversation, some of it heated, "Donut" and Perkins drove off in the Monte Carlo, and Parker and the 4th guy drove off in the Pontiac. With the continued assistance of "Aerial 1" we were able to continue the surveillance on both vehicles at the same time. Both were heading east towards the same general direction of the residence they had cased Saturday evening. We didn't know what "Charlie" may have been upset about, but for the time being it seemed as if our bad guys intended to follow through with their original plan.

When both vehicles continued on past the residential area where the target house was located, without even slowing down a little, our optimism and positive thinking quickly evaporated into almost nothing. It was as if they wanted to get out of the area as fast as they could. Once again though, I was confident none of these jerks had any inclination at all they were being followed. I have no idea what may have spooked them, but I'm sure it was not our presence in the area. We were absolutely certain that when "Donut" and Perkins made this trip tonight down to the Lums restaurant they fully intended to commit a home invasion robbery at the residence they had cased Saturday evening. The fact both men brought extra clothes with them only reinforced this belief that much more. Something apparently happened at the rear of Lums to change their minds, and from the way the 4th subject acted, the guy we thought was "Charlie," it seemed a good guess that he was the damn fly in the ointment. While "Aerial 1" maintained the surveillance on the Monte Carlo with "Donut" and Perkins in it, our ground units stayed with the 4th guy's Pontiac. "Donut" and Perkins drove to an all-night restaurant located on Biscayne Boulevard near downtown

Miami. They exited their vehicle and went inside. Instead of getting either a booth or a table they decided to sit at the counter. Meanwhile, the 4th guy dropped Parker off at his residence, and then he apparently went home himself.

The ground units didn't stay with the 4th guy however, because as soon as "Charlie" had left Parker's residence, Parker got into his own vehicle and drove to the same all-night restaurant where "Donut" and Perkins had gone. Parker joined Perkins and "Donut" at the restaurant and the three of them sat there at the counter talking. Sergeant Gerwens decided to try something a little different, and maybe even downright ingenious and bold. The sergeant and a female plainclothes officer, Denise Carpenter who was assisting us during this surveillance, would enter the restaurant and sit down somewhere close to the three suspects. With any luck at all the three suspects wouldn't give Joe and Officer Carpenter even a second thought. And, hopefully they might just be able to overhear some of what the three bad guys were talking about. After all, we could speculate all we wanted about what was happening, and why things were unfolding the way they were, but to hear something firsthand from the suspects themselves, now that would be almost more than we could ever wish for.

Sergeant Gerwens and Officer Carpenter also sat down at the restaurant's counter, right next to our three bad guys. We didn't know this until later, of course, but the sergeant and the female officer were able to hear tantalizing bits and pieces of the suspect's conversation. They heard talk of a house, and also talk about people being home, and although there weren't any specific details overheard, it definitely sounded as if the three suspects were discussing a crime they intended to commit. One of the subjects also said he was 90% sure of something, but Sergeant Gerwens and Officer Carpenter unfortunately weren't able to overhear what that "something" was. Wow, talk about being left hanging! Was our bad guy, and Sergeant Gerwens never did tell us which one of the three mentioned this, but was our bad guy 90% sure they were being followed? Or, maybe he was 90% sure "Charlie" was a damn pussy for backing out at the last minute! Again, we could speculate all we wanted, but there really was no way for us to know for sure. One other thing Sergeant Gerwens overheard seemed to confirm my previous opinion that our three bad guys did not know they were being followed. According to Joe, all three of the suspects seemed to agree that they would do "it" in one or two days. I don't think they would have this kind of attitude if they thought the police were aware of their activities. Now, we just had to make damn sure we were going to be there when "it" actually happened!

When Parker, Perkins and "Donut" finally left the restaurant they walked over to where their vehicles were parked and then they continued their conversation for another 10-15 minutes. As they stood there in the parking lot talking, they continued to look all around at every vehicle and person that passed by them. Eventually, Parker got into his Torino and drove off. When he began heading in the same general direction of his residence this portion of our surveillance on him and his vehicle was dropped. "Donut" and Perkins drove to the trailer park that was located not to far from the all-night restaurant and this was the one "Donut" had been to several times before. They only stayed there a few minutes and then "Donut" took the subject Perkins home. I still couldn't figure out who, or what, was at the trailer park. Before, after the first time "Donut" visited it, I thought he may have had a girlfriend there. But now, I just didn't know. Who knows, maybe they were there to buy drugs. Anything was possible.

After the surveillances on Parker and Perkins were terminated for the night we were still stuck with the subject Cannonier. And, instead of being a good boy and going home for the night he began to drive around aimlessly all by himself. But, because we knew there wasn't going to be any robbery tonight, thanks to Sergeant Gerwens' very efficient eaves dropping at the restaurant, the decision was made to terminate the surveillance on "Donut" too. Tomorrow would be another day and why continue to follow "Donut" around tonight if we were relatively certain all three bad guys weren't going to get back together later. Why needlessly take the chance he might spot the surveillance? Sure, he might go out and do some more prowling, like he'd done before, but our main objective was still to catch him and his buddies in a robbery in-progress, so it made very good sense to call it quits for the night. It was approximately 10:30 p.m. when we finally pulled off the subject Cannonier.

March 2nd (Tuesday) was an unusual day. "Donut" didn't leave his home until 7:00 p.m. and when he did he was accompanied by two unknown white females and another white male we didn't know. They drove directly to Broward General Hospital which is located just south of downtown Fort Lauderdale and remained there at the hospital until approximately 9:30 p.m. Why they were there, or who they may have visited, is unknown. They drove home and "Donut" went inside his residence and stayed there. Because it appeared our bad guy was in for the night we pulled the plug at 11:00 p.m.

March 3rd (Wednesday) was a very frustrating day. We couldn't locate any of our bad guys and we had no idea what they might be up to, if anything. His Monte Carlo and Honda motorcycle were parked out front where they should have been so we had every reason to believe "Donut" was there too. But, around 8:30 we began to get a little bit concerned. At 6:30 the suspect's wife had left in the Monte Carlo. She was alone and we were pretty sure she was just going to work at *Dania Jai alai*. The lights inside the apartment remained on though and it appeared as if someone else was still inside. But, we still hadn't seen "Donut" so at 8:45 one of our tac guys called the residence to see if he was there. A young female answered the phone and this was probably his teenage daughter. Our tac guy asked her, "Is your daddy home?" She said he wasn't. Shit! It became painfully obvious "Donut" had left his residence sometime before we began today's surveillance at four o'clock.

We immediately began checking on the whereabouts of our other three bad guys; Parker, Perkins and the new guy "Charlie." When we checked Parker's Miami residence we found that his Ford Torino was not there and he did not appear to be home either. When we called the Hallandale residence of Charlie Middleworth there was no answer. Finally, when we drove by Perkins' Opa Locka residence we did observe his Olds Cutlass parked there in the driveway. This heartened us just a little, but it still didn't mean Perkins was inside the damn house. For all we knew, and suspected, our four bad guys were together in Parker's Torino and they were probably out somewhere committing an armed robbery. By the time we had put all of this information together we realized it was more than likely already to late. If the four subjects had gone down to Coral Gables again, without us tagging along this time, they would have already done their thing by now. Parker was known to prefer dinnertime and early evening hours to commit his crimes, so we just had to hope and pray nothing bad had happened tonight while we weren't there with them.

Except for one very important new development, March 4th (Thursday) was another depressing and frustrating day and there wasn't that much activity to report. But, this new development made up for this lack of activity in a big way! It also apparently signaled a major change in the way "Donut" and Perkins now intended to conduct their business. What was this new development that got us so excited? It was simple; our two bad boys had gone out and rented themselves a new vehicle, a maroon over white 1976 Ford Elite. One day we couldn't find these two bastards to save our souls, and then out of the blue there they were, driving a brand new rental vehicle. We first saw the rental car when

Perkins dropped "Donut" off at his Sunrise residence. Then, we followed Perkins to his own place down in Opa Locka. He was driving the rented Ford.

This unexpected appearance of a rental vehicle necessitated a sudden change in our own strategy and tactics. We could think of only two good reasons why "Donut" and Perkins would go out and rent a vehicle. Reason Number One: they definitely planned to do a job in the very near future and they didn't want to use one of their own vehicles. This made sense to us, but we didn't know if this was how they sometimes liked to operate, or was this just unique to our surveillance. We'd never heard about them renting a vehicle before, but that didn't mean that they hadn't. Reason Number Two: maybe they had picked up on the fact we were following them around and now they were so nervous neither one of them wanted to drive his own car. I still doubted this though because I just couldn't believe any of us had been made. We were good, and with the help of our police plane and the cop pilots that flew it, I didn't see how we could have been burnt. But, anything's possible and we still had to consider this just the same.

Our supervisors now made the decision we would extend our normal surveillance hours. Instead of us beginning each day's surveillance in the late afternoon we would now start bright and early each morning. This meant T.I.U. would be watching and following "Donut" and his associates, when appropriate, from early morning until late each night. We planned to be there at Cannonier's apartment when he awoke each morning and then stay with him until we were absolutely certain he and his three buddies weren't up to any hanky-panky. This meant we would more than likely continue to put "Donut" to bed each night, before we secured ourselves. And, this meant in most cases T.I.U. would be working at least twelve-hour days and probably a lot longer than that. It didn't take a damn mathematician to figure out that from 9:00 a.m. to midnight was a fifteen-hour day and that's what I suspected would be the norm. These long hours didn't bother me though and I know none of the other tac guys cared either. After all, we all took the sudden appearance of a rental car to be a very positive sign. We believed "Donut" and Perkins, and maybe even Parker and "Charlie" too, were very close to pulling another job. So, all of us in T.I.U., and the men of the Aviation Unit too, were prepared to work as many hours as it took to eliminate this filthy scum from our streets!

For a variety of reasons our supervisors elected to divide T.I.U.'s manpower into two different shifts. Some of us would work the morning to early afternoon shift and some the late afternoon to evening shift. By doing it this way they hoped none of us would have to work an excessive number of hours. I give them credit for this, because they apparently were trying to get the job done, yet still look out for the welfare of their men too. They knew a man who was tired was much more prone to make mistakes than someone who was rested. And, in our deadly business, where the wrong move could easily blow an important surveillance, a serious mistake could even get you killed! None of us had a crystal ball, including our T.I.U. supervisors, and no one knew for sure just how long this surveillance was going to last. It might end in a day or two, another week or so, or it might never come to a successful conclusion. Therefore, it made good sense to evenly distribute our manpower because 12-15 hour days had a way of tearing down a man rather quickly.

March 5th (Friday) became one of the most interesting and intriguing days of the entire surveillance! Several very important things happened today and even though these individual events may have been totally unrelated, their cumulative effect was staggering! Today also happened to be our first multi-shift, fifteen-hour, surveillance day. I'm sure when this single piece of T.I.U. trivia is viewed all by itself it probably isn't that impressive or even noteworthy. But, it was a new milestone for the men of T.I.U. Because

Perkins had taken the rental vehicle home with him last night, the surveillance this morning began bright and early at his Opa Locka residence, not at Cannonier's Sunrise apartment, where we had started every other day. Our tac guys in Opa Locka began today's work right around 9:00 a.m. I wasn't with them however, because I was assigned to help cover the evening portion of the surveillance. Al Smith and George Long were the two tac officers watching Perkins' residence and both men were original members of T.I.U. when it was created back in 1974. At approximately 11:20 a.m. they observed Perkins exit his residence and get into the rental vehicle. He was followed northbound into Broward County and he eventually ended up at Cannonier's apartment in Sunrise. He arrived there right around 11:40. Perkins and "Donut" didn't stay at Cannonier's apartment very long though and after about ten minutes they left together in the rental vehicle. They drove eastbound towards Fort Lauderdale but ended up at a well known steak joint in the City of Oakland Park. It was now approximately 12:15 and they apparently had stopped there to have lunch.

Our two bad guys left the restaurant at 12:40. Lunch was apparently now over. They drove another mile or two due east on Oakland Park Boulevard until they finally came to Fort Lauderdale itself. The first major intersection they came to was U.S. Highway #1. On the northeast corner of this massive intersection was a medium-sized shopping center and its various parking lots. In addition to a very busy Publix supermarket, which was in a building all by itself, there were also several major department stores located in one huge mall-like building. "Donut" and Perkins pulled their rental vehicle into one of these parking lots and then they both went inside the Publix. They remained inside the store for about ten minutes and when they exited it was easy to see they hadn't bought a thing. It seemed obvious they hadn't gone inside the supermarket just to look at the damn fruit! They moved their rental car to another part of the parking lot nearer the south end of the shopping center property and then both of them disappeared inside the Coral Ridge Mall building. Our tac guys decided not to get out on foot and follow them into the mall itself but they did maintain an "eye" on the subject's now empty vehicle.

"Donut" and Perkins remained inside the mall from about 1:00 p.m. until 2:00 p.m. When they finally came out, our guys were right there waiting for them. They left the mall property and drove northbound to a very nice neighborhood along beautiful Bayview Drive, just north of Commercial Boulevard. They ended up at an apartment complex which appeared to have mostly well-to-do people living there. Several expensive looking cars were parked at the complex but the majority of parking spaces were vacant. During the next fifteen minutes or so our two overgrown delinquents did their thing around this apartment complex. At one point, while "Donut" remained in the rental vehicle, Perkins got out on foot and our tac guys thought he may have even committed a larceny of mail from one of the mail boxes. Then, after Perkins got back into the rental, our two bad guys drove south again, back to the Coral Ridge Shopping Center and Mall. They arrived there at approximately 2:35 p.m. and they parked their vehicle in a lot located at the east side of the building. This time when "Donut" and Perkins entered the mall, Al Smith, Jim Kriner and George Long followed them.

Our tac guys initially lost sight of "Donut" and Perkins after they entered the mall building but it didn't take them very long to locate these two dirt bags again. They were both walking aimlessly around the ground floor of *Brackman's*, the popular department store located at the extreme south end of the mall building. Most of the time they didn't walk together and it seemed as if they were trying to act as if they didn't even know each other. But, every so often they would come together for a brief moment or two, say a few words and then separate again. Like most major department stores, *Brackman's* had more than one level.

"Donut" and Perkins seemed content to stay on the ground floor though. The two subjects remained inside the department store for almost one full hour and we really didn't have a clue to what they were up to. Then, at about 3:40, "Donut" left the store and returned to their rental vehicle. Alone! He started the car up and began to move, and he now drove from the east side where they had originally been parked, around to the west side. Perkins now exited *Brackman's* and he quickly walked to where "Donut" was stopped and waiting.

We still didn't know what they were up to, or why they were just sitting there in their vehicle and waiting. What were they waiting for? This location at the west side of *Brackman's* was where city buses would stop to load and unload their passengers. After about fifteen minutes of waiting a city bus stopped and a handful of people got on, and off. Most of these people were senior citizen types. Some of these new passengers on the bus had been inside the mall shopping and now they apparently needed a ride to wherever they were going. When the bus began to move southbound through the shopping center parking lots, towards Oakland Park Boulevard, "Donut" and Perkins in their rental vehicle began to move too. It suddenly became very obvious our two bad guys were interested in one of the people who had just gotten on the bus. In fact, there was almost a frantic silent panic associated with some of their efforts to follow this bus and its unknown object of their intense desire. When several other cars unexpectedly got between them and this city bus, this created a situation where they might get caught by the red light at Oakland Park, but the bus would make it through the intersection on green. When they realized they might lose their intended prey Perkins quickly got out on foot and briefly played the traffic cop role as he directed "Donut" and their rental vehicle around these other cars. Then, as the bus slowly headed eastbound on Oakland Park Boulevard, towards Fort Lauderdale's north beach area, "Donut" and Perkins followed along behind. Our tac guys, of course, were also part of this strange parade, but they brought up the rear.

The bus and its unsuspecting occupants continued eastbound over the Oakland Park Bridge and then it headed south on A1A. This area was a combination of residences, motels and hotels, and a few large condos thrown in for good measure. T.I.U. was already very familiar with this territory because this was the same general area where much of the Bill Mason surveillance had taken place just a month ago. Now, as the bus headed southbound, every few blocks it would stop and a passenger or two would get off. And, when the bus would stop, so would the subject's rental vehicle. They would usually stop right behind the bus and it didn't seem they were even trying to disguise their intentions. Man, what balls! They probably figured no one would notice them anyway, but if someone did, with the rental tag on their vehicle they looked like just another "snow-bird" who was lost in paradise.

At N.E. 22nd Street an elderly female got off the bus and began walking southbound. Perkins exited their rental vehicle and he began to follow along behind her. "Donut" remained in their vehicle and he slowly kept pace with both of them. At one point "Donut" passed by Perkins and then stopped and when Perkins walked by the vehicle "Donut" exited and also got out on foot. Now, they both began to walk south behind their unsuspecting female target. When the female got to the *Sea Breeze Motel*, located in the 2000 block of North Atlantic Boulevard, she left the sidewalk and walked up to apartment #3, which she then entered. Perkins stopped there on the sidewalk by the front of the building and he continued to watch the female until she disappeared in her apartment. Meanwhile, "Donut" passed by the building itself as he continued walking south along North Atlantic Blvd. He eventually turned around and walked back north until he finally got to the spot where Perkins waited for him. "Donut" and Perkins now both walked into the motel complex, toward where the female had entered her apartment. Our tac officers briefly lost sight of them, but then after a few minutes "Donut" reappeared at the front of the motel. He quickly walked to their rental vehicle and in a few more moments he was also joined by the subject Perkins. It was approximately 4:15 p.m. when the two subjects left the area.

Because we wanted to make sure the female target was alright, and she hadn't been victimized by our two bad guys, Al Smith made contact with her at apartment #3. She advised Al she had just returned home from shopping and immediately upon entering her apartment she had gotten in the shower. Therefore, if anyone had knocked on her door, like our two bad guys, she wouldn't have heard it, so she wouldn't have answered the door. It appeared that her desire to have a shower had possibly saved her from being a robbery victim. When Al inspected the front door to the female's apartment he observed that the jalousies in the door, directly to the right of the door knob, had been pushed up at one corner. Was this the work of our two bad guys? Probably!

"Donut" and Perkins spent the next two hours visiting several other locations and then shortly after 6:00 p.m. they ended up back at Perkins' Opa Locka residence. At approximately 7:45 p.m. our two thugs, and Perkins' wife too, drove off in the subject's rental vehicle. They headed back north towards Broward County and eventually they arrived at Fort Lauderdale's north beach area. The vehicle was followed northbound on A1A and it drove directly to the same area where the two subjects had been during the day. They parked their car in the 2000 block of North Atlantic Boulevard, directly across the street from the *Sea Breeze Motel*. Almost immediately the subject Perkins exited the vehicle and he crossed the street walking east towards the motel. Perkins eventually entered the motel grounds and we momentarily lost sight of him. But, after several more seconds, Perkins reappeared as he walked away from the motel back to the sidewalk out in front. Now, he just stood there and looked all around and it was very obvious he was checking out the entire area.

Perkins eventually walked back to the rental and re-joined his wife and the subject Cannonier. The vehicle and subjects then drove south past the motel, and then south on A1A. They continued southbound until the 1700 block of North Atlantic Blvd. where they suddenly made a U-turn and then parked there on the beach side of A1A. The rental's dome light came on and we could now see that "Donut" was exiting the vehicle. I was hiding in some bushes on the beach and I had a very good view of "Donut" as he walked northbound along the sand. As he did, he looked all around. He eventually came abreast of the *Sea Breeze Motel* and this is when he turned and walked westward away from the beach.

When "Donut" entered the motel grounds I lost the "eye" but Sergeant Joe Gerwens and another tac officer were positioned so they could watch the front door of the subject's intended target, apartment #3. "Donut" walked up to #3 and looked into the apartment through the window. He then walked around to the rear door, stayed there for only a few moments, and then again came back to the apartment's front door. The probable robbery victim, the elderly female they had followed home from the mall, was obviously not in her apartment so "Donut" now walked back to the beach, and then back south to where Perkins and his wife patiently waited.

As the three subjects left the area several things now became abundantly clear. First of all, it was obvious that "Donut" and Perkins now intended to do their thing without their previous partner Henry C. Parker. For whatever reasons, Parker was no longer a major player! Second, Perkins' wife apparently was just as bad and rotten as he was!

21

"DONUT" and PUSSYWILLOW

Perkins and his wife dropped off "Donut" at his Sunrise apartment and then they headed back south to their own residence in Opa Locka. The surveillance on them was terminated and we elected to maintain the watch on Cannonier's apartment, just in case he decided to move again later. This turned out to be a good decision on our part because "Donut" did move again, but this time he was alone and on his motorcycle. He headed east on Oakland Park Boulevard and eventually came to the City of Wilton Manors. At Andrews Avenue and Oakland Park he stopped at the *Mr. Donut* located there in a small strip mall, at the southwest corner of that busy intersection.

Cannonier had just entered the *Mr. Donut* and sat down when the phone at the business apparently rang. From my vantage point across Andrews Avenue I watched as the waitress answered the phone, which hung on the wall at the end of the counter. There weren't any other customers in the donut shop and as far as I could see it was just "Donut" and the one waitress. She said something to him, which I obviously couldn't hear, and then he got up from his stool at the counter and he walked over to where she was standing and he took the telephone from her outstretched hand. He put the receiver up to his ear and listened. I was watching him with my binoculars and I never saw him say a word. After about thirty seconds he hung the phone up, sat back down at the counter and then he quickly finished his coffee. Then, he just as quickly exited the *Mr. Donut*.

I was surprised to see him leave so quickly. On all his other stops at donut shops he spent much more time inside than he had done tonight. Now, after he exited the *Mr. Donut* he just stood there in front and he looked all around. As I continued to watch him I sensed that something very wrong had just happened! I could feel it in my bones. He stood there quietly, intently watching everything and everyone around him. His motorcycle helmet dangled there by his side, as he tightly clutched the helmet's long thin chin strap in his strong right hand. Even though he had suddenly and unexpectedly left the donut shop he still didn't seem to be in any real hurry and he made no immediate effort to put his helmet back on. "Donut" seemed to be paying extra special attention to the numerous vehicles heading north and south on Andrews Avenue and also those going east and west on Oakland Park Boulevard. He also appeared to be looking at the few parked cars still remaining in the shopping center's parking lot. All these parked vehicles looked as if they were empty and this seemed to satisfy him for the time being.

When "Donut" first climbed onto his motorcycle to-night, a little while ago, and he headed eastbound for this late night rendezvous with a donut and coffee, he appeared to not have a care in the world. Sure, there were a few times since the surveillance started several weeks ago that our boy got a little tail conscious, and he took us on a grand tour of the county, but for the most part he was usually pretty predictable and easy to follow. Now however, he seemed to be deeply troubled and disturbed and it was very obvious this sudden and dramatic change of attitude was the direct result of the mysterious phone call he had just received.

I wasn't much of a betting man, in fact, almost every time I tried to play a friendly game of poker I usually went home a loser. But, if someone had asked me to bet with them tonight, reference what had just happened to our friend Cannonier, I would have bet a year's salary the phone call he just received was from some low life scum who had tipped him off that the police were watching and following him. After all, anyone could go out and buy an inexpensive scanner and then monitor all of our police radio channels. We knew for a fact there were many private citizens around the county who liked to spend at least a part of their evenings listening to real-life police action on their scanners. It was often better entertainment than damn television. Most of these people were very pro-police and therefore harmless, and they just liked to hear the exciting things that were going on in their city.

Unfortunately though, bad guys and anti-police crud could also listen to police scanners too. I was sure this was what had happened now. Some lazy crum out there in the real world, who probably had a hard on for all cops, was listening to our surveillance and heard that "Donut" had stopped at the *Mr. Donut* at Andrews and Oakland Park. This person, whoever he or she was, didn't like cops, so he looked up the donut shop's phone number in the phone book. When the girl behind the counter answered the phone our caller merely asked to talk with the guy who had just come in. The caller really didn't have to say that much to Cannonier; just something like, "Hey man, the fucking cops are following you! Be careful!" I was also certain the caller didn't even know "Donut" himself, and there probably wasn't any bond between these two jerks, other than the fact they were both assholes and neither one could tell the difference between right and wrong!

Cannonier got on his motorcycle and he eventually slowly drove out of the parking lot. Now, for approximately the next thirty minutes, "Donut" drove around the area aimlessly, like a man once again possessed with paranoia. He made a number of turns, stops and other movements, which were all obviously an effort by him to see if he was being followed. Once, when he headed westbound on Oakland Park Blvd., he suddenly stopped in the center median and began watching all the cars going by him. Eventually though, he headed home, and when he got there we decided to drop him for the remainder of the night. Because of the apparent warning he had received we doubted he would come back out later.

On <u>March 6th (Saturday)</u> Perkins, his wife, and several other unidentified subjects arrived at Cannonier's Sunrise apartment. They were in the rental vehicle. "Donut" eventually drove Perkins and his friends back to Dade County, and then he returned home to Sunrise, still driving the rental. Our surveillance continued through the evening hours of <u>March 7th (Sunday)</u>, and the rental vehicle remained at Cannonier's residence. It soon became very apparent "Donut" was now keeping the rental vehicle at his Sunrise apartment. This did seem a bit odd, especially since Perkins' name was on the actual rental agreement. We also noted that since "Donut" had been warned he now only drove the rental and he apparently was purposely staying away from his motorcycle. We speculated that even if "Donut" did believe that the police were interested in him, he definitely did not know the extent. He may think we knew of his motorcycle and his Monte Carlo, but he probably didn't have a clue that we also knew about the rental vehicle too.

* The Surveillance (Week Four) *

Cannonier's initial concern that he may be under police scrutiny didn't seem to last for very long and he and Perkins quickly returned back to their twisted and wicked ways. Even so, T.I.U. immediately took steps to make sure "Donut" wouldn't be warned again. Sergeant Dierkzon quickly put together an elaborate code that we hoped would prevent any would-be listeners from knowing where we were at. The code was very complex and there was even a secondary version, if we really wanted to get fancy. All of the major streets were given fictitious names and we also gave new names to the places that "Donut" liked to frequent. Now, when he again visited his favorite *Mr. Donut*, at Andrews and Oakland Park, the message that would go out over the radio was, "'Donut' is at the graveyard at Boxer and Judd." Perkins' code name now became "Pussywillow," and I never did know why he was given that nickname. I speculated that they would have liked to call him just "Pussy" but decided our brass probably wouldn't take kindly to us using that name over the public radio channels. We all also now took nicknames and my partner Mike became "Smokey," because of the cigars he sometimes like to smoke. When I couldn't immediately think of a nickname that I liked Sergeant Joe Gerwens said that I would be called "Snake." I never did figure out if he meant this as a compliment, or what.

On March 8th (Monday) "Donut" drove down to Opa Locka and picked up his buddy in crime. They drove back north, but by-passed Broward County entirely, and ended up in Palm Beach County. They drove around a number of different beach side towns with quaint little names like; Gulfstream, Highland Beaches and Briny Breezes. We were almost sure they intended to do a burglary at one specific residence they parked at, but they were scared off by another individual before they could and they left the area. This is when they drove to nearby Lantana. Nothing panned out for them though and Perkins, now a.k.a. "Pussywillow," eventually dropped "Donut" off at his Sunrise residence. This time however, Perkins kept the rental himself. Our evening shift tac guys later observed "Donut" as he prowled around, and he even peeped in a few bedroom windows, in his own neighborhood. He did this for about an hour, from 10:45 p.m. to 11:45 p.m.

On March 9th (Tuesday) our ground units watched Cannonier's residence while "Aerial 1" maintained a watch on Perkins' place in Opa Locka. The subject Perkins eventually drove north and picked up "Donut" and then they spent several hours driving around and doing what appeared to be personal business. The high point of the day came when "Donut" drove down to Miami and visited Henry C. Parker. "Charlie" Middleworth was also there. Parker, "Donut" and "Charlie" went to the rear yard of Parker's residence and talked and then they eventually moved to a nearby boat dock. "Donut" was doing most of the talking and it seemed as if he was trying to convince Parker and "Charlie" about something. The subject Middleworth apparently didn't want any part of what "Donut" suggested. He shook his head "No!" a few times, and then he left. Parker and "Donut" talked for another hour and then "Donut" left too.

On <u>March 10th (Wednesday)</u> "Donut" drove to *Lester's Diner* on State Road #84. When he got there, right around 11:45 a.m., we saw that Perkins was inside the diner waiting for him. They eventually went to the airport and turned their rental vehicle in at the car rental agency and then they drove off in Perkins' car. We now also observed that Perkins' wife was in the vehicle too. "Donut" was dropped off at his residence but left again later, this time on his motorcycle. He and Perkins then met up again in the City of Hollywood and Perkins was riding a motorcycle too.

"Donut" and Perkins rode their motorcycles south to Miami and eventually ended up at the rear of a *Burger King* located on Biscayne Boulevard. They seemed to be waiting for someone and then at approximately 5:00 p.m. the subject Henry C. Parker showed up. Parker walked up to where "Donut" and Perkins were standing and we assumed he had parked his vehicle somewhere nearby. All three bad guys talked for about an hour. Once again, it appeared as if "Donut" and Perkins were trying to talk Parker into something, but it also seemed that Parker was not buying whatever it was the other two were selling. We could only speculate what that "something" was, but I think we were all thoroughly convinced it involved some sort of criminal activity.

The remainder of this week's surveillance was filled with an almost total lack of noteworthy activity. Perkins did visit with "Donut" on both <u>March 12th (Friday)</u> and <u>March 14th (Sunday)</u>, but these two visits to Cannonier's Sunrise apartment seemed to be more social than business related.

* The Surveillance (Week Five) *

The majority of this week's surveillance was mostly boring and uneventful. On <u>March 15th (Monday)</u>, after his wife left for work, "Donut" did some more prowling and peeping in his own neighborhood. This was during daylight and I think all of us were a little surprised by Cannonier's boldness. Later, he drove to Fort Lauderdale's beautiful beach on his motorcycle and then he did some sun bathing and girl watching. On his way home he made his usual stop at the *Mr. Donut* at Andrews and Oakland Park Boulevard ("...the graveyard at Boxer and Judd.").

On <u>March 16th (Tuesday)</u>, again after his wife left for work, "Donut" got on his motorcycle and drove to Fort Lauderdale's Sunrise Shopping Center. There, he met up with Perkins. "Pussywillow" was on his motorcycle too. The two subjects cruised around the shopping center's parking lots, apparently looking for potential targets they might be able to follow home. They eventually cruised around Fort Lauderdale's beach area too, but then they split up and went there separate ways. Once again, on his way home, Cannonier made a stop at his favorite *Mr. Donut*.

On <u>March 17th (Wednesday)</u>, and <u>March 18th (Thursday)</u>, the surveillance again took us to Palm Beach County. On both days "Donut" took his wife to the Town of Ocean Ridge, and they went to the beach. This was also part of the same general area where "Donut" and Perkins had cased the week before. Wednesday's excursion to the beach seemed to be merely for pleasure, but Thursday's trip appeared to be a combination of pleasure and business. "Donut" left his wife for a period of time and began walking south along the beach and he eventually appeared to be very interested in one specific beach front residence.

"Donut" visited Perkins' Opa Locka residence on March 19th (Friday), but that visit didn't last very long, and no more noteworthy activity was observed for the remainder of the week.

* The Surveillance (Week Six) *

Henry C. Parker's probation officer made contact with us again and she informed us that Parker was apparently scared and he had decided he would lay low for a while. He had also apparently backed out of a job because something just didn't feel right. We assumed he meant the Coral Gables Caper. Now, it appeared that our conclusion that Parker wanted nothing to do with whatever "Donut" and Perkins had in mind was indeed correct. Once again, Parker was no longer a major player!

March 23rd (Tuesday) became a very important date. Around 10:30 a.m. Perkins arrived at Cannonier's apartment. He was driving a new Monte Carlo, white in color. We quickly realized this was another rented vehicle. "Donut" transferred some items from the trunk of his own personal vehicle to the trunk of the rental. He also carried some extra clothes with him too. Then, at approximately 10:45 a.m., both subjects entered the rental and drove off, eventually heading eastbound on Oakland Park Boulevard. For the next several hours they cruised and scouted a number of different locations. It was very apparent they had some potential targets already in mind but they were also looking for some new ones too.

At approximately 2:00 p.m. "Donut" and Perkins arrived in the area of Fort Lauderdale's north beach and they parked their rented Monte Carlo almost directly across the street from the *Sea Breeze Motel*, which had been the location of one of their past targets. Both subjects exited the rental and walked east towards the motel itself. They returned to their vehicle ten minutes later and then left the area. We speculated that they were checking to see if their previous target was still staying at the motel. We knew she wasn't though, and she had already checked out and returned home.

Several more hours passed and then "Donut" and Perkins eventually led us back to *Brackman's* at the Coral Ridge Mall. They had been there before on March 5th and that was when they had followed the elderly female back to her apartment at the *Sea Breeze Motel*. The large expensive-looking ring on her finger apparently had attracted them and now our two bad guys were back at *Brackman's* looking for another potential target. Yes indeed, things today were definitely looking very, very good!

"Donut" and Perkins entered *Brackman's* and when I went into the store to look for them I found them seated at the counter area of the store's snack bar. They were having some coffee and talking. Once they left the snack bar they began walking around the huge department store and like before they seemed content to remain on the first floor. After approximately 10-15 minutes it appeared as if the two subjects may have picked out a new target. "Donut" quickly left *Brackman's* by way of the building's southernmost exit. He briskly walked to their rental vehicle, got in, and then he pulled the Monte Carlo around to the west side of the store, abreast of the westernmost exit.

Shortly after "Donut" parked his car in the crowded parking lot I observed two elderly females exiting *Brackman's* by way of this same west side door. Perkins was right behind them! As these two unsuspecting women walked slowly westward through the lot, Perkins entered the rental and joined his buddy Cannonier. The two women eventually got into their vehicle, a white over blue Plymouth. When they finally started to drive away "Donut" and Perkins followed them. When our two bad guys got caught in a little bit of traffic Perkins quickly exited the rental and then he ran through the parking lot on foot so he would not lose sight of their new target's vehicle. Once again, like he did back on March 5th, Perkins played like a traffic cop and he directed several other vehicles through the lot so "Donut" could catch up to him. Perkins quickly got back into the rental and then our two thugs headed eastbound on Oakland Park, following right along behind their new target's Plymouth.

The two women in the Plymouth crossed over the I.C.W. and eventually ended up at a small beach front residence located in the 2500 block of North Atlantic Boulevard. As they exited their vehicle and entered the residence, "Donut" and Perkins slowly drove by them. We eventually learned that one of these two women lived at the residence and her name was Beatrice Hand. Ms. Hand was 75 and she was wearing a large diamond ring that appeared to be of considerable value. I'm sure that ring is what first attracted our two rock hounds and caused them to follow Ms. Hand and her friend home.

For the next thirty minutes "Donut" and Perkins cased Ms. Hand's residence. They initially stopped their rental at a small park located about a half block to the north of their target and then they went and parked about a block south of it, near some busy hotels and motels. They left their vehicle at one of these hotels and then both of them walked northward along the beach. They eventually arrived at the rear of Ms. Hand's house and studied it for a few minutes. Then, they returned to their vehicle and drove off out of the area.

For the next two hours our two bad guys drove around apparently just killing time and waiting for it to get dark. When it finally did they headed back to the area where Ms. Hand's residence was located. But, what they didn't know was that Sergeant Dierkzon, Al Smith and I were inside her residence awaiting their return. "Donut" and Perkins made several slow passes by the residence and then eventually they parked their vehicle at the small park located just to the north, about a half block away. "Aerial 1" had the "eye" and advised that both subjects were now out on foot and walking south. Because of the nearby houses and heavy foliage in the area, and the fact none of our ground units wanted to get spotted, from time to time "Aerial 1" and our men on foot lost sight of the two subjects.

Although we were less than certain about where Perkins had gone, "Donut" was observed as he walked all the way around Ms. Hand's residence, and at one point he even stopped and peered into the living room through a large plate glass window that faced east towards the beach and the ocean. Just as we were almost sure "Donut" and Perkins were about to do their thing, two additional females arrived at Ms. Hand's residence, in two separate vehicles. The two visitors were unexpected guests and they clearly unnerved our two bad boys who didn't know what to make of their sudden appearance. One of these ladies left her vehicle's parking lights on and when we spoke with her after she came inside, she indicated that she had seen our two suspects standing on the sidewalk out in front of the residence. Even though we got these two women visitors to quickly leave the area, the damage had apparently already been done! "Donut" and Perkins were obviously hinky and they left the area too.

"Donut" drove Perkins down to Opa Locka and then he went home himself. He was still driving the rental and we all took this as a very good sign. When he got home he parked the rental in a spot that was away from his own apartment. Now, as we put "Donut" to bed for the night, the big question became: Would they eventually return to Ms. Hand's residence to complete their illicit work, or would they move on to something else? It was a question none of us could answer.

22

MARCH 25, 1976

"Well, what do you think?" Sergeant Joe Gerwens asked softly, as he and I sat there alone in the T.I.U. office. I had just finished my shift and was about ready to secure for the night but I sensed that Joe was frustrated and slightly bewildered, just like the rest of us were. "Donut" and Perkins had picked out their latest target two days ago and they had even spent some time casing Ms. Hand's residence too, but since that night they hadn't moved against it again and we all wondered why they hadn't. Would this latest caper end negatively like the Coral Gables Caper had, or, like their first intended victim from *Brackman's*? Only time would tell but the clock was ticking and we all knew that our department's upper-brass wouldn't let us follow these two bad guys around forever. Sooner or later, if we didn't catch them in the act, we would have to pull off and return to our normal T.I.U. duties. After all, T.I.U. was working under a federal grant and statistics were unfortunately very important. And, while we were following "Donut" and Perkins around, almost exclusively, we weren't making any other arrests. Our brass couldn't allow this to continue forever. So, this is why Joe Gerwens was slightly frustrated. I understood and I could feel his pain!

I was just about ready to respond to Joe's question when the police radio's tactical channel suddenly sputtered to life. "Donut" was once again on the move! At approximately 6:30 p.m., Officer Jim Kriner ("Crash"), one of the tac guys who relieved me, observed "Donut" leave his apartment and walk to the driver's side of the rental vehicle. He appeared to remove a small object from his waistband, near the front of his pants. This unknown object, which could have been a gun, had been concealed underneath Cannonier's t-shirt. "Donut" entered the rental and then he eventually drove off southbound away from his residence. "Crash" alerted "Aerial 1" and the other ground units.

As "Donut" began heading eastbound, in the general direction of Fort Lauderdale, Joe and I continued to listen to the surveillance and although it sounded promising we also tried to contain our excitement too. But, when it finally became apparent "Donut" was headed for *Lester's Diner* on State Road #84, we both realized that tonight might just be the night! Parker's M.O., which "Donut" and Perkins had adopted, was to meet at a restaurant and then proceed to the target and do their thing. So, when "Donut" finally arrived at *Lester's* at approximately 7:15 p.m. we all felt we might really have something tonight.

"Donut" went inside and sat down at the counter. About five minutes later the subject Perkins ("Pussywillow"), along with his wife ("Pinky"), also arrived at the diner. They were in their Olds Cutlass. Perkins and his wife went inside the diner and sat down with Cannonier. They all stayed there for approximately thirty minutes. When they exited the diner "Donut" opened the trunk of the rental and took out a small unidentified object and placed it in the passenger compartment, at the driver's side. Perkins also took an unknown object from his own vehicle and he too placed it inside of the rental. Then, Perkins gave his wife a kiss.

"Looks like he's kissing his wife good-bye," Bill Stewart ("Broker") advised matter-of-factly. Several more seconds went by before another voice advised almost solemnly, "He sure is!"

As both subjects and their rental now headed eastbound towards Fort Lauderdale's beach area the observer in "Aerial 1" advised, "Wilbur's got the eye."

While "Aerial 1" continued to maintain the "eye" from about 500 feet overhead almost all of our unmarked ground units didn't stay behind the surveillance. Instead, they took any shortcuts they could and sped around the two subject's vehicle which was now apparently headed to the target location on North Atlantic Boulevard. Saying they "sped" was probably a gross understatement! Sergeant Gerwens and I had also left the P.D. and headed towards Ms. Hand's residence and I know we "sped" too. We wanted to get to the target location ahead of the suspects and that meant we had to violate a few traffic laws along the way.

"Hawk to all units, when I get to the target I'll open up a land line to the bureau. Let's not give them a reason not to." Sergeant Gerwens may have named me "Snake" but he took the nickname "Hawk" for himself. I had to admit it fit him pretty well. He was an aggressive supervisor, not afraid to take chances or to make waves and he was always the hunter, and never the hunted!

"Smokey to Hawk," Mike called out, "you want to clear the marked units away from that (target) area?"

"I've already taken care of that, let's just not US give them a reason."

I'm sure Mike, and the rest of the tactical units too, knew exactly what Joe meant!

Even though most of the tactical units got way ahead of the surveillance, and arrived at the target location ahead of the suspects, thankfully not everyone did this. One or two, and this included my partner Mike, dutifully stayed behind the surveillance just in case they might be needed. And, as it turned out, they were! "Aerial 1" almost always did an outstanding job but they weren't infallible and every now and then mistakes did occur. Tonight was one of those nights. Flying at 500 feet could sometimes be a rather bumpy experience and when you're trying to watch a vehicle down below with a pair of binoculars it was sometimes easy to mistake one vehicle for another. If there happened to be two white cars side-by-side, that looked similar, in the blink of an eye, and a bump from some unfriendly air, you could end up watching the wrong car. This is what happened tonight. Somewhere after they had pulled away from *Lester's Diner* "Aerial 1" lost track of our suspect's vehicle ("Candy Box") and they began reporting the whereabouts of an entirely different vehicle that had nothing at all to do with our caper. Luckily for us though, these two cars were both headed in the same general direction, so this momentary slip didn't last for very long. The ground units that were still behind the surveillance suddenly pulled up abreast of the suspect's vehicle and they quickly realized that "Aerial 1" was watching a car that was about a quarter mile ahead of them. Once alerted to their error, it didn't take "Aerial 1" very long for them to reacquire the suspect's vehicle.

"How's it looking?" one of our off-duty tac guys asked.

"Gooooood!" Mike responded quickly, then added confidently, "We're 51 (enroute) target."

Almost immediately this off-duty officer advised, "I'm enroute."

He wasn't the only off-duty tac guy to respond though, and at least one or two others did too. We had all lived and breathed this surveillance for six weeks now, and no one wanted to miss out on the finale when it finally did occur. And, it looked more and more like tonight might just be the night, so it didn't surprise me at all to hear our off-duty tac guys advising they were also enroute to the target location. After all, I was off-duty too.

"Okay," Mike began again, "we're gonna have to be real strict on the code, we got a lot of C.B.er's in this area."

Most of our tac units, and "Aerial 1" too, were already trying to stick strictly to the code so Mike's warning may have seemed unnecessary to a few. But, every so often one of the guys would slip and mention a landmark or a street by name, and these minor deviations from the code might just give a listener a clue to where we were all headed. None of us wanted to take the chance that "Donut" and Perkins might be warned again, as "Donut" had been back on March 5th, during week number three of the surveillance. So, Mike's warning, whether it was necessary or not, served as a gentle reminder that we all needed to be extra vigilant and careful.

Sergeant Gerwens and I were among the first tac officers to arrive in the target area and as I parked our vehicle in an out of the way location, where it wouldn't be noticed by the two suspects, "Hawk" made contact with their intended victim and advised her that company was once again coming to visit! It was now approximately 8:15 p.m. Ms. Hand seemed to be a very resilient individual, courageous and not easily frightened. She advised us that she would do whatever we wanted and she had complete faith in our ability to handle the situation. She was a remarkable woman!

"55 on the D.O.T.," "Aerial 1" reported. No one else knew what this meant, but we all knew it meant the two subjects were still headed our way, and they were getting closer by the second.

Ms. Hand's residence was very simple and unobtrusive looking, in fact, the beach front property it was located on probably was worth much more than the actual structure itself. Unlike some of the more expensive homes in the area it was only a single-story structure and the house's no-frills floor plan was basically in the shape of a square. There were three points of entry into the home; the main front door which faced the street to the west, and two side doors, one on the north side of the residence, and the other one at the south side. Joe and I knew that we would have to position ourselves in such a way that all three doors could be watched at the same time. Initially, this presented us with a bit of a challenge.

The front door opened into a large open foyer area that quickly became the living room and then the family room.

The door at the south side also opened into this large family room area. A chest-high wall separated the smaller kitchen area, and the door at the north side, from the living room and family room areas. There was also a very small hallway leading away from this kitchen area that led to Ms. Hand's bedroom located at the N.W. corner of the squared-shape structure. Joe put Ms. Hand and her female friend in this bedroom and advised them not to come out until they heard from us that everything was all right. I took up a position in the kitchen area from which I could watch both the front door, which faced west towards the street, and the side door located at the north side of the residence. Sergeant Gerwens was in the hallway approximately five feet away from me and he was in a position to see if anyone entered the residence by way of the side door at the south side. He couldn't really see the door itself, but if someone came into the residence he would be able to see them once they entered the family room.

We decided we wanted to make things as easy for our two crooks as possible. And, we also wanted to be the ones to control where they would enter the residence. We locked both the front door and the side door at the north side that entered onto the kitchen. Now, to enter the home by either of these two doors the subjects would have to physically make a forced entry and we didn't think they would do that, not if they were given a better alternative. The main inside door at the south side was left wide open and only the unlocked screen door prevented them from making entry. Also, to make them believe that they had caught the victim unaware and completely vulnerable, I turned on the shower in the small bathroom that was located just off of the living room and family room areas, near the south side door. Hopefully, they would see the open unlocked door, hear the shower, and then enter thinking they had their unsuspecting victim right where they wanted her. Little did they know that they would be walking into a trap!

We established phone contact with the detective monitoring the radio in the bureau and then we turned off our own hand held radios. We didn't want our two bad guys to hear the crackle of a police radio. Initially, after we first took up our concealed positions within the residence, I was armed with one of our departmental pump-action shotguns, plus my own S&W 9mm automatic. Sergeant Gerwens had only his automatic handgun and I eventually learned that this was a new weapon that Joe had, and he hadn't even qualified with it yet. I suggested that Joe might want to use my shotgun instead of a weapon he hadn't even qualified with, and although at first he resisted my suggestion, he did come around to my way of thinking and eventually he took the shotgun from me. My thinking was very simple; if this went down tonight, and it appeared that it might, we didn't want to give anyone anything to second guess, and Joe using an unauthorized weapon might just muddy the water, even if only a little bit.

With our police radios now off our only real link to the outside world was the open phone line to our detective bureau. Things were happening outside of the residence but for the most part Joe and I were in the dark, literally! We crouched there in our darkened hiding places and awaited the arrival of "Donut" and Perkins. Outside, our tac units on the ground were moving into position and we knew there were at least a half dozen men now secreted in the bushes and yards that surrounded Ms. Hand's residence. None of them were on Ms. Hand's property itself though, and they were around the houses across the street, and in some of the other neighboring yards nearby. Two of the off-duty tac guys also would cover the suspect's vehicle when it finally stopped moving.

"Wilbur if you can, get rid of the beacon," one of our tac guys requested. I'm sure the officers in "Aerial 1" didn't like flying with their navigation lights turned off and I don't even know if they might have been breaking some F.A.A. regulations by doing this, but we all knew we didn't want our bad guys to look up and see a plane circling there overhead. Without lights, it seemed less likely that "Aerial 1" might be noticed.

"A little wider please, a little wider," Mike also eventually requested.

"We'll do," Wilbur answered back immediately.

The two suspects made a few slow passes by Ms. Hand's residence and then they eventually stopped and turned their lights off. Officer Ron Ray ("Troll") was one of the tac guys watching the suspect's rental vehicle when it finally stopped moving. When "Aerial 1" reported that the "Candy Box" was now stopped in the 2300 block of North Atlantic Boulevard, which was south of Ms. Hand's residence, Ron hid behind a bush at the corner of an apartment building located on the N.W. corner of Atlantic and 23rd Street. Ron was only about 25-30 feet west and south of the suspect's vehicle which was parked facing north on the east side of Atlantic Blvd. Ron watched as "Donut" exited the vehicle and then walked northbound towards Ms. Hand's residence. Initially, Perkins remained seated in the driver's seat, with the vehicle's headlights turned off.

Approximately 3-5 minutes later the suspect Perkins also exited the vehicle. For the next several minutes he just stood there in the street and looked up and down Atlantic Boulevard. Then, when he was apparently convinced that everything was cool, he walked around to the passenger's side of the rental and he opened the door. Perkins reached inside the vehicle and Ron observed him retrieve something that looked like a piece of clothing apparel. Ron watched as the suspect now put on a dark colored pull over type shirt, and then just like "Donut" had done moments before, he started walking north in the general direction of Ms. Hand's residence.

"Crash" and "Broker" were hiding in the bushes of the house located directly across the street from Ms. Hand's residence. They had watched as the suspect's rental vehicle made several slow passes by the target location and now they observed "Donut" walking northbound along the east side of Atlantic Blvd. He was looking all around and he also kept looking over his shoulder behind him. "Donut" also carried what looked like a black cloth bag in his right hand. When he reached Ms. Hand's residence he quickly entered the southern side of her property and disappeared. Shortly after they lost sight of "Donut" "Crash" and "Broker" observed the subject Perkins now also walking northbound on Atlantic towards the residence. Just like "Donut" had done moments before, when Perkins reached Ms. Hand's property he also headed east and disappeared somewhere around the south side of the structure.

Joe and I could hear movement outside and knew that at least one of the subjects was walking around the residence. The detective on the phone then advised me that the subject Cannonier was walking up to the front of the house. I carefully stole a peek at the front plate glass window and observed "Donut" looking inside. I saw him, but he couldn't see me! "Donut" eventually walked away from the front of the residence, back towards the street. Several more minutes passed and then I heard a weird clicking sound on the phone. After several seconds of this clicking the phone suddenly went dead and I could no longer communicate with the detective at the bureau. Almost immediately I observed and heard one subject running from the N.W. corner of the residence. This was where the phone lines to the residence were located. The subject ran eastward along the house's north side towards the beach and as he passed by the glass jalousie door, which led from the kitchen to the outside, I observed his form go by. I immediately realized that the subjects had cut the phone lines to the residence and this meant that they would be coming soon! I motioned to Sergeant Gerwens and with hand gestures I advised him that the phone line had just been cut. He silently nodded his head indicating that he understood. He also made his weapon ready as he clicked the safety off so the shotgun would be ready to fire.

I've always been amazed, and even amused too, by some of the totally absurd and irrelevant thoughts that dance through a man's mind just before he is about to do battle, and maybe even face death head-on. Tonight, as I hid there in Ms. Hand's kitchen, clutching my 9mm automatic in my right hand, my thoughts reverted back to my early childhood in Oakland. My mom and dad divorced when I was just a baby and although it was sometimes very difficult for her she did the best she could to provide me with a stable and safe home. But, she was still a young and attractive woman and every now and then she would go out at night and leave me all alone in our apartment. I'm not really sure how old I was, but I think I was probably about ten. My mom always asked me if I was going to be all right alone and the macho cockiness that is inside of almost every young boy always confidently assured her that I would be.

Sometimes I would be okay; other times I wouldn't be! More than once I laid there on the living room couch, watching television, and I imagined that there was a big bad nasty monster in the kitchen waiting for me. I couldn't see the kitchen from the living room couch, but I was sure that monster was there just the same. Unfortunately, if I needed to go to the bathroom I had to pass by the kitchen to get there. More than once I felt like my bladder would explode as I prayed that my mom would get home soon so I could go to the bathroom. Sometimes I made it; sometimes I didn't! But, as far as I can recall, I never was brave enough to get up from that couch and confront that monster in the kitchen face-to-face. A young boy's imagination can be a wonderful, yet a very terrible thing. Now, all these years later, I was the one hiding in the kitchen, waiting for a different kind of two-legged monster that was about to invade Ms. Hand's home!

At about 8:40 p.m. Sergeant Gerwens slowly peeked around the hallway wall towards the family room and the south side door. As Joe later recounted, "I noticed movement in the family room by the rear door and observed two subjects standing inside the house approx. 12 feet from the rear door. Both subjects were wearing dark clothing and had dark masks covering their heads and face." Joe also noticed that both of these individuals were wearing dark colored gloves. And, the subject to Joe's right, that appeared to be our bad guy Perkins, also carried a briefcase in one hand and a large automatic pistol in the other.

Sgt. Gerwens felt that he had to act immediately and he didn't think he had the time to alert me to the subject's presence inside of the residence. If he had tried to do this the subjects may have seen him first and tried to flee, or they may have even started shooting. So, Joe jumped to his feet and he yelled "Freeze, police!" He also pointed his shotgun at the two suspects as he began to move forward towards them. When Joe jumped up and yelled, this was my first clue that some very serious shit was now happening! I also jumped up to my feet and looked over the wall that separated the kitchen from the living room and family room areas.

Even though only a few precious seconds had elapsed since Joe yelled for the two subjects to "freeze," by the time I jumped up and saw them they had already turned around and were heading back towards their point of entry, the south side door. They were also both crouched down into a squat and each appeared to be doing a duck walk as they made their way to the door as fast as they could. At least one of the subjects, thought to be Perkins, was still armed, and it was very, very obvious that neither had any intentions of surrendering!

Okay Officer, It's Decision Time!

(Situation #19)

"Donut" and Perkins have illegally entered Ms. Hand's residence (a Felony), with the obvious intent to commit a home invasion robbery. At least one of the subjects is armed with an automatic handgun. Sgt. Gerwens has ordered the suspects to "freeze" but neither appears willing to surrender. If you were me, OR, if you were Sgt. Gerwens, what should you do next?

What is your answer? (put an "X" in the space in front of your answer)

❏ _____ Because they are both running away from you, you hold your fire and you decide to let the other tactical officers outside of the residence deal with the two subjects.

❏ _____ Because they haven't given up, and at least one is still armed and they are attempting to flee the residence, even though they are both still running away from you, you shoot at the two subjects.

An analysis of this situation appears at the end of the book

(Do not go there until you have finished reading this chapter)

I brought my 9mm up and quickly aimed it in the general direction of the two suspects. Joe was off to my right but I could also see that he was still moving forward, away from the hallway and into the living room area. I intended to fire, in fact, I had already begun to squeeze my automatic's trigger when Joe suddenly and unexpectedly appeared right there in front of me. Now, there was no way at all that I could safely fire my weapon. If I tried to shoot at the two fleeing suspects I would have to take the chance that I might just hit Sergeant Gerwens in the back by mistake. This risk was totally unacceptable, so I reluctantly held my fire and watched as "Donut" and Perkins continued their mad dash towards the door.

Joe had moved in front of me because he knew he needed to be in that specific spot to have the best shot possible. If he had fired from the hallway there was a better than 50-50 chance he would have missed both of the fleeing suspects entirely. But, from his present position in the living room, in front of me, he now had a perfect shot. He was now just thirteen feet away from the two subjects. The first blast from Joe's shotgun seemed to be extremely loud and I think the fact we were inside of a house only helped to exaggerate the overall sound of the weapon's report. A split second after Joe fired this first round one of the two suspects squealed loudly like a stuck pig. Even though they both still continued to scurry duck walk style towards the open door it was very obvious that at least one of them had been wounded. Joe now fired off a second round from his shotgun, but by the time he did this both "Donut" and Perkins had already reached the door and quickly disappeared into the darkness.

Jim Kriner and Bill Stewart, who were positioned across the street from Ms. Hand's residence, heard the two blasts from Sgt. Gerwens' shotgun. They immediately ran to the street where they now observed both of the suspects running away from the south side of Ms. Hand's residence. Jim

Kriner yelled, "Freeze, Police Officer!" but "Donut" and Perkins turned south and now ran along the east side of the street. The two subjects were running side by side, each man had an object in his hand and it was obvious they were trying to make it back to their own vehicle.

When Mike Gillo heard the loud reports from Sgt. Gerwens' shotgun he also immediately moved towards the street in an effort to intercept any of the subjects that may have been able to get away from Joe and I. To be honest though, most of the tac guys outside the house, and this included Mike, were almost certain that Joe and I would probably capture or kill at least one of the two suspects inside the target residence, and that meant they would more than likely only have to deal with one subject at the most. If Joe and I were lucky, both bad guys would be successfully apprehended inside Ms. Hand's residence, and neither one would make it to the street. So, when "Donut" and Perkins both suddenly appeared at the street I think all of our guys, including Mike, were probably just a little bit surprised.

Now that "Donut" and Perkins were running southbound towards their vehicle, as fast as they could, the only remaining tac officer they needed to get by was Mike. Each man still wore his hooded mask that covered his face and at least one of the two men, the subject Perkins, also had a large caliber automatic in his hand. As Mike stepped boldly into the street to confront the two subjects, the armed subject Perkins was to Mike's right, approximately 28 feet away. Mike was armed with one of our department's pump-action shotguns.

Okay Officer, It's Decision Time!

(Situation #20)

"Donut" and Perkins have been caught in the act of trying to commit a home invasion robbery. Shots have already been fired (in the home) and now you are face-to-face with the two suspects. Neither subject appears willing to surrender and at least one of the two subjects is armed with a large caliber automatic. If you were in Mike Gillo's place, what would you do next?

What is your answer? (put an "X" in the space in front of your answer)

❑ _____ You want to give the two subjects one last chance to peacefully surrender. So, you hold your fire and yell for them to give up.

❑ _____ Giving the two subjects one more chance to surrender clearly puts you at a distinct disadvantage. Therefore, because you fear that you may be fired upon at any moment, you do NOT shout out a warning, and instead you open fire on the suspect with the large caliber automatic in his hand.

An analysis of this situation appears at the end of the book

(Do not go there until you have finished reading this chapter)

Mike yelled out loudly, "Halt, Police!" But, instead of taking this last opportunity to surrender the subject Perkins, who still had that automatic pistol in his hand, fired off one quick shot from the hip as he continued running towards Mike's exposed location. Mike immediately fired his shotgun and he hit Perkins in the groin area. Perkins fell to his knees and then he spun around in a circle and after he made this complete turn he once again ended up facing Mike with the gun still in his hand. Mike saw that the automatic was still pointed at him so he quickly fired off yet another round from his shotgun. Perkins was hit again, this time in the head, and now he fell backwards to the ground.

Mike now turned his attention to the subject "Donut" who had stopped running and was in a crouched position in the middle of the street. It also appeared as if he intended to change his direction of flight and run back north towards Officers Jim Kriner and Bill Stewart. "Donut" still had something in his hands and the logical and prudent thing to assume was that he was armed with a handgun, just like his now fallen buddy Perkins had been. And, because "Donut" still wasn't ready to give up, and he also had this unknown object hidden in his hands, the tac officers surrounding him all felt that they had no other choice but to open fire. While Mike fired off two more deadly rounds of OO buck from his shotgun, both Kriner and Stewart each fired once with their shotguns too. Jim and Bill had been approximately 43 feet from "Donut" when they fired, while Mike had been a little bit closer. Most, if not all, of these projectiles violently struck "Donut" and he quickly fell to the pavement, right there in the middle of the street.

Once "Donut" had been neutralized Mike again looked back at Perkins and observed that he was still moving. Later, in Mike's sworn statement to our detectives he indicated, "I could not see his hands or the weapon I knew that he had. Being afraid that he would again fire, I fired at him." After this fifth and final round from Mike's shotgun there was no further movement from the subject Perkins. When Mike moved closer to the now motionless suspect he got his first good look at the gun that Perkins had been carrying. It was a .45 caliber Colt automatic, model 1911, with the words "Springfield Armory" and "U.S. Army" engraved on the side. The gun was fully loaded with one round in the chamber and six rounds in the clip. The hammer was back in a cocked position. One .45 cal. casing was also about five feet from the head of the subject Perkins. This was the spent casing from the bullet that he had fired at Mike.

Although Perkins seemed to be dead, Mike remained there by him until he was officially relieved by one of the detectives assigned to secure and gather evidence. Mike didn't want to take any chances that this .45 caliber automatic might pull a disappearing act as had happened before reference some of our other capers. Perkins' body lay about 37 feet south of Ms. Hand's property and "Donut" lay in the middle of the street just 27 feet away from her driveway. But, even though Perkins was dead, "Donut" was still very much alive, although he was obviously hurting and in a great deal of pain. After all, he had been riddled by shotgun blasts from Sgt. Gerwens in the house, and then Mike, Jim and Bill outside. It seemed almost a miracle that he was still alive.

After E.M.S. gave him emergency treatment at the scene, and just before we shipped his bleeding ass off to the hospital, "Donut" was thoroughly searched. In his pant's pockets detectives found an open switch blade knife and a police-type slap stick. Later, I was told that when he hit the pavement after being shot, "Donut" fell on his own open switch blade knife and cut himself. If this was really true, and I don't know for a fact that it was, how appropriate! Also taken from him was a pair of bloodstained black leather gloves he had been wearing and the homemade mask he used to cover his face. This mask appeared to be made from a woman's underwear tights. It had two holes cut out so he could see and it was also knotted at the top so it would stay on his head.

Some of the evidence taken from Perkins was just as revealing. In his right rear pants pocket detectives found a pair of needle nose pliers. He had used these pliers to cut the telephone lines outside of Ms. Hand's residence. There were some small splotches of white paint on the pliers and this matched the white paint covering the phone lines. Perkins had also been carrying a small brown leather brief case type pouch and after all the shooting had ended it was found on the ground between his legs. Besides some obvious burglar tools the case contained a ¼ pound can of liquid ether. This can of ether had apparently been hit by one of Mike's OO buckshot projectiles, which went through the can, and through and through the leather pouch. Although we could still detect the faint smell of ether, the can itself was now empty. We could only speculate what these two thugs had in mind, as far as the ether was concerned, but we were sure it wasn't something good! Finally, the homemade mask that Perkins wore was also removed from his head and taken into evidence. It was made of a light blue denim material and like the mask "Donut" wore it also had two holes cut out so Perkins could see. It now contained a large amount of blood and some human flesh too.

When "Donut" first arrived at the hospital emergency room, under police guard, the doctors quickly determined that he had approximately twenty-four (24) penetrations from gunshot wounds to his body. And, they weren't even sure that they would be able to save him. After he was x-rayed he received intravenous feedings, plus a quantity of blood, and then he was rushed to surgery. By the next day he was still listed as critical, but at least he was still alive.

Perkins hadn't been hit as many times as "Donut" had, but his wounds had definitely been much more lethal. There were seven entrance wounds in his genitals and left leg area alongside his genitals. Only one of these shotgun pellets exited the back of his left leg in the middle of the thigh area. The immediate cause of Perkins' death though were two shotgun pellets to the head that entered his brain. One of these shotgun pellets hit him almost in the center of his forehead and the other one was approximately 1¼ inch left of the mid-line. These two shotgun pellets from Perkins' brain were later recovered and placed into evidence.

Like most Americans, police officers believe in doing what's right, instead of doing what's wrong; they also favor justice, not injustice; and they want ALL bad guys to eventually be held accountable for their actions. Unfortunately, as we all know, real life doesn't always work out this way. Henry C. Parker's case was the perfect example of this. For whatever reasons, Parker had decided that he would lay low for a while and he did not participate in the latest caper that "Donut" and Perkins had tried to pull off. Lucky for him! Now, as we gathered at the detective bureau, after we gave our sworn statements, a few of us discussed how much of a damn shame it was that Parker had missed out on the party we had just thrown for "Donut" and Perkins. We would have really liked for him to be there too!

"Dallas" was one of the detectives that had been assigned by the bureau to work portions of this surveillance with us. So, even though he had not actually participated in the fireworks tonight he still had been in the area nearby and ready to act just in case we may have needed additional back-up. And, like the rest of us in T.I.U., he too was unhappy with the fact that Henry C. Parker had been able to escape his own personal judgment day. "Dallas" felt that Parker now deserved some special attention and he decided to do something about it – now!

"Dallas" suddenly picked up the telephone and he silently dialed Parker's Dade County number. After a few more seconds someone finally answered and "Dallas" quickly inquired, "Is this Henry C. Parker?" His voice was loud and clear, and very authoritative sounding.

"Yes," Parker responded, with a hint of uncertainty in his voice.

"Mr. Parker, I want you to listen to me very carefully," "Dallas" began again sternly. "I don't know if you've heard, but Robert Perkins is dead and Ricky Cannonier is dying!"

Now, there was only just silence at the other end of the phone line.

"Mr. Parker," "Dallas" continued unabated, "there's already been enough blood shed tonight and there's no need for YOU to die too! We have your house surrounded and we want you to surrender!"

There was still only silence at the other end of the line.

"Parker," the detective began again firmly, "do you understand what I've just told you?"

"Yes," Parker responded dejectedly, then quickly added, "I understand! What do you want me to do?"

"I want you to strip down completely, so we can see that you don't have any weapons on you. Then, I want you to go outside to your front yard and make contact with the officers there. Do you understand?"

"Yes sir," Parker answered back immediately. "You promise they won't shoot me if I do as you say?"

"I promise, now do it! Now!"

"Yes sir."

The phone line went dead.

"Dallas" hung the phone up and then he looked over at the three tac guys that were crowded around his desk. Each of us looked at one another with a quiet kind of satisfaction. Then, almost as if on cue, we all burst out laughing at the exact same moment. There weren't, of course, any police officers surrounding Parker's house and when he went out and stood in his front yard butt naked, pleading to be taken into custody, there wouldn't be anyone there to hear him yelling. Except, of course, maybe his neighbors.

==

Ricky Cannonier (a.k.a. "Donut") survived for a couple of weeks but then he eventually died as a result of his wounds.

*   *   *   *   *

Henry C. Parker eventually had his Parole violated because he had associated with Cannonier and Perkins, who were known felons. He was sent back to Florida's State Prison at Raiford.

23

EPILOGUE

PRESENT DAY

I have always been extremely proud of my chosen profession. The men and women of law enforcement are, for the most part, dedicated and decent individuals who try to do a very difficult job most other ordinary Americans would never want to do. Now, with the enormously successful completion of T.I.U.'s six week surveillance involving Parker, "Donut" and Perkins, the overall pride I felt in my profession, my department and my fellow officers, was at a new all time high.

Mike Gillo and I remained partners until we both left T.I.U. in 1977 and transferred to the detective bureau. Before we left though, we were named Police Officers of the Year by two different south Florida organizations. B'nai B'rith's Fort Lauderdale Lodge #1438 named Mike and I their 1975-76 Policemen of the Year. The fact that slain F.L.P.D. Officer Walter Ilyankoff had been the award's previous recipient only made Mike and I more humble and proud that we had been chosen to receive this tremendous honor. We also received the 1976 J. Lester Holt Memorial Award from the Fort Lauderdale Jaycees for "Courageous Service to the Community." Again, we were both very honored to be selected.

Mike and I ended up as partners again in the Homicide Squad, but that's a totally different story for another time. Eventually, Mike left F.L.P.D. and he went to the Broward County State Attorney's Office as an investigator, and then as their Chief Investigator. I remained with F.L.P.D. and in 1981 I was promoted to the rank of sergeant. Even though I was very happy with my promotion to sergeant, 1981 was still a dreadful year for F.L.P.D. On August 3, 1981, "Aerial 1" crashed while on routine patrol over the southwest section of the City. Kenneth Petersen, one of the original members of our department's Aviation Unit, and another officer pilot/observer, John Alexander, were both killed instantly.

Joe Gerwens, one of my sergeants from my old T.I.U. days became Chief of Police of Fort Lauderdale P.D. in 1987. Unfortunately, Joe also had to endure the unthinkable during his tenure as Chief and on May 25, 1989, tragedy again struck F.L.P.D. when "Aerial 1" crashed during a return flight from the City of Tallahassee. Both the pilot, Officer Frank Mastrangelo Jr., and his passenger, Detective Norman Eddy, were killed. In 1992, Chief Gerwens retired from F.L.P.D. and he accepted a new law enforcement manger's position with the Broward County Sheriff's Office. Joe Gerwens, a cop's cop, died in 2006. He was just 60.

In the summer of 1993, with the rank of Captain, and after twenty-six years as an officer with Fort Lauderdale P.D., I retired. I remained active in law enforcement however, but again, that's another story for a different time. When I look back on my career with F.L.P.D. I do so fondly and with an immense sense of pride and personal satisfaction. I also feel confident in laying claim to two very unofficial departmental records during this twenty-six years; the most high-speed vehicle pursuits and involvement in the most "Shots Fired!" kind of incidents. I'm definitely not trying to brag when I say this, but I am very proud of the positive attitude I always tried to maintain, and the proactive way I usually went about my daily duties and responsibilities. The end result was my eventual involvement in many, many high profile police activities.

But, even more important to me than the overall quantity of my work, was the quality! I was involved in almost a dozen incidents where I had to fire my weapon and use deadly force, but there were many more times when I would have been justified using deadly force, and I didn't. I am not unique by any means and the overall majority of law enforcement officers today exhibit this same professionalism and courageous restraint. In this book there were twenty (20) different situations the reader was asked to evaluate and then decide what specific course of action would be appropriate. Police work is an immensely complicated animal, and things are never just black or white. There is always a tremendous amount of gray area too, and hopefully, by analyzing and completing these twenty different situations, the reader will have a new appreciation of just how difficult the law enforcement profession really is.

In 1971 Doctor Pike told me I would never be a police officer again. I've always been extremely proud of what I have been able to accomplish, and being named Police Officer of the Year was obviously the ultimate honor, but my biggest reward has always been my being able to prove Doctor Pike wrong!

24

SITUATION ANALYSIS SECTION

Situation #1
(Chapter 1)

Even though I fired three shots at the suspect's vehicle I quickly realized "this was just a waste of good ammunition." I had already given my partner all my extra rounds, plus my second back-up weapon too, and I should have saved all the bullets in MY own gun for when we finally got the subjects stopped. Although I was legally justified to shoot, and was also in line with our Departmental policy, I do not think I used my best judgment when I fired at the suspect's vehicle.

Therefore, the correct answer is: "No! I would not fire at this time."

If this was your choice, then congratulations! You did better than I did in real life. Give yourself one (1) point for good judgment and for coolness under fire. You get zero points if you fired your weapon (like I did). If you would have fired all six shots in your gun; shame on you, because now you have an empty weapon, and no ammunition to reload it with!

Situation #2
(Chapter 1)

You definitely don't want to let go of the suspect and just "back away from him." You already have one of his hands cuffed, so if you let him go and back away, he can then use your own handcuffs as a possible weapon. Sorry, but you are committed! Why are the other officers kicking and punching the suspect? You don't know! But, you also don't see any weapons, so you're really not justified in using any additional force (like hitting him yourself).

Therefore, the correct answer is: "I would continue my efforts to handcuff the suspect."

If this was your choice, give yourself one (1) point for good judgment and for successfully maintaining your own self-control. You lose one (1) point if you decided to back away from the subject before you completed cuffing him, but you lose two (2) points if you joined in the feeding frenzy and began to hit and punch the suspect too.

Situation #3
(Chapter 3)

Leaving your post without permission, and driving around the neighboring residential area, is <u>not</u> a proper thing to do. If something bad happened at the store and you weren't there to see it, and you should have been, you could get disciplined, and maybe even fired. The department's laser-sighted machine gun is not a toy! Using it like one is <u>not</u> professional conduct. This type of misconduct, if detected by a supervisor, most likely would result in discipline and/or a transfer out of the tactical unit. Also, biting the bullet and sticking it out might seem to be the macho thing to do, but if you're not 100% alert, you definitely need to advise your supervisor.

Therefore, the best answer is: "I would ask my supervisor for relief."

If this was your choice, give yourself one (1) point for good judgment. You lose one (1) point if you left the store without permission, or if you improperly used the laser-sighted machine gun for fun and games. You get no points for biting the bullet, but you don't lose a point either.

The answer to this situation is a definite no-brainer! There is really only one correct thing you should do. You follow the sergeant's instructions, you stay out of sight, and you let the bad guy go by you. You might be frustrated and disappointed that you're going to miss out on the action, but that still does not justify you intentionally disregarding your supervisor's orders, and then lying to him too.

Therefore, the only possible correct answer is: "I would follow the sergeant's orders...."

If this was your choice, good! However, you don't get points just because you do the right thing. You're expected to follow orders, and anything else is totally unacceptable, and unprofessional!

If you decided to "disobey the sergeant's orders" you lose two (2) points, and if you didn't know what you would do, you lose one (1) point. Also, I strongly suggest that you probably should consider a career that doesn't involve either the military or law enforcement.

Situation #5
(Chapter 5)

In a perfect world you definitely wouldn't have to worry about sergeants trying to get you in trouble and you could concentrate entirely on just catching the bad guys! But, as we all know, this isn't a perfect world! If it was, then society wouldn't need cops to protect it. So, as much as you might like to move forward, and then intercept the second suspect, you need to remember your previous encounter with the K-9 sergeant.

Therefore, the best answer is: "You attempt to raise the K-9 sergeant on the radio, to ask his permission to move east along the sidewalk."

There really isn't a "right" or a "wrong" answer for this situation. Instead, this is one of those situations you really can't win. If you move without asking permission, you run the risk of making the K-9 sergeant's hit list again (like I did). If you play it safe, and you don't move, you're going to feel like you could have done more to catch the second suspect, but didn't. If you try to raise the K-9 sergeant on the radio, chances are he won't answer, or he'll just tell you to stay put where you are. You can't win!

No points involved.

Situation #6
(Chapter 7)

There are some situations where the use of deadly force is unfortunately almost unavoidable. I don't think any sane individual really wants to kill another human being, but sometimes, sadly, there is no other alternative. Now, with the suspect's vehicle still bearing down on you at a high rate of speed, and with it appearing as if they do intend to ram you, the use of deadly force is almost required.

Therefore, the correct answer is: "Yes! I would fire my weapon."

If this was your choice, give yourself one (1) point for good judgment. But if you decided not to fire your weapon, I would suggest you seriously ask yourself "Why?" If your religious and/or moral beliefs prevented you from firing, then you definitely should seek out another profession other than law enforcement. Your motives are noble and pure, but your failure to be able to fire in some future encounter may cost you your life, or the life of a fellow officer.

Situation #7
(Chapter 7)

As indicated in Chapter 7's narrative, "you can't kill a car" so the vehicle itself should <u>not</u> be the target. Your goal is to stop the vehicle, and the only sure way to do that is to take out the driver.

Therefore, the best answer is: "I would fire at the vehicle's driver."

A good argument can also be made that the passenger is a legitimate target too. This is true and even though my own personal preference would be the driver, if you decided to fire at the passenger instead that would <u>not</u> be considered the wrong thing to do. If you decided to fire at either the driver or the passenger, then give yourself one (1) point for good judgment and for picking the right target to shoot at. If you decided to fire at the vehicle's tires, you don't get any points at all.

Situation #8
(Chapter 8)

You always want to do everything you can to avoid a hostage type situation, but you also need to act aggressively when it is appropriate. If you wait for the two subjects to leave the store before you "Move in!" there is a good chance you won't be able to pick the ground where you finally do engage them. You, <u>not</u> the bad guys, should always be in control of the situation (when and where you confront them). It also wouldn't be wise to let them run back to their vehicle, which is parked across the busy boulevard. Although one tactical officer is on the way to cover their vehicle, no one is there yet.

Therefore, the best answer is: "Most robberies are over in less than one minute, so I would immediately advise all our units to 'Move in!'"

The wild card in all of this are the two tactical officers on the west side of the store. You don't have a clue what they may have witnessed, or where they are located, or what they may be doing. So, even if you don't give the word to "Move in!" they may "Move in!" on their own.

If you chose to "Move in!" immediately, give yourself one (1) point for good judgment.

Situation #9
(Chapter 8)

You definitely should <u>not</u> "retreat backwards away from the advancing suspect." If he was walking, and he had a knife, then this might be an option. But, the suspect is running towards you at full speed and you're worried he might have a gun in the paper bag. Trying to back up away from him only puts you on the defensive, and at a disadvantage. You may think the subject might have a gun in the paper bag, but if you don't see it in his hands, you're really not justified in shooting the suspect at this point. You might be able to convince a grand jury that you needed to shoot him, but ethically and/or morally I don't believe the use of deadly force is appropriate yet. Many agencies frown on warning shots (what goes up, must eventually come down), so it would <u>not</u> be appropriate to fire a warning shot either.

Therefore, the best answer is: "I would give him one more chance to surrender."

If you chose this response, then give yourself one (1) point for good judgment. If you decided to shoot the suspect, because he wouldn't drop the paper bag, you lose two (2) points instead. The other answers (backing away from the suspect, or firing a warning shot), although <u>not</u> the best things to do, are somewhat acceptable and you do not lose, or gain, any points.

Situation #10
(Chapter 9)

The best answer is: "I would continue to chase after the suspect, and Officer Smith who is behind him, but I would do nothing else at this time."

If this is the decision you made, you earn one (1) point for good judgment.

Just because you won't be able to catch the fleeing suspect is <u>not</u> a reason to stop chasing after him. Officer Smith is still there in front of you and he seems to be gaining on the subject. If you stop and return to your partner's location you won't be able to provide a back-up for Officer Smith if he needs it. You are committed and as long as Officer Smith is chasing after the bad guy, you need to be there too! Under these circumstances, firing a warning shot is also <u>not</u> appropriate either. Officer Smith is out in front of you and if you fire a warning shot he won't know if it's just a warning shot and he might think you're shooting at the suspect. This might make him worry about you hitting him instead of the bad guy. Also, besides the obvious danger that you might miss the bad guy, and hit Officer Smith, you've seen nothing that would justify the use of deadly force. You lose one (1) point if you fired a warning shot, or if you stopped the chase and returned to your partner. You lose two (2) points if you shot at the suspect himself.

Situation #11
(Chapter 10)

This is another one of those no-brainers!

The only acceptable answer is: "I radio the dispatcher and give her the vehicle's description, location, direction and why I want it stopped (to arrest the subject Pee Wee). I then let the vehicle go and I would <u>not</u> attempt to follow it." If this is the decision you made, you earn one (1) point for good judgment.

No matter how much you might want to follow after the subject's vehicle, this is <u>not</u> a smart thing to do, not with your wife and kids in the car with you. If you were alone it would be different, but you should never take a chance with your family's safety! Never! If you decided to follow along after the subjects (like I did), you lose one (1) point.

Situation #12
(Chapter 11)

This is another one of those situations where there really isn't a "right" or a "wrong" answer, not unless things turn totally bad for you, and then everybody and their brother will be saying you did the wrong thing!

I suppose it really comes down to a matter of personal preference. Some officers would probably choose to wait at their vehicle, to see what happens next. Others would be more aggressive and would want to "take the high ground" before the enemy could.

I'll leave it up to the reader to decide what course of action is best, and why.

No points involved.

Situation #13
(Chapter 11)

This is another one of those situations where the use of deadly force is not only justified, unfortunately it almost becomes a requirement! After all, this is what police officers do; they protect society from a criminal element that is sometimes very ruthless and vicious. If these two guys in the Camero dared to challenge us, armed law enforcement officers, what chance would an unarmed citizen have, if they were to cross paths with them later?

No, the acceptable answer would be: "Yes! I would fire my weapon."

However, if you decided not to fire because the suspect's vehicle was racing backwards straight towards you, and you were worried you might be run over, this is indeed a legitimate concern. Only the person standing there in the path of the vehicle can really judge how much time they have. Do they have enough time to fire, or do they need to jump out of the way now? If you did not fire for this reason (the fear of being run over), you don't get any points, but you don't lose any either. If you decided to stand your ground and you fired your weapon before you jumped out of the way, you get two (2) points for exceptional coolness under fire. If you decided not to fire for any other reason, then you lose two (2) points.

In most "normal" situations you would <u>not</u> continue to fire if a fleeing vehicle was headed away from you. After all, the immediate threat to you is now over, so there no longer is a need for you to use deadly force to protect yourself. Many police departments have policies and procedures that address this specific issue.

However, as they say, there are exceptions to every rule. This incident in Lauderhill was not one of your "normal" situations. These two guys in the Camero had just tried to kill us, so there was still a very real threat to any other police officers they might encounter, as well as the general public too.

Therefore, the right answer would be: "Yes! I would continue to shoot at the two suspects in the still fleeing vehicle."

If you decided to continue firing your weapon, give yourself one (1) point for good judgment. However, if you decided <u>not</u> to continue to fire, then you didn't make the best decision you could, and you lose one (1) point.

Situation 15
(Chapter 13)

This is another one of those complicated situations where there really isn't a "right" or a "wrong" answer. Because the lieutenant found in your favor you definitely "won the battle," but you also probably "lost the war" too. No matter what you do it is doubtful Sergeant Dierkzon will forgive and forget, so it would be best to end this matter as soon as possible.

Therefore, the choice you should make is: "You've won! Say 'Thank you!' and then leave the lieutenant's office a.s.a.p. without any further comment. Consider yourself fortunate that the lieutenant is a fair and objective supervisor."

You get one (1) point for good judgment if you decided to leave the lieutenant's office without any further comment.

If, because of this incident you really don't want the overtime, just don't turn the overtime card in like you would normally do. Tearing the card up in front of the sergeant and lieutenant might make you feel better, but it's really not a smart thing to do.

Situation 16
(Chapter 14)

Because it's dark and you can't see the subject's right side, and it appears he may be reaching for a weapon, you probably would be legally justified to shoot him. But, what if it turned out he did <u>not</u> have a weapon? A grand jury might clear you, but how would you feel shooting an unarmed man? No, unless I actually saw a weapon in a suspect's hands, I usually tried to hold my fire, if at all possible.

Waiting to see what he does next might seem like the best thing to do, but it's really not. By waiting you surrender the initiative to the suspect and you never want to do this. You need to act aggressively, so either of the following two decisions would be correct:

"As much as you didn't want to come into physical contact with the subject, you rush and tackle him, and take him down to the ground."

- or -

"You strike the subject in the head with your gun and this makes him fall to the ground."

If you made either one of these decisions you earn one (1) point for good judgment.

Situation 17
(Chapter 15)

___

If possible, you should always do everything within your power to avoid a hostage type situation. However, waiting to see what happens next is now no longer an option. You observed the two female clerks being taken to the back of the store, and now their immediate safety becomes your primary concern. If you wait, or if you try to raise your supervisor on the radio, to see what he wants you to do, you're wasting precious seconds.

While you wait the two clerks may be injured or killed, so the only correct answer is: "Fearing for the safety of the two female clerks you decide you must immediately take action and you give the order to 'Move in!'"

If this is the decision you made you earn one (1) point for good judgment. If you decided to wait, for any reason, you lose one (1) point.

Situation 18
(Chapter 15)

The subject in front of you hasn't given up yet and he continues to try and hide behind the clerk's vehicle. You're also sure that he has something in his hands so you might be legally justified to shoot him. Yes, the shooting might be legally justified, but would it be morally and/or ethically right too?

The simple answer is "No!" Although you're not sure, you believe the unknown object in the suspect's hands is a bottle of wine. Under these circumstances shooting him just wouldn't be right.

Firing a warning shot would also <u>not</u> be the best thing to do. Even though it would obviously be preferable to shooting the suspect himself, other officers moving in on the store would not know who was shooting at who, and this might cause them to react in a more aggressive and/or undesirable manner.

Therefore, because the suspect is trapped, and you have him in your sights, you can afford to be a little generous and wait. Therefore, the best decision to make is: "You wait. You want to see what he does next."

If this is the decision you made you earn one (1) point for good judgment. If you decided to shoot the suspect, even though you suspected he only had a bottle of wine in his hands, you lose two (2) points.

Situation #19
(Chapter 22)

The correct answer is: "Because they haven't given up, and at least one is still armed and they are attempting to flee the residence, even though they are both still running away from you, you shoot at the two subjects."

If this is the decision you made, you earn two (2) points for keeping a cool head during a very stressful situation, and for exercising good judgment.

If you decided that you would hold your fire "to let the other tactical officers outside of the residence deal with the two subjects" you lose two (2) points.

By choosing this course of action you clearly endanger the lives of the officers outside. At least one suspect is armed and it is very obvious they do not intend to surrender peacefully. You have an obligation to immediately stop them if you can. And, if that means shooting them in the back, as they are running away from you, then that's what you should do!

<u>**Situation #20**</u>
(Chapter 22)

Legally, either answer would probably be considered correct. Under these circumstances it would be legally defensible to fire first, without giving any more warnings. However, there would definitely be those who would say the subjects should have been given another warning and a chance to surrender, regardless of the additional risks to the officers.

Therefore, if you did NOT immediately fire, and you gave the subjects one more last warning, you earn two (2) points. If you decided to fire first without any more warnings, you earn one (1) point.

If your moral and/or ethical principals would have prevented you from firing at the subjects, no matter what they did, then you probably would end up dead.

SITUATION ANALYSIS POINTS

POINTS YOU EARNED   **YOUR FINAL RANK**

20 points …………….....………Chief of Police/or Sheriff

19 points…………………….….Assistant Chief/or Colonel

18 points}.
17 points}……………………………….……………….Major
16 points}.

15 points}.
14 points}……….[author scored 14 points]……...Captain
13 points}.

12 points}.
11 points}…………………………...............………Lieutenant
10 points}.

09 points}.
08 points}……………….…...………………......………Sergeant
07 points}.

06 points}.
05 points}…………………………………………….Detective
04 points}.

03 points}.
02 points}………………….....……Patrol Officer/or Deputy
01 points}.

Note: If your overall score ended up minus points, you should definitely find another career path to pursue.